Cooking Light

LOW-FAT
LOW-CALORIE

quick & easy cookbook

Cooking Light.

LOW-FAT LOW-CALORIE

quick & easy cookbook

Oxmoor House.

Cooking Light® Low-Fat, Low-Calorie
quick & easy cookbook

© 1998 by Oxmoor House, Inc.
Book Division of Southern Progress Corporation
P.O. Box 2463, Birmingham, Alabama 35201

Library of Congress Catalog Card Number: 98-65944
ISBN: 0-8487-1591-8
Manufactured in the United States of America
First Printing 1998
Be sure to check with your health-care provider before making any changes in your diet.

EDITOR-IN-CHIEF: Nancy Fitzpatrick Wyatt

SENIOR FOODS EDITOR: Katherine M. Eakin

SENIOR EDITOR, EDITORIAL SERVICES: Olivia Kindig Wells

ART DIRECTOR: James Boone

LOW-FAT, LOW-CALORIE • quick & easy cookbook

EDITOR: Deborah Garrison Lowery

ASSOCIATE EDITOR: Anne Chappell Cain, M.S., M.P.H., R.D.

COPY EDITORS: Jacqueline Giovanelli, Catherine S. Ritter

DESIGNER: Carol O. Loria

EDITORIAL ASSISTANTS: Alison Rich Lewis, Kaye Howard Smith

DIRECTOR, TEST KITCHENS: Kathleen Royal Phillips

ASSISTANT DIRECTOR, TEST KITCHENS: Gayle Hays Sadler

TEST KITCHENS STAFF: Molly Baldwin, Susan Hall Bellows,
      Julie Christopher, Michele Brown Fuller,
      Natalie E. King, Elizabeth Tyler Luckett, Jan Jacks Moon,
      Iris Crawley O'Brien, Jan A. Smith

PHOTOGRAPHER: Brit Huckabay

PHOTO STYLIST: Virginia R. Cravens

PUBLISHING SYSTEMS ADMINISTRATOR: Rick Tucker

PRODUCTION DIRECTOR: Phillip Lee

ASSOCIATE PRODUCTION MANAGER: Vanessa Cobbs Richardson

PRODUCTION ASSISTANT: Faye Porter Bonner

RECIPE DEVELOPMENT: Susan Dosier, Jean Kressy, Karen Levin,
      Karen Mangum, Debby Maugans Nakos, Greg Patent,
      Susan Reeves, Donna Shields, Elizabeth J. Taliaferro

COVER: Grilled Texas Ranch Burgers with Zippy Corn Relish (page 18)
PAGE 1: Baked Ravioli and Vegetables (page 113)
PAGE 2: Grilled Orange Roughy with Pineapple-Cucumber Salsa (page 10)
PAGE 4: No-Chop Antipasto Tray (page 38)

We're Here for You!
We at Oxmoor House are dedicated to serving you with reliable information that expands your imagination and enriches your life. We welcome your comments and suggestions.
Please write to us at:

Oxmoor House, Inc.
Editor: LOW-FAT, LOW-CALORIE
quick & easy cookbook
2100 Lakeshore Drive
Birmingham, AL 35209

To order additional publications,
call 1-205-877-6560.

Contents

Our Top 10 Timesaving Tips

In the Oxmoor House test kitchens we use dozens of techniques and tricks to avoid cleanup and to save time in the kitchen. Here are 10 of our favorite tips so you can do the same. For more secrets to cooking quickly, turn to page 224.

1 Buy bags of fresh baby carrots, celery sticks, cauliflower flowerets, broccoli flowerets, and presliced mushrooms in the produce section to save chopping and slicing time.

◄ **2** Chop and freeze ½-cup portions of red or green pepper, onion, and parsley in heavy-duty, zip-top freezer bags, or buy prepackaged frozen chopped onion and green pepper. When you're preparing breadcrumbs or toasting nuts for a recipe, prepare extra and freeze it in heavy-duty, zip-top bags.

3 Keep chopped cooked chicken in the freezer. You can now find packages of precooked chopped chicken in the freezer section of supermarkets.

◄ **4** Use a pizza cutter to cut dough or to cut day-old bread into cubes for croutons. It's faster than using a knife.

5 To remove the papery skin from garlic, press a clove with the flat side of a knife blade; ▶ the clove will slip out from the skin. Or, roll the clove inside a rubber lid opener to pull the skin off.

6 Use a slow cooker to help with advance preparation of meals that are hot and ready when you need them.

7 Cooking on the grill, especially a gas grill, saves time and cleanup because there are fewer cooking dishes to wash. The smoke also ▶ flavors the food.

8 To skim fat from broth or gravy, pour it into a zip-top bag, and seal the bag. Snip a hole in one corner and allow the broth or gravy to drip out into a measuring cup. The fat will rise to the top in the zip-top bag. When the broth or gravy has dripped out, pinch closed the hole and discard the bag with the remaining fat.

9 To open a vacuum-packed jar, insert the pointed end of a can opener church key (the part you use to open juice cans) under the lid to break the vacuum. The lid will open easily.

10 Use kitchen scissors to make many kitchen ▶ jobs faster and easier. Use them to chop tomatoes in a can, snip fresh herbs in a measuring cup, cut pita bread into wedges, and trim skin and fat from chicken or meat. Spray the scissors with vegetable cooking spray, and you'll find it easy to cut sticky foods like dried fruit.

from the grill

Grilled Herbed Corn on the Cob (page 28)

Creole Catfish Grill

prep: 4 minutes   marinate: 30 minutes   cook: 16 minutes

¼ cup fat-free Italian dressing

¼ cup fresh lemon juice
(about 1 large lemon)

1 teaspoon salt-free Creole
seasoning

6 (4-ounce) farm-raised
catfish fillets

Vegetable cooking spray

Dash of paprika (optional)

Lemon slices (optional)

1 Combine first 3 ingredients in a shallow dish; place fish in a single layer over dressing mixture, turning to coat fish. Cover and marinate in refrigerator 30 minutes, turning fish once.

2 Remove fish from marinade, discarding marinade. Arrange fish in a large wire grilling basket coated with cooking spray; place basket on grill rack over medium-hot coals (350° to 400°). Grill, covered, 8 minutes on each side or until fish flakes easily when tested with a fork. If desired, sprinkle with paprika and serve with lemon slices.
Yield: 6 servings.

PER SERVING: CALORIES 137 (34% FROM FAT)   FAT 5.1G (SAT 1.1G)   PROTEIN 20.6G   CARBOHYDRATE 0.8G   FIBER 0.0G   CHOLESTEROL 66MG   SODIUM 112MG
EXCHANGES PER SERVING: 3 Lean Meat

Serve with rice, broccoli sprinkled with lemon juice, and French bread.

Spicy Grilled Tuna

prep: 5 minutes   marinate: 30 minutes   cook: 8 minutes

¼ cup nonfat mayonnaise

1 tablespoon fresh lime juice
(about 1 small lime)

½ teaspoon ground red
pepper

½ teaspoon ground cumin

¼ teaspoon minced garlic
(about ½ clove)

4 (4-ounce) tuna steaks

Vegetable cooking spray

1 Combine first 5 ingredients in a small bowl. Brush mayonnaise mixture on both sides of fish. Place fish in a shallow dish; cover and marinate in refrigerator 30 minutes.

2 Coat grill rack with cooking spray; place on grill over medium-hot coals (350° to 400°). Arrange fish on rack; grill, covered, 4 to 5 minutes on each side or until fish flakes easily when tested with a fork.
Yield: 4 servings.

PER SERVING: CALORIES 179 (29% FROM FAT)   FAT 5.8G (SAT 1.4G)   PROTEIN 26.6G   CARBOHYDRATE 3.6G   FIBER 0.1G   CHOLESTEROL 43MG   SODIUM 235MG
EXCHANGES PER SERVING: 4 Very Lean Meat

Serve with couscous, asparagus, and/or grilled tomato slices.

RECIPE tip

When you're in a time bind, marinating the tuna steaks is optional. The fish won't be quite as flavorful if you don't marinate it, but you can add mesquite chips to the coals for a delicious flavor boost.

Grilled Orange Roughy with Pineapple-Cucumber Salsa

prep: 6 minutes   marinate: 30 minutes   cook: 8 minutes

Pineapple-Cucumber Salsa

4 (4-ounce) orange roughy
   or flounder fillets

½ cup low-sodium soy sauce

¼ cup fresh lime juice
   (about 1 large lime)

3 tablespoons rum (optional)

2 tablespoons honey

   Dash of hot sauce

   Vegetable cooking spray

   Sliced cucumber (optional)

1 Prepare Pineapple-Cucumber Salsa; cover and refrigerate, if desired, until ready to serve.

2 Place fish in a large heavy-duty, zip-top plastic bag. Combine soy sauce and next 4 ingredients; pour over fish. Seal bag; turn to coat fish. Marinate in refrigerator 30 minutes.

3 Coat grill rack with cooking spray; place on grill over medium-hot coals (350° to 400°). Remove fish from marinade, discarding marinade. Place fish on rack; grill, covered, 4 minutes on each side or until fish flakes easily when tested with a fork. Place fish on 4 individual serving plates; top each serving with ½ cup Pineapple-Cucumber Salsa. Garnish with cucumber slices, if desired.
Yield: 4 servings.

PER SERVING: CALORIES 216 (29% FROM FAT) FAT 6.9G (SAT 1.0G) PROTEIN 22.0G
CARBOHYDRATE 14.5G FIBER 0.3G CHOLESTEROL 68MG SODIUM 159MG
EXCHANGES PER SERVING: 3 LEAN MEAT, 1 FRUIT

Serve with *rice pilaf and grilled vegetable kabobs.*

Pineapple-Cucumber Salsa

1 (20-ounce) can pineapple
   tidbits in juice, drained

1½ cups peeled, finely chopped
   cucumber

⅓ cup finely chopped purple
   onion

2 tablespoons sugar

3 tablespoons fresh lime juice
   (about 1 large lime)

⅛ teaspoon dried crushed red
   pepper

1 Combine all ingredients in a large bowl; serve immediately or cover and chill, if desired. Serve with grilled fish, chicken, or pork.
Yield: 3½ cups.

PER ½ CUP: CALORIES 54 (2% FROM FAT) FAT 0.1G (SAT 0.0G) PROTEIN 0.3G
CARBOHYDRATE 13.6G FIBER 0.3G CHOLESTEROL 0MG SODIUM 3MG
EXCHANGE PER ½ CUP: 1 FRUIT

Grilled Orange Roughy with Pineapple-Cucumber Salsa

Barbecued Shrimp Grill

prep: 9 minutes   chill: 15 minutes   cook: 6 minutes

20 unpeeled large fresh shrimp
    (about 1 pound)

1 cup ketchup

1 cup low-sugar orange
   marmalade

3 tablespoons cider vinegar

1 tablespoon low-sodium
   Worcestershire sauce

¾ teaspoon chili powder

2 tablespoons reduced-fat
   mayonnaise

   Vegetable cooking spray

1 Peel and devein shrimp, leaving tails intact; set aside.

2 Combine ketchup and next 4 ingredients in a small bowl. Microwave at HIGH 5 minutes, stirring after every minute. Let cool. Combine mayonnaise and half of ketchup mixture, stirring well; cover and chill mayonnaise mixture at least 15 minutes. Set aside remaining half of ketchup mixture.

3 Thread shrimp onto 3 (10-inch) metal skewers. Coat grill rack with cooking spray; place on grill over medium-hot coals (350° to 400°). Place skewers on rack; grill, covered, 3 to 4 minutes on each side or until shrimp turn pink, basting frequently with reserved ketchup mixture. Remove shrimp from skewers. Place on a serving platter, and serve with reserved mayonnaise mixture.
Yield: 10 appetizer servings (2 shrimp and 2 tablespoons sauce per serving).

PER SERVING: CALORIES 79 (18% FROM FAT) FAT 1.6G (SAT 0.1G) PROTEIN 7.6G
CARBOHYDRATE 8.8G FIBER 0.5G CHOLESTEROL 53MG SODIUM 349MG
EXCHANGES PER SERVING: 1 VERY LEAN MEAT, ½ FRUIT

Serve with *an appetizer buffet menu of grilled chicken-pineapple kabobs, black bean salsa with tortilla chips, spinach-stuffed mushrooms, and assorted fresh vegetables with reduced-fat Ranch-style dip.*

RECIPE tip

To broil shrimp, place skewers on rack of a broiler pan coated with vegetable cooking spray. Broil 3 inches from heat (with electric oven door partially opened) 3 minutes on each side or until shrimp turn pink, basting frequently with reserved ketchup mixture.

Grilled Grecian Chicken

prep: 10 minutes   cook: 10 minutes

¼ cup reduced-fat mayonnaise

2½ teaspoons grated lemon rind

1½ tablespoons fresh lemon juice
(about 1 small lemon)

1 tablespoon chopped fresh
oregano or 1 teaspoon
dried oregano

½ teaspoon minced garlic
(about 1 clove)

4 (4-ounce) skinned, boned
chicken breast halves

Vegetable cooking spray

1 Combine first 5 ingredients in a small bowl, stirring until smooth. Brush mayonnaise mixture on both sides of chicken breast halves.

2 Coat grill rack with cooking spray; place on grill over medium-hot coals (350° to 400°). Place chicken on rack; grill, covered, 5 to 6 minutes on each side or until done.
Yield: 4 servings.

PER SERVING: CALORIES 181 (35% FROM FAT) FAT 7.1G (SAT 1.4G) PROTEIN 26.0G
CARBOHYDRATE 2.2G FIBER 0.1G CHOLESTEROL 75MG SODIUM 173MG
EXCHANGES PER SERVING: 4 VERY LEAN MEAT

Serve with *couscous and a spinach salad with tomatoes and feta cheese.*

Maple-Mustard Grilled Chicken

prep: 4 minutes   cook: 30 minutes

½ cup Dijon mustard

¼ cup maple-flavored syrup

2 tablespoons white vinegar

4 (6-ounce) skinned chicken
breast halves

Vegetable cooking spray

½ teaspoon ground pepper

⅛ teaspoon salt

1 Combine first 3 ingredients in a small bowl, stirring well; set aside.

2 Coat chicken lightly with cooking spray; sprinkle with pepper and salt.

3 Coat grill rack with cooking spray; place on grill over medium-hot coals (350° to 400°). Place chicken on rack; grill, uncovered, 15 minutes, basting often with mustard mixture. Turn chicken, and grill 15 additional minutes or until meat thermometer inserted into thickest part of chicken registers 180°, basting often with mustard mixture.
Yield: 4 servings.

PER SERVING: CALORIES 194 (19% FROM FAT) FAT 4.2G (SAT 0.8G) PROTEIN 25.1G
CARBOHYDRATE 11.3G FIBER 0.1G CHOLESTEROL 69MG SODIUM 580MG
EXCHANGES PER SERVING: 3 VERY LEAN MEAT, 1 STARCH

Serve with *herbed red potatoes and grilled yellow squash-zucchini kabobs.*

TIME-saver

Boneless chicken breast halves cook much faster than bone-in breasts. If you use boned chicken breast halves, grill them about 5 to 6 minutes on each side or until done.

Grilled Tomato-Basil Chicken

prep: 15 minutes   marinate: 8 hours   cook: 10 minutes

½ teaspoon minced garlic
      (about 1 clove)

 4 plum tomatoes, quartered

¾ cup balsamic vinegar

¼ cup fresh basil leaves

½ teaspoon ground pepper

¼ teaspoon salt

 4 (4-ounce) skinned, boned
      chicken breast halves

      Vegetable cooking spray

 4 plum tomatoes, halved

1 Position knife blade in food processor bowl. Combine first 6 ingredients in processor bowl. Process until smooth. Set aside ¼ cup tomato mixture.

2 Place chicken in a large heavy-duty, zip-top plastic bag. Pour remaining tomato mixture over chicken. Seal bag; turn bag to coat chicken. Marinate in refrigerator 8 hours.

3 Coat grill rack with cooking spray; place on grill over medium-hot coals (350° to 400°). Remove chicken from marinade, discarding marinade. Coat tomato halves with cooking spray. Place chicken and tomato halves on rack; grill, covered, 5 to 6 minutes on each side or until chicken is done and tomato is cooked but still slightly firm. Place chicken on 4 individual serving plates; top each chicken breast half with 1 tablespoon reserved tomato mixture. Arrange 2 grilled tomato halves on each plate with chicken.
Yield: 4 servings.

Per Serving: Calories 160 (20% from fat)   Fat 3.6g (Sat 0.9g)   Protein 26.5g
Carbohydrate 4.7g   Fiber 1.2g   Cholesterol 70mg   Sodium 143mg
Exchanges Per Serving: 3½ Very Lean Meat, 1 Vegetable

Serve with *a tossed green salad with fat-free zesty Italian dressing and French bread.*

WORK-saver

To mince garlic in the food processor, drop it through the food chute with the processor running and process until it's minced. Then add other ingredients to chop.

Grilled Tomato-Basil Chicken

Grilled Curry-Thyme Chicken

prep: 7 minutes   cook: 10 minutes

Curry-Thyme Rub

4 (4-ounce) skinned, boned
   chicken breast halves

Vegetable cooking spray

1 Prepare Curry-Thyme Rub.

2 Rub 1 teaspoon rub evenly over both sides of each chicken breast half, reserving remaining rub for other uses.

3 Coat grill rack with cooking spray; place on grill over medium-hot coals (350° to 400°). Place chicken on rack; grill, covered, 5 to 6 minutes on each side or until chicken is done.
Yield: 4 servings.

PER SERVING: CALORIES 146 (20% FROM FAT) FAT 3.3G (SAT 0.9G) PROTEIN 26.0G
CARBOHYDRATE 1.6G FIBER 0.5G CHOLESTEROL 70MG SODIUM 119MG
EXCHANGES PER SERVING: 4 VERY LEAN MEAT

Serve with parslied rice and glazed carrots.

Curry-Thyme Rub

3 tablespoons dried thyme

3 tablespoons garlic powder

3 tablespoons curry powder

3 tablespoons paprika

1 teaspoon poultry seasoning

1 teaspoon ground red pepper

1 teaspoon ground black
   pepper

½ teaspoon salt

1 Combine all ingredients in a small bowl, stirring well. Store in an airtight container. Use to season chicken, turkey, rice, vegetables, and soups.
Yield: ⅔ cup.

PER TEASPOON: CALORIES 8 (23% FAT) FAT 0.2G (SAT 0.0G) PROTEIN 0.4G
CARBOHYDRATE 1.6G FIBER 0.5G CHOLESTEROL 0MG SODIUM 38MG
EXCHANGE PER TEASPOON: FREE

Grilled Pineapple-Chicken Pockets

prep: 16 minutes   cook: 11 minutes

1 (8-ounce) can pineapple
    slices in juice, undrained

⅓ cup hot pepper jelly

3 (4-ounce) skinned, boned
    chicken breast halves

    Vegetable cooking spray

2 (7-inch) pita bread rounds,
    cut in half

¼ cup nonfat cream cheese

1 tablespoon plus 1 teaspoon
    hot pepper jelly

8 large, fresh spinach leaves

1 Drain pineapple slices, reserving 3 tablespoons juice. Set pineapple aside. Combine reserved juice and ⅓ cup jelly, stirring until smooth. Place chicken breast halves in a large heavy-duty, zip-top plastic bag; add jelly mixture. Seal bag, and shake until chicken is well coated. Remove chicken from jelly mixture. Pour jelly mixture into a small saucepan; bring to a boil. Remove from heat; set aside.

2 Coat grill rack with cooking spray; place on grill over medium-hot coals (350° to 400°). Place chicken on rack. Grill, covered, 5 minutes, basting once with reserved jelly mixture. Turn chicken, and place pineapple slices on grill with chicken; baste with remaining jelly mixture. Grill, covered, 6 minutes or until chicken is done and pineapple is thoroughly heated. Remove chicken and pineapple from grill. Cut chicken into thin slices.

3 Spread inside of each pita pocket with 1 tablespoon cream cheese and 1 teaspoon jelly; place 2 spinach leaves and 1 pineapple slice in each pocket. Arrange chicken evenly in pockets. Serve immediately. Yield: 4 servings.

PER SERVING: CALORIES 277 (11% FROM FAT)   FAT 3.4G (SAT 0.6G)   PROTEIN 23.7G
CARBOHYDRATE 35.2G   FIBER 4.2G   CHOLESTEROL 56MG   SODIUM 260MG
EXCHANGES PER SERVING: 3 VERY LEAN MEAT, 1 STARCH, 1 FRUIT

Serve with fresh strawberries and sliced mango.

Sweet Ginger-Grilled Flank Steak

make ahead

prep: 4 minutes   marinate: 8 hours   cook: 12 minutes

1 (1½-pound) flank steak

½ cup firmly packed brown
    sugar

½ cup low-sodium soy sauce

¼ cup dry red wine

1 teaspoon peeled, minced
    gingerroot or 1 teaspoon
    ground ginger

2 cloves garlic, crushed

    Vegetable cooking spray

1 Trim fat from steak. Place steak in a large heavy-duty, zip-top plastic bag. Combine brown sugar and next 4 ingredients; pour over steak. Seal bag; turn bag to coat steak. Marinate in refrigerator 8 hours, turning bag occasionally.

2 Coat grill rack with cooking spray; place on grill over medium-hot coals (350° to 400°). Remove steak from marinade, discarding marinade. Place steak on rack; grill, covered, 6 to 8 minutes on each side or to desired degree of doneness. Let steak stand 5 minutes. Cut diagonally across grain into thin slices.
Yield: 6 servings.

PER SERVING: CALORIES 217 (55% FROM FAT)   FAT 13.2G (SAT 5.6G)   PROTEIN 22.2G
CARBOHYDRATE 0.8G   FIBER 0.0G   CHOLESTEROL 61MG   SODIUM 105MG
EXCHANGES PER SERVING: 3 MEDIUM-FAT MEAT

Serve with rice and stir-fried peppers.

Grilled Texas Ranch Burgers with Zippy Corn Relish (photo on cover)

prep: 12 minutes   cook: 8 minutes

Zippy Corn Relish

1   pound lean ground round

2   tablespoons chili powder

    Vegetable cooking spray

6   whole wheat hamburger
    buns

6   lettuce leaves

12 slices tomato

¾   cup hot salsa

1   Prepare Zippy Corn Relish; cover and chill until ready to serve.

2   Combine ground round and chili powder, mixing well. Shape mixture into 6 (½-inch-thick) patties.

3   Coat grill rack with cooking spray; place on grill over medium-hot coals (350° to 400°). Place meat patties on rack; grill, covered, 4 minutes on each side or until done. Grill bun halves, cut sides down, 1 minute or just until toasted, if desired.

4   To serve, line bottom half of each bun with 1 lettuce leaf; top with 2 tomato slices and a meat patty. Top each patty with 2 tablespoons salsa and 2 tablespoons Zippy Corn Relish. Reserve remaining corn relish for other uses. Top with remaining bun halves.
Yield: 6 servings.

PER SERVING: CALORIES 304 (27% FROM FAT) FAT 9.1G (SAT 2.8G) PROTEIN 22.5G
CARBOHYDRATE 33.8G FIBER 3.9G CHOLESTEROL 64MG SODIUM 537MG
EXCHANGES PER SERVING: 2 MEDIUM-FAT MEAT, 2 STARCH, 1 VEGETABLE

Serve with roasted potato wedges.

Zippy Corn Relish

1   (11-ounce) can Mexican-
    style corn, drained

3   tablespoons hot salsa

2   tablespoons fresh lime juice
    (about 1 medium lime)

1   teaspoon ground cumin

1   Combine all ingredients; cover and chill until ready to serve. Serve with beef or turkey burgers, or grilled chicken.
Yield: 1½ cups.

PER TABLESPOON: CALORIES 11 (8% FROM FAT) FAT 0.1G (SAT 0.0G) PROTEIN 0.3G
CARBOHYDRATE 2.3G FIBER 0.1G CHOLESTEROL 0MG SODIUM 41MG
EXCHANGE PER TABLESPOON: FREE

*Grilled Texas Ranch Burgers
with Zippy Corn Relish*

Grilled Barbecued Pork with Vegetable Kabobs

prep: 18 minutes   marinate: 8 hours   cook: 15 minutes

6 (4-ounce) lean, boneless
    loin pork chops

½ cup maple-flavored syrup

¼ cup red wine vinegar

3 tablespoons barbecue sauce

3 tablespoons finely chopped
    onion

2 teaspoons minced garlic
    (about 4 cloves)

6 frozen half-ears corn on
    the cob, thawed and
    cut in half

2 sweet red peppers, seeded
    and cut into 2-inch
    pieces

1 large onion, cut into 6
    wedges

   Vegetable cooking spray

1 Cut each pork chop into ½-inch-thick strips; place pork in a large heavy-duty, zip-top plastic bag. Combine syrup and next 4 ingredients; pour over pork. Seal bag; turn bag to coat pork. Marinate in refrigerator 8 hours, turning occasionally.

2 Remove pork from marinade, reserving marinade. Place marinade in a small saucepan; bring to a boil, and remove from heat. Thread pork, corn, and pepper alternately onto 8 (10-inch) metal skewers. Thread onion separately onto 1 (10-inch) skewer.

3 Coat grill rack with cooking spray; place on grill over medium-hot coals (350° to 400°). Place pork and vegetable kabobs and onion kabob on rack; grill, covered, 12 minutes or until meat is done, turning once and basting with reserved marinade. Remove pork and vegetable kabobs from grill. Grill onion kabob, covered, 3 to 5 additional minutes or until tender, turning once and basting with reserved marinade.
Yield: 6 servings.

PER SERVING: CALORIES 332 (31% FROM FAT) FAT 11.6G (SAT 3.8G) PROTEIN 25.2G CARBOHYDRATE 32.5G FIBER 2.4G CHOLESTEROL 74MG SODIUM 131MG EXCHANGES PER SERVING: 3 MEDIUM-FAT MEAT, 2 STARCH

Serve with crusty French bread and grilled fat-free pound cake topped with strawberries.

Molasses-Grilled Chops with Horseradish Sauce

Molasses-Grilled Chops with Horseradish Sauce

prep: 8 minutes   marinate: 4 hours   cook: 10 minutes

4 (4-ounce) lean, boneless center-cut loin pork chops (½ inch thick)

½ cup low-sodium soy sauce

¼ cup molasses

1 teaspoon garlic powder

Vegetable cooking spray

¼ cup nonfat mayonnaise

3 tablespoons fat-free milk

1 tablespoon prepared horseradish

2 teaspoons finely chopped onion

¼ teaspoon ground pepper

1 Place pork chops in a large heavy-duty, zip-top plastic bag. Combine soy sauce, molasses, and garlic powder; stir well, and pour over pork chops. Seal bag; turn bag to coat chops. Marinate in refrigerator 4 to 8 hours, turning occasionally.

2 Coat grill rack with cooking spray; place on grill over medium-hot coals (350° to 400°). Remove pork chops from marinade, discarding marinade. Place pork chops on rack; grill, covered, 5 minutes on each side or until meat is done. Remove from grill, and keep warm.

3 Combine mayonnaise and remaining 4 ingredients in a small saucepan. Cook over low heat, stirring constantly, until thoroughly heated. Spoon horseradish sauce evenly over pork chops.
Yield: 4 servings.

PER SERVING: CALORIES 231 (42% FROM FAT) FAT 10.9G (SAT 3.7G) PROTEIN 23.7G
CARBOHYDRATE 7.7G FIBER 0.1G CHOLESTEROL 75MG SODIUM 355MG
EXCHANGES PER SERVING: 3 LEAN MEAT, ½ STARCH

***Serve with** herbed roasted potato wedges.*

WORK-saver

Spray the measuring cup with vegetable cooking spray or rinse it in cold water before measuring sticky molasses. The molasses will slide right out of the cup.

Grilled Cumin-Cornmeal Pork Tenderloins

prep: 3 minutes   cook: 20 minutes

Cumin-Cornmeal Rub

2 (¾-pound) pork tenderloins

2 tablespoons low-sodium soy
    sauce

Vegetable cooking spray

1 Prepare Cumin-Cornmeal Rub.

2 Brush tenderloins with soy sauce. Rub 2 tablespoons rub evenly over each tenderloin, pressing rub onto tenderloins. Reserve remaining rub for other uses.

3 Coat grill rack with cooking spray; place on grill over medium-hot coals (350° to 400°). Place tenderloins on rack; grill, covered, 15 minutes or until meat thermometer inserted into thickest part of tenderloins registers 160°, turning occasionally. Allow tenderloins to stand 5 minutes; cut into slices.
Yield: 6 servings.

PER SERVING: CALORIES 165 (25% FROM FAT)   FAT 4.6G (SAT 1.5G)   PROTEIN 26.3G
CARBOHYDRATE 2.9G   FIBER 0.5G   CHOLESTEROL 83MG   SODIUM 193MG
EXCHANGES PER SERVING: 3½ VERY LEAN MEAT

***Serve with** garlic-seasoned turnip greens, red potatoes, and corn sticks.*

RECIPE tip

For more intense flavor, allow the precoated pork to stand in the refrigerator up to 8 hours.

Cumin-Cornmeal Rub

3 tablespoons yellow
    cornmeal

2 tablespoons ground cumin

2 tablespoons dried thyme

1 tablespoon garlic powder

1 Combine all ingredients in a small bowl; stir well. Store in an airtight container. Use rub to season pork, beef, or chicken.
Yield: ½ cup.

PER TABLESPOON: CALORIES 22 (21% FROM FAT)   FAT 0.5G (SAT 0.1G)   PROTEIN 0.8G
CARBOHYDRATE 4.3G   FIBER 0.7G   CHOLESTEROL 0MG   SODIUM 4MG
EXCHANGE PER TABLESPOON: FREE

Grilled Ham Steaks

prep: 5 minutes   cook: 6 minutes

⅓ cup apple jelly

2 tablespoons no-salt-added
     tomato sauce

1 tablespoon cider vinegar

   Dash of ground red pepper

1 (1-pound) lean, boneless
     ham steak (about ½ inch
     thick)

   Vegetable cooking spray

1 Combine first 4 ingredients in a small saucepan; cook over medium heat until smooth, stirring often. Cut ham in half lengthwise. Slice each half horizontally into 2 (¼-inch-thick) slices.

2 Coat grill rack with cooking spray; place on grill over medium-hot coals (350° to 400°). Baste ham with jelly mixture; place on grill. Grill, covered, 3 to 4 minutes on each side or until ham is thoroughly heated, basting with remaining jelly mixture.
Yield: 4 servings.

PER SERVING: CALORIES 147 (24% FROM FAT) FAT 3.9G (SAT 1.3G) PROTEIN 14.8G
CARBOHYDRATE 13.0G FIBER 0.1G CHOLESTEROL 35MG SODIUM 1,087MG
EXCHANGES PER SERVING: 1½ LEAN MEAT, 1 STARCH

Serve with baked sweet potatoes and green beans.

RECIPE tip

If sodium is a concern, use a 33⅓%-less-sodium center-cut ham slice instead of a boneless ham steak. But be aware that calories and fat are higher in the lower sodium ham slices.

Grilled Venison Steaks

prep: 5 minutes   marinate: 4 hours   cook: 10 minutes

4 (4-ounce) lean, boneless
     venison loin steaks
     (1 inch thick)

1 cup cranberry-orange
     crushed fruit for chicken
     (Ocean Spray), divided

½ cup dry red wine

2 tablespoons Dijon mustard

2 teaspoons minced garlic
     (about 4 cloves)

2 teaspoons dried rosemary,
     crushed

½ teaspoon ground pepper

   Vegetable cooking spray

1 Trim fat from steaks. Place steaks in a large heavy-duty, zip-top plastic bag. Combine ½ cup cranberry-orange sauce, red wine, and next 4 ingredients; pour over steaks. Seal bag; turn to coat steaks. Marinate in refrigerator 4 to 8 hours, turning bag occasionally.

2 Coat grill rack with cooking spray; place on grill over medium-hot coals (350° to 400°). Remove steaks from marinade, discarding marinade. Place steaks on rack; grill, covered, 5 minutes on each side or to desired degree of doneness. Serve with remaining ½ cup cranberry-orange sauce.
Yield: 4 servings (1 steak and 2 tablespoons sauce per serving).

PER SERVING: CALORIES 237 (13% FROM FAT) FAT 3.4G (SAT 1.1G) PROTEIN 25.8G
CARBOHYDRATE 20.7G FIBER 0.8G CHOLESTEROL 95MG SODIUM 733MG
EXCHANGES PER SERVING: 4 VERY LEAN MEAT, 1 FRUIT

Serve with garlic mashed potatoes and asparagus.

Grill-and-Chill Taco Salad

Grill-and-Chill Taco Salad

prep: 10 minutes   chill: 10 minutes to 8 hours   cook: 8 minutes

1 large sweet red pepper

1 teaspoon chili powder

¼ teaspoon salt

¼ teaspoon ground black pepper

4 (4-ounce) skinned, boned chicken breast halves

Vegetable cooking spray

1 (15-ounce) can black beans, drained and rinsed

¼ cup finely chopped onion

¼ cup fat-free Catalina dressing

¼ cup chutney

4 cups shredded iceberg lettuce

½ cup (2 ounces) shredded reduced-fat Cheddar cheese

24 no-oil baked tortilla chips

1 Cut four sides lengthwise from red pepper, leaving stem ends and seeds intact. Discard stem and seeds. Combine chili powder, salt, and ¼ teaspoon black pepper; sprinkle evenly over chicken and pepper quarters.

2 Coat grill rack with cooking spray; place on grill over medium-hot coals (350° to 400°). Place chicken and pepper quarters on rack; grill, covered, 4 to 5 minutes on each side or until chicken is done and pepper is tender. Cool slightly; slice chicken and pepper quarters into strips.

3 Combine chicken and pepper strips, beans, and next 3 ingredients in a large bowl; toss well. Cover and chill 10 minutes or until ready to serve. To serve, place 1 cup lettuce on each of 4 individual serving plates. Arrange chicken mixture evenly over lettuce, and sprinkle each serving with 2 tablespoons cheese. Arrange 6 tortilla chips on each salad plate.
Yield: 4 servings.

PER SERVING: CALORIES 433 (15% FROM FAT) FAT 7.2G (SAT 2.6G) PROTEIN 38.6G CARBOHYDRATE 53.3G FIBER 5.7G CHOLESTEROL 79MG SODIUM 770MG EXCHANGES PER SERVING: 3 LEAN MEAT, 3 STARCH, 2 VEGETABLE

Serve with *a fresh fruit compote.*

the easy way to cut red pepper strips

You won't find this technique in many books, but it's a fast, mess-free way to cut strips from peppers.

Slice off 4 sides of the pepper, being careful not to cut into the seedy center. Discard the stem and the seeds. Cut the quarters into strips.

Grilled Potato Salad

prep: 6 minutes   cook: 27 minutes

1½ pounds small round red
   potatoes, quartered

2 tablespoons water

¼ cup plus 2 tablespoons
   white vinegar

¼ cup plus 2 tablespoons
   no-salt-added chicken
   broth

2 tablespoons vegetable oil

1 teaspoon minced garlic
   (about 2 cloves)

1 small onion, thinly sliced

1 medium-size sweet red
   pepper, cut into
   1-inch-wide strips

1 medium-size green pepper,
   cut into 1-inch-wide
   strips

   Vegetable cooking spray

4 slices turkey bacon

1 Place potato in a 2-quart baking dish; add water. Cover with plastic wrap, and microwave at HIGH 7 to 9 minutes or until potato is almost tender, stirring once. Drain and pat dry with paper towels.

2 While potato is cooking, combine vinegar and next 3 ingredients in a jar; cover tightly, and shake vigorously. Set aside.

3 Place potato, onion, and pepper strips in a grill basket coated with cooking spray; coat vegetables with cooking spray. Place turkey bacon slices over vegetables. Place grill basket on grill rack, bacon side up, over medium-hot coals (350° to 400°). Grill, covered, 15 to 20 minutes or until vegetables are tender, turning once.

4 Place grilled vegetables in a large bowl; crumble bacon slices over vegetables. Shake vinegar dressing to mix, and pour over vegetables; toss well. Let stand 5 minutes before serving, stirring occasionally. Yield: 10 (½-cup) servings.

PER SERVING: CALORIES 93 (25% FROM FAT) FAT 2.6G (SAT 0.5G) PROTEIN 2.9G
CARBOHYDRATE 15.3G FIBER 2.1G CHOLESTEROL 4MG SODIUM 92MG
EXCHANGES PER SERVING: 1 STARCH, ½ FAT

Serve with *oven-fried chicken and creamy coleslaw.*

technique for grilling vegetables

A grill basket is the key to adding a smoky grilled flavor to cut vegetables. Here's how:

Coat a grill basket with vegetable cooking spray to prevent the vegetables from sticking.

Place strips of turkey bacon over the vegetables. Extra flavor drizzles over the vegetables as the bacon cooks.

Squash and Onion Grill

prep: 5 minutes   cook: 10 minutes

½ cup reduced-fat Italian
   dressing

½ teaspoon dried tarragon

½ teaspoon garlic powder

   Vegetable cooking spray

2 medium-size yellow squash
   (about 5 inches long),
   cut in half lengthwise

2 medium zucchini (about
   5 inches long), cut in
   half lengthwise

1 medium-size purple onion,
   cut into 4 slices

1 Combine first 3 ingredients; stir well. Set aside.

2 Coat grill rack with cooking spray; place on grill over medium-hot coals (350° to 400°). Place yellow squash, zucchini, and onion on rack; grill, covered, 5 minutes on each side, basting occasionally with dressing mixture.
Yield: 4 servings (1 squash half, 1 zucchini half, and 1 onion slice per serving).

PER SERVING: CALORIES 68 (16% FROM FAT) FAT 1.2G (SAT 0.2G) PROTEIN 3.3G
CARBOHYDRATE 13.4G FIBER 3.4G CHOLESTEROL 0MG SODIUM 327MG
EXCHANGES PER SERVING: 2 VEGETABLE

Serve with *grilled or broiled lemon chicken and basmati rice.*

Grilled Mushroom Kabobs

prep: 5 minutes   cook: 4 minutes

12 large, fresh mushrooms

 3 tablespoons low-sodium
    soy sauce

 2 tablespoons reduced-calorie
    margarine, melted

½ teaspoon garlic powder

   Vegetable cooking spray

1 Thread mushrooms on 4 (8-inch) metal skewers; set aside. Combine soy sauce, margarine, and garlic powder. Brush half of soy sauce mixture on mushrooms.

2 Coat grill rack with cooking spray; place on grill over medium-hot coals (350° to 400°). Place kabobs on rack; grill, covered, 4 to 5 minutes or until mushrooms are tender, turning and basting occasionally with remaining soy sauce mixture.
Yield: 4 servings.

PER SERVING: CALORIES 35 (57% FROM FAT) FAT 2.2G (SAT 0.3G) PROTEIN 1.2G
CARBOHYDRATE 2.9G FIBER 0.7G CHOLESTEROL 0MG SODIUM 225MG
EXCHANGES PER SERVING: 1 VEGETABLE, ½ FAT

Serve with *grilled flank steak, red potatoes, and a tossed green salad with fat-free vinaigrette dressing.*

Grilled Herbed Corn on the Cob

Grilled Herbed Corn on the Cob

prep: 15 minutes   cook: 15 minutes

6   ears fresh corn in husks

3   tablespoons reduced-calorie
    margarine, melted

1½ tablespoons finely chopped
    fresh oregano or 1½
    teaspoons dried oregano
    or thyme

¾   teaspoon ground pepper

¼   teaspoon salt

1 Carefully peel back husks, exposing corn and leaving husks attached. Remove and discard silks. Soak corn and husks in cold water 5 minutes to prevent husks from burning. Remove corn from water; drain and pat excess water from corn and husks with paper towels.

2 Combine margarine and remaining 3 ingredients; stir well. Brush evenly over corn, using all of margarine mixture. Return husks to original position, and tie tips with heavy string.

3 Grill corn, covered, over medium-hot coals (350° to 400°) 15 minutes or until tender, turning occasionally.
Yield: 6 servings.

PER SERVING: CALORIES 101 (41% FROM FAT) FAT 4.6G (SAT 0.7G) PROTEIN 2.7G
CARBOHYDRATE 15.8G FIBER 2.7G CHOLESTEROL 0MG SODIUM 165MG
EXCHANGES PER SERVING: 1 STARCH, 1 FAT

Serve with spicy grilled fish and broccoli with lemon wedges.

Grilled Balsamic Onions with Pineapple Chutney

prep: 7 minutes   cook: 15 minutes

2 large onions
  (about 1½ pounds)

Vegetable cooking spray

¼ cup mango chutney
  (such as Major Grey)

¼ cup drained, crushed
  pineapple in juice

3 tablespoons balsamic
  vinegar, divided

1 Peel onions, and slice each into 4 slices. Place onion slices in a single layer in a 13- x 9- x 2-inch baking dish coated with cooking spray. Cover and microwave at HIGH 5 minutes.

2 While onion cooks, combine chutney and pineapple; stir well. Set aside.

3 Remove onion slices from dish, and place in a single layer on 2 large pieces of aluminum foil coated with cooking spray. Brush onion slices evenly with half of vinegar; wrap tightly in aluminum foil.

4 Place foil packets, seam sides down, on grill rack over medium-hot coals (350° to 400°). Grill, covered, 10 minutes; turn packets. Open packets, and brush onion slices evenly with remaining vinegar. Top each slice with 1 tablespoon chutney mixture. Loosely wrap slices; grill 5 additional minutes or until onion is glazed and crisp-tender.
Yield: 4 servings.

PER SERVING: CALORIES 115 (5% FROM FAT)   FAT 0.6G (SAT 0.1G)   PROTEIN 2.2G   CARBOHYDRATE 27.1G   FIBER 3.4G   CHOLESTEROL 0MG   SODIUM 40MG   EXCHANGES PER SERVING: 2 VEGETABLE, 1 FRUIT

Serve with *grilled pork tenderloin and squash strips.*

foil packets for grilling

Vegetables that are difficult to cook directly on the grill can be cooked in foil packets. They still pick up some smoky flavor, and you can open the packets for basting and adding ingredients.

Place onion slices on foil sheets the size of a large paper towel. Bring the sides together and fold them together to seal. Place the foil packets directly on the grill rack.

Grilled Pound Cake with Peach Sauce

prep: 5 minutes   cook: 2 minutes

1 (16-ounce) package frozen peaches, thawed, or 3 cups sliced fresh peaches

¼ cup honey

½ teaspoon almond extract

1 (16-ounce) loaf fat-free pound cake

Vegetable cooking spray

1 cup fat-free frozen whipped topping, thawed

1 Combine first 3 ingredients; set aside.

2 Cut cake into 8 slices. Coat grill rack with cooking spray; place on grill over medium-hot coals (350° to 400°). Place cake slices on rack; grill, covered, 1 minute on each side or until toasted. Place 1 cake slice on each of 8 individual serving plates. Top cake slices evenly with peach mixture and whipped topping.
Yield: 8 servings.

PER SERVING: CALORIES 202 (0% FROM FAT) FAT 0.1G (SAT 0.0G) PROTEIN 2.4G
CARBOHYDRATE 46.0G FIBER 0.9G CHOLESTEROL 0MG SODIUM 165MG
EXCHANGES PER SERVING: 1 STARCH, 2 FRUIT

***Serve with** grilled beef or turkey burgers and coleslaw.*

Grilled Pear Fantasia

prep: 6 minutes   cook: 8 minutes

3 firm, ripe, unpeeled pears

3 tablespoons honey

2 tablespoons unsweetened orange juice

Vegetable cooking spray

¾ cup seedless raspberry jam

1½ cups vanilla low-fat frozen yogurt

1 Core pears; cut each in half lengthwise. Combine honey and orange juice; brush some of the honey mixture over cut surfaces of pear halves, reserving remaining honey mixture.

2 Coat grill rack with cooking spray; place on grill over medium-hot coals (350° to 400°). Place pears on rack; grill, covered, 4 to 5 minutes on each side or until tender, basting occasionally with remaining honey mixture. While pears grill, spoon raspberry jam into a small saucepan; cook over low heat, stirring constantly, until melted.

3 Place hot or room temperature pear halves onto 6 individual plates. Top each with 2 tablespoons melted raspberry jam and ¼ cup frozen yogurt.
Yield: 6 servings.

PER SERVING: CALORIES 149 (8% FROM FAT) FAT 1.3G (SAT 0.6G) PROTEIN 1.6G
CARBOHYDRATE 34.9G FIBER 2.0G CHOLESTEROL 4MG SODIUM 25MG
EXCHANGES PER SERVING: 1 STARCH, 1 FRUIT

***Serve with** grilled herbed chicken breast halves and a spinach salad with fat-free red wine vinaigrette dressing.*

Grilled Pound Cake with Peach Sauce

appetizers & beverages

No-Chop Antipasto Tray (page 38)

Festive Cranberry-Cream Cheese Spread

prep: 5 minutes

1 (8-ounce) package nonfat
cream cheese

1 (12-ounce) container
cranberry-raspberry
crushed fruit for chicken
(Ocean Spray)

2 tablespoons amaretto
(optional)

2 tablespoons chopped
pecans

1 Place cream cheese on a serving plate. Combine crushed fruit and amaretto, if desired, and spoon over cream cheese.

2 Spread pecans in a pieplate, and microwave, uncovered, at HIGH 1 to 2 minutes, or until lightly toasted, stirring once. Sprinkle pecans over crushed fruit mixture. Serve immediately.
Yield: 2 cups.

PER TABLESPOON: CALORIES 31 (9% FROM FAT) FAT 0.3G (SAT 0.0G) PROTEIN 1.0G
CARBOHYDRATE 5.1G FIBER 0.3G CHOLESTEROL 1MG SODIUM 48MG
EXCHANGE PER TABLESPOON (UP TO 3 TABLESPOONS): FREE

Serve with fat-free crackers in an appetizer menu of sliced roast turkey with mustard and miniature rolls and fresh-cut vegetables with a creamy reduced-fat dressing dip.

RECIPE tip

For a creamier texture, you can substitute reduced-fat cream cheese for nonfat, but calories and fat will be higher.

Tuna Salad Spread

prep: 17 minutes

1 (6½-ounce) can solid white
tuna in spring water,
drained and flaked

1 cup canned cannellini
beans, rinsed and
drained

½ cup seeded, finely chopped
tomato

¼ cup finely chopped onion

1 teaspoon finely chopped
fresh basil or ¼
teaspoon dried basil

1 teaspoon olive oil

1 tablespoon Dijon mustard

1 tablespoon balsamic vinegar

1 Combine all ingredients; stir well. Serve immediately or cover and chill up to 1 hour.
Yield: 2½ cups.

PER TABLESPOON: CALORIES 13 (21% FROM FAT) FAT 0.3G (SAT 0.0G) PROTEIN 1.3G
CARBOHYDRATE 1.1G FIBER 0.2G CHOLESTEROL 2MG SODIUM 26MG
EXCHANGE PER TABLESPOON (UP TO 4 TABLESPOONS): FREE

Serve with toast rounds, fat-free wheat crackers, or endive leaves in an appetizer menu of a low-fat antipasto tray and fresh fruit with reduced-fat cream cheese mixed with pineapple preserves.

Blue Cheese-Almond Pears

prep: 14 minutes

¼ cup chopped almonds

1 (8-ounce) package nonfat
    cream cheese, softened

¼ cup nonfat sour cream

¼ cup crumbled blue cheese

1 tablespoon honey

6 firm, ripe, unpeeled pears

¼ cup lemon juice

1 Spread almonds in a pieplate, and microwave, uncovered, at HIGH 2 to 3 minutes or until lightly toasted, stirring after every minute. Set aside.

2 Beat cream cheese at medium speed of an electric mixer until creamy. Add sour cream, blue cheese, and honey, beating until smooth. Serve immediately or cover and chill, if desired.

3 Core pears; cut each into 10 wedges. Brush cut sides of pears with lemon juice. Spoon 1 teaspoon blue cheese mixture onto each pear wedge; top evenly with almonds.
Yield: 60 appetizers.

PER APPETIZER: CALORIES 19 (24% FROM FAT)   FAT 0.6G (SAT 0.1G)   PROTEIN 0.9G
CARBOHYDRATE 3.1G   FIBER 0.5G   CHOLESTEROL 1MG   SODIUM 30MG
EXCHANGE PER APPETIZER (UP TO 3 APPETIZERS): FREE

Serve with an appetizer menu of ham-wrapped steamed asparagus, chilled potato slices topped with nonfat sour cream and pimiento, spinach-stuffed mushrooms, and strawberries with lemon yogurt dip.

RECIPE tip

For variety, serve the blue cheese mixture on endive leaves, and sprinkle with almonds. Or use it as a sandwich topping on turkey burgers. The blue cheese mixture is 20 calories per tablespoon.

Pineapple-Raisin Cream Cheese Dip

prep: 4 minutes

½ (8-ounce) package nonfat
    cream cheese, softened

¼ cup pineapple preserves

1 tablespoon raisins

1 In a small bowl, beat cream cheese at medium speed of an electric mixer until creamy. Add preserves, mixing well. Stir in raisins. Serve immediately, or, if desired, cover and chill.
Yield: ¾ cup.

PER TABLESPOON: CALORIES 27 (0% FROM FAT)   FAT 0.0G (SAT 0.0G)   PROTEIN 1.4G
CARBOHYDRATE 5.3G   FIBER 0.0G   CHOLESTEROL 2MG   SODIUM 60MG
EXCHANGE PER TABLESPOON (UP TO 3 TABLESPOONS): FREE

Serve with apple and pear wedges, bagels, or gingersnaps in a tailgate appetizer menu of chicken salad, chilled spinach tortellini with marinara sauce, and red and green grapes.

Fruit Kabobs with Lemon Curd Dip

prep: 15 minutes

1 large lemon

1 (8-ounce) carton vanilla nonfat yogurt

2 tablespoons lemon curd

2 large bananas

2 kiwifruit, peeled

2 cups fresh or canned pineapple chunks, drained

8 fresh strawberries, halved

1 tablespoon sugar

1 Grate and juice lemon, reserving juice and 2 teaspoons rind.

2 Combine 1 teaspoon lemon rind, yogurt, and lemon curd in a small bowl.

3 Peel bananas, and cut into 1-inch slices; add lemon juice, and toss well. Cut kiwifruit in half lengthwise; cut into ½-inch slices. Thread banana, kiwifruit, pineapple, and strawberries on 6-inch bamboo skewers. Combine sugar and remaining 1 teaspoon lemon rind; sprinkle over fruit kabobs, coating evenly. Serve with lemon curd dip. Yield: 8 appetizer servings (1 skewer of fruit and 2 tablespoons dip per serving).

PER APPETIZER SERVING: CALORIES 107 (5% FROM FAT)   FAT 0.6G (SAT 0.1G)
PROTEIN 2.5G CARBOHYDRATE 24.8G   FIBER 2.9G   CHOLESTEROL 1MG   SODIUM 23MG
EXCHANGES PER SERVING: 1 STARCH, ½ FRUIT

***Serve with** a tea party menu of cucumber-cream cheese finger sandwiches, miniature currant muffins, and hot tea with honey and lemon.*

WORK-saver

To make the best use of a fresh lemon, first grate the rind, and then extract the juice. To get the most juice from a lemon, let it come to room temperature, and then roll it on the counter with your palm, pressing firmly on the lemon.

Fruit Kabobs with Lemon Curd Dip

Roasted Pepper Salsa Dip

prep: 13 minutes   chill: 30 minutes

1 (14.5-ounce) can chunky pasta-style tomatoes, undrained

⅔ cup drained finely chopped roasted sweet red pepper (packed in water)

½ cup thinly sliced green onions (about 2 large)

¼ cup finely chopped fresh cilantro or parsley

1 teaspoon minced garlic (about 2 cloves)

1 to 2 teaspoons hot sauce

1 Combine all ingredients, stirring well. Cover and chill at least 30 minutes.
Yield: 2½ cups.

PER TABLESPOON: CALORIES 6 (0% FROM FAT)   FAT 0.0G (SAT 0.0G)   PROTEIN 0.1G
CARBOHYDRATE 1.5G   FIBER 0.2G   CHOLESTEROL 0MG   SODIUM 58MG
EXCHANGE PER TABLESPOON (UP TO 3 TABLESPOONS): FREE

***Serve with** no-oil baked tortilla chips in a lunch menu of chicken salad and fresh fruit slices.*

Baked Greek-Style Bean Dip

prep: 7 minutes   cook: 25 minutes

2 (15.8-ounce) cans Great Northern beans, drained and rinsed

1 (8-ounce) package nonfat cream cheese

4 ounces crumbled reduced-fat feta cheese

1½ teaspoons minced garlic (about 3 cloves)

2 tablespoons lemon juice

1 tablespoon chopped fresh oregano or 1 teaspoon dried oregano

½ teaspoon ground pepper

¼ teaspoon salt

½ cup seeded, finely chopped tomato

¼ cup sliced ripe olives

1 Position knife blade in food processor bowl. Add first 8 ingredients, and process until smooth, scraping sides of processor bowl once. Spoon into a 1½-quart baking dish. Cover and bake at 350° for 25 minutes or until thoroughly heated.

2 Sprinkle tomato and olives over dip before serving.
Yield: 3¾ cups.

PER TABLESPOON: CALORIES 19 (19% FROM FAT)   FAT 0.4G (SAT 0.2G)   PROTEIN 1.7G
CARBOHYDRATE 2.3G   FIBER 0.4G   CHOLESTEROL 1MG   SODIUM 86MG
EXCHANGE PER TABLESPOON (UP TO 3 TABLESPOONS): FREE

***Serve with** pita wedges or bagel chips in an appetizer menu of tabbouleh-stuffed cherry tomatoes, marinated artichokes, garlic breadsticks with marinara sauce, and low-fat lemon cookies.*

TIME-saver

You can make this recipe up to 24 hours in advance. Prepare the bean mixture; cover and chill. Let mixture stand at room temperature 30 minutes, and bake at 350° for 35 to 40 minutes.

Layered Black Bean Dip

prep: 20 minutes   chill: 8 hours

1 teaspoon minced garlic
(about 2 cloves)

2 (15-ounce) cans no-salt-
added black beans,
rinsed and drained

¼ cup canned no-salt-added
chicken broth

3 tablespoons lemon juice

1 teaspoon ground cumin

1 (8-ounce) carton nonfat
sour cream

¾ cup (3 ounces) shredded
fat-free Cheddar cheese

½ cup seeded, finely chopped
tomato

½ cup thinly sliced green
onions (about 2 large)

¼ cup loosely packed fresh
cilantro or parsley
leaves, finely chopped

1 Position knife blade in food processor bowl; top with cover. Drop garlic through food chute with processor running; process until garlic is minced. Add beans and next 3 ingredients; process until smooth, stopping once to scrape down sides.

2 Spread bean mixture in a shallow serving dish. Spread sour cream over mixture. Cover and chill at least 8 hours.

3 Just before serving, layer cheese and remaining 3 ingredients over sour cream.
Yield: 2½ cups.

PER TABLESPOON: CALORIES 36 (3% FROM FAT) FAT 0.1G (SAT 0.0G) PROTEIN 2.9G CARBOHYDRATE 5.7G FIBER 0.9G CHOLESTEROL 0MG SODIUM 30MG
EXCHANGE PER TABLESPOON: 1 VEGETABLE

Serve with no-oil baked tortilla chips in an appetizer menu of fresh vegetable dippers with turkey salad spread, sliced fresh fruit with lime-poppy seed dip, and brownies.

South-of-the-Border Dip

prep: 5 minutes   cook: 15 minutes

1 (16-ounce) can fat-free
refried beans

½ cup hot salsa

Vegetable cooking spray

¼ cup (1 ounce) shredded
reduced-fat sharp
Cheddar cheese

1 Combine beans and salsa; stir well. Spoon mixture into an 11- x 7- x 1½-inch baking dish coated with cooking spray. Cover and bake at 350° for 10 minutes. Uncover, sprinkle with cheese, and bake at 350° for 5 minutes or until cheese melts.
Yield: 1½ cups.

PER TABLESPOON: CALORIES 34 (8% FROM FAT) FAT 0.3G (SAT 0.1G) PROTEIN 2.2G CARBOHYDRATE 5.6G FIBER 1.9G CHOLESTEROL 1MG SODIUM 163MG
EXCHANGE PER TABLESPOON: 1 VEGETABLE

Serve with vegetables or no-oil baked tortilla chips in a dinner menu of fajitas with chopped fresh vegetables and fat-free flour tortillas, and a fresh citrus salad.

No-Chop Antipasto Tray

prep: 8 minutes   cook: 6 minutes

1 (9-ounce) package
   refrigerated spinach
   tortellini

1 (12-ounce) jar pepperoncini
   peppers, undrained

1 (16-ounce) package fresh
   broccoli flowerets

1 (16-ounce) package fresh
   baby carrots

1 (14-ounce) can quartered
   artichoke hearts, drained

1 (8.5-ounce) package sliced
   turkey pepperoni

2 tablespoons Dijon mustard

1 tablespoon olive oil

18 (6-inch-long) thin
   breadsticks

1 Cook tortellini according to package directions, omitting salt and fat; drain. Drain peppers, reserving 3 tablespoons liquid.

2 Arrange peppers, tortellini, broccoli, and next 3 ingredients on a large platter. Combine reserved pepper liquid, mustard, and olive oil; stir well. Drizzle mustard mixture over antipasto; serve immediately with breadsticks or, if desired, cover and chill.
Yield: 18 appetizer servings.

PER APPETIZER SERVING: CALORIES 121 (27% FROM FAT) FAT 3.6G (SAT 1.0G)
PROTEIN 7.4G CARBOHYDRATE 15.2G FIBER 1.3G CHOLESTEROL 13MG SODIUM 508MG
EXCHANGES PER SERVING: ½ HIGH-FAT MEAT, 1 STARCH

Serve with *a dinner party menu of grilled chicken with marinara sauce, garlic green beans, fresh tomato slices, and Italian bread.*

Note: Using convenience products makes this easy appetizer tray higher in sodium than most. Still, it's light compared to 747 milligrams of sodium and 20.6 grams of fat for a traditional antipasto serving.

Skewered Tortellini with Ranch-Style Dip

prep: 21 minutes   cook: 6 minutes   chill: 1 hour

1 (16-ounce) carton nonfat
   sour cream

1 (1-ounce) envelope Ranch-
   style dressing mix

½ cup fresh basil leaves

3 tablespoons fat-free milk

36 refrigerated cheese-filled
   tortellini (about half
   of a 9-ounce package)

3 medium-size sweet red
   peppers, seeded and
   cut into 1-inch pieces

3 medium zucchini, cut into
   ½-inch-thick slices

1 Combine first 4 ingredients in container of an electric blender or food processor; cover and process until smooth. Transfer mixture to a bowl; cover and chill at least 1 hour.

2 Cook tortellini according to package directions, omitting salt and fat. Drain; rinse with cold water, and drain again. Thread 2 tortellini alternately with pepper pieces and zucchini slices onto 18 (6-inch) wooden skewers. Serve with Ranch-style dip.
Yield: 18 appetizer servings (1 skewer and 1½ tablespoons dip per serving).

PER APPETIZER SERVING: CALORIES 51 (7% FROM FAT) FAT 0.4G (SAT 0.2G)
PROTEIN 3.4G CARBOHYDRATE 7.5G FIBER 0.3G CHOLESTEROL 0MG SODIUM 162MG
EXCHANGE PER SERVING: ½ STARCH

Serve with *an appetizer menu of warm crostini with herbed chopped tomato and reduced-fat mozzarella cheese, marinated mushrooms, and spinach dip with low-fat crackers.*

No-Chop Antipasto Tray

Black Bean and Corn Quesadillas

1 cup (4 ounces) shredded reduced-fat Monterey Jack cheese

¾ cup canned no-salt-added black beans, rinsed and drained

½ cup frozen whole-kernel corn, thawed

⅓ cup chopped onion

⅓ cup finely chopped fresh cilantro

4 (8-inch) fat-free flour tortillas

¾ cup seeded, finely chopped tomato

¾ cup salsa

¼ cup nonfat sour cream

¼ cup finely chopped fresh cilantro

prep: 16 minutes   cook: 8 minutes

1 Combine first 5 ingredients in a small bowl; toss lightly. Lightly brush tortillas with water. Divide bean mixture evenly among tortillas, arranging just off-center of each. Fold tortilla in half. Place on a large baking sheet. Bake at 400° for 8 to 10 minutes or until cheese melts and tortillas are crisp.

2 Cut each quesadilla into 3 wedges. Top each wedge with 1 tablespoon tomato, 1 tablespoon salsa, 1 teaspoon sour cream, and 1 teaspoon cilantro.
Yield: 12 appetizers.

PER APPETIZER: CALORIES 94 (19% FROM FAT)   FAT 2.0G (SAT 1.1G)   PROTEIN 5.5G CARBOHYDRATE 13.8G   FIBER 1.5G   CHOLESTEROL 6MG   SODIUM 223MG
EXCHANGES PER APPETIZER: ½ LEAN MEAT, 1 STARCH

Serve with a dinner menu of chicken stew, jicama-orange salad, and corn sticks.

Black Bean and Corn Quesadillas

Zucchini and Cheddar Puffs

prep: 15 minutes   cook: 22 minutes

1 cup water

2 tablespoons reduced-calorie margarine

1 cup all-purpose flour

1 teaspoon garlic salt

¾ cup fat-free egg substitute

½ cup finely shredded zucchini

¼ cup (1 ounce) shredded reduced-fat Cheddar cheese

Vegetable cooking spray

1 Combine water and margarine in a medium saucepan; bring to a boil. Reduce heat; add flour and garlic salt, stirring vigorously over low heat until mixture leaves sides of pan and forms a smooth ball, about 1 minute. Remove from heat.

2 Add egg substitute to flour mixture, beating with a wooden spoon until smooth. Stir in zucchini and cheese.

3 Drop by heaping tablespoonfuls onto a baking sheet coated with cooking spray. Bake at 400° for 22 to 24 minutes or until puffed and golden.
Yield: 2 dozen appetizers.

PER APPETIZER: CALORIES 32 (25% FROM FAT)   FAT 0.9G (SAT 0.2G)   PROTEIN 1.7G   CARBOHYDRATE 4.2G   FIBER 0.2G   CHOLESTEROL 1MG   SODIUM 116MG   EXCHANGE PER APPETIZER: 1 VEGETABLE

Serve with a brunch menu of ham frittata, melon balls with poppy seed dressing, and banana bread.

Bruschetta with Tomato and Garlic

superquick

prep: 7 minutes   cook: 3 minutes

8 (½-inch-thick) slices French bread

1 teaspoon olive oil

1¼ cups chopped plum tomato (about 3)

1½ teaspoons minced garlic (about 3 cloves)

1 teaspoon balsamic vinegar

½ teaspoon dried basil or 1½ teaspoons finely chopped fresh basil

¼ teaspoon sugar

¼ teaspoon ground pepper

1 Place bread slices on an ungreased baking sheet; brush bread slices evenly with olive oil. Bake at 500° for 3 to 4 minutes or until lightly browned.

2 While bread bakes, combine tomato and remaining 5 ingredients in a small bowl; stir well. Spoon mixture evenly over toasted bread slices.
Yield: 8 appetizers.

PER APPETIZER: CALORIES 72 (14% FROM FAT)   FAT 1.1G (SAT 0.2G)   PROTEIN 2.1G   CARBOHYDRATE 13.0G   FIBER 0.9G   CHOLESTEROL 1MG   SODIUM 121MG   EXCHANGE PER APPETIZER: 1 STARCH

Serve with an appetizer menu of boiled, chilled shrimp, spinach-cheese dip with crackers, and marinated mushrooms.

5 Fast Lemonade Drinks

With one recipe of lemonade syrup that's stored in the fridge you can make five beverages—from steaming to frozen—in just 10 minutes or less.

Make-Ahead Lemonade Syrup

prep: 10 minutes   chill: 4 hours

2½ cups water
1⅓ cups sugar
1⅓ cups fresh lemon juice

Combine water and sugar in a heavy saucepan; cook over medium heat, stirring constantly, until sugar dissolves. Remove from heat, and cool to room temperature. Stir in fresh lemon juice; cover and chill at least 4 hours. Store in refrigerator up to 4 days.
Yield: 4½ cups.

Pucker Up Lemonade

prep: 2 minutes

Combine ½ cup chilled Make-Ahead Lemonade Syrup and ½ cup water. Pour into a glass filled with crushed ice. Garnish with a fresh lemon slice, if desired.
Yield: 1 (1-cup) serving.

Per Serving: Calories 123 (0% from fat) Fat 0.0g (Sat 0.0g) Protein 0.1g Carbohydrate 32.6g Fiber 0.0g Cholesterol 0mg Sodium 1mg
Exchanges Per Serving: 1 Starch, 1 Fruit

Pucker Up Lemonade Spritzer

prep: 5 minutes

Combine ½ cup chilled Make-Ahead Lemonade Syrup and ½ cup chilled club soda. Serve over ice cubes, and garnish with fresh mint leaves, if desired. Serve immediately.
Yield: 1 (1-cup) serving.

Per Serving: Calories 123 (0% from fat) Fat 0.0g (Sat 0.0g) Protein 0.1g Carbohydrate 32.6g Fiber 0.0g Cholesterol 0mg Sodium 26mg
Exchanges Per Serving: 1 Starch, 1 Fruit

Strawberry-Lemonade Slush

prep: 10 minutes

Combine 1½ cups sliced fresh strawberries, ⅔ cup chilled Make-Ahead Lemonade Syrup, and 1 tablespoon sifted powdered sugar in container of an electric blender. Add 2 cups ice cubes; cover and process until smooth. Pour mixture evenly into chilled glasses.
Yield: 3 (1-cup) servings.

PER SERVING: CALORIES 92 (3% FROM FAT) FAT 0.3G (SAT 0.0G) PROTEIN 0.6G CARBOHYDRATE 23.5G FIBER 2.4G CHOLESTEROL 0MG SODIUM 1MG **EXCHANGES PER SERVING:** 1½ FRUIT

Lemon Dessert Float

prep: 5 minutes

Place ½ cup vanilla nonfat frozen yogurt in a tall glass; pour ½ cup chilled Make-Ahead Lemonade Syrup and ½ cup club soda over yogurt. Garnish with a maraschino cherry, if desired. Serve immediately.
Yield: 1 (1-cup) serving.

PER SERVING: CALORIES 198 (0% FROM FAT) FAT 0.0G (SAT 0.0G) PROTEIN 3.3G CARBOHYDRATE 49.2G FIBER 0.0G CHOLESTEROL 0MG SODIUM 81MG **EXCHANGES PER SERVING:** 3 STARCH

Warm Bourbon Lemonade

prep: 5 minutes   cook: 1 minute

Combine 1 cup Make-Ahead Lemonade Syrup and ¾ cup plus 2 tablespoons water in a 4-cup glass measure; microwave at HIGH 1 to 1½ minutes or until hot. Stir in 2 tablespoons bourbon. Garnish with a cinnamon stick, if desired.
Yield: 2 (1-cup) servings.

PER SERVING: CALORIES 156 (0% FROM FAT) FAT 0.0G (SAT 0.0G) PROTEIN 0.1G CARBOHYDRATE 32.6G FIBER 0.0G CHOLESTEROL 0MG SODIUM 1MG **EXCHANGES PER SERVING:** 1 STARCH, 1 FRUIT

Lemon-Ginger Tea Cooler

prep: 5 minutes   chill: 1 hour

1 lemon, thinly sliced

1½ cups water

3 regular-size red zinger tea bags

3 (⅛-inch) slices peeled gingerroot

¼ cup sugar

2⅔ cups ginger ale, chilled

Ice cubes

1 Reserve 4 lemon slices, and set aside. Combine remaining lemon slices, water, tea bags, and gingerroot in a medium saucepan. Bring to a boil; cover, reduce heat, and simmer 5 minutes. Remove from heat, and stir in sugar. Let cool completely; chill at least 1 hour.

2 Strain tea mixture, discarding tea bags, lemon slices, and gingerroot. Stir in ginger ale. Place ice cubes and reserved lemon slices in 4 glasses; pour tea over ice. Serve immediately.
Yield: 4 (1-cup) servings.

PER SERVING: CALORIES 103 (0% FROM FAT)   FAT 0.0G (SAT 0.0G)   PROTEIN 0.1G   CARBOHYDRATE 27.6G   FIBER 0.0G   CHOLESTEROL 0MG   SODIUM 9MG   **EXCHANGES PER SERVING:** 2 STARCH

RECIPE tip

Look for fresh gingerroot in the produce section of your supermarket. Peel only what you need, and then wrap the remainder of the root tightly in plastic wrap, and store it in the freezer. You can grate or slice it right from the freezer.

Limeade Sunset Slush

superquick

prep: 10 minutes

1 cup cranberry juice cocktail

1 (6-ounce) can frozen limeade concentrate, undiluted

2 cups ice cubes

1 cup ginger ale

1 Place ¼ cup cranberry juice in each of 4 glasses; set aside.

2 Place limeade in container of an electric blender. Add ice cubes; cover and process until smooth. Divide evenly among prepared glasses. Top each serving with ¼ cup ginger ale.
Yield: 4 (1-cup) servings.

PER SERVING: CALORIES 134 (1% FROM FAT)   FAT 0.1G (SAT 0.0G)   PROTEIN 0.1G   CARBOHYDRATE 34.9G   FIBER 0.2G   CHOLESTEROL 0MG   SODIUM 8MG   **EXCHANGES PER SERVING:** 2½ FRUIT

Pineapple-Banana Shake

prep: 9 minutes   freeze: 1 hour

1 (15¼-ounce) can pineapple chunks in juice, drained

1 large ripe banana, peeled and sliced

1½ cups vanilla nonfat frozen yogurt

1 cup fat-free milk

½ teaspoon vanilla extract

1 Combine pineapple and banana in an 8-inch square dish; toss well. Cover and freeze at least 1 hour.

2 Combine frozen fruit, yogurt, milk, and vanilla in container of an electric blender; cover and process until smooth, stopping once to scrape down sides. Serve immediately.
Yield: 4 (1-cup) servings.

PER SERVING: CALORIES 149 (4% FROM FAT) FAT 0.6G (SAT 0.2G) PROTEIN 5.1G CARBOHYDRATE 33.1G FIBER 2.2G CHOLESTEROL 1MG SODIUM 75MG EXCHANGES PER SERVING: 1 STARCH, 1 FRUIT

Papaya Cooler

superquick

prep: 11 minutes

1 ripe papaya (about 1 pound), peeled, seeded, and chopped

2 (12-ounce) cans apricot nectar, chilled

1¼ cups unsweetened orange juice, chilled

3 tablespoons fresh lime juice

⅓ cup sugar

½ cup light rum (for a non-alcoholic drink, omit rum and increase orange juice to 1¾ cups)

1½ cups sparkling water, chilled

1 Combine first 5 ingredients in container of an electric blender; cover and process until mixture is smooth and sugar is dissolved. Add rum. Cover and chill, if desired.

2 Just before serving, stir in sparkling water. Serve over ice cubes.
Yield: 8 (1-cup) servings.

PER SERVING: CALORIES 142 (1% FROM FAT) FAT 0.1G (SAT 0.0G) PROTEIN 0.8G CARBOHYDRATE 27.6G FIBER 1.0G CHOLESTEROL 0MG SODIUM 4MG EXCHANGES PER SERVING: 2 FRUIT

TIME-saver

For a cool make-ahead slush, freeze the pureed mixture for 8 hours. Spoon the mixture into glasses, and add sparkling water.

Chocolate-Caramel Royale Coffee

prep: 4 minutes

3¾ cups strongly brewed hot coffee

2 tablespoons fat-free caramel-flavored syrup

2 tablespoons chocolate-flavored syrup

½ teaspoon vanilla extract

1 Combine all ingredients, stirring until syrups dissolve. Pour 1 cup coffee mixture into each mug. Serve hot.
Yield: 4 (1-cup) servings.

PER SERVING: CALORIES 58 (2% FROM FAT) FAT 0.1G (SAT 0.0G) PROTEIN 0.5G CARBOHYDRATE 13.2G FIBER 0.0G CHOLESTEROL 0MG SODIUM 28MG EXCHANGE PER SERVING: 1 STARCH

RECIPE tip

Combine 2 tablespoons plus 1 teaspoon instant coffee granules and 3¾ cups hot water to make 3¾ cups strongly brewed coffee.

Chocolate-Caramel Café au Lait

prep: 3 minutes   cook: 9 minutes

¾ cup reduced-fat milk

2 tablespoons fat-free caramel-flavored syrup

2 tablespoons chocolate-flavored syrup

½ teaspoon vanilla extract

3 cups strongly brewed hot coffee

1 Combine first 3 ingredients in a small saucepan. Bring to a simmer over medium heat, stirring constantly. Remove from heat; stir in vanilla.

2 Pour ¾ cup brewed coffee into each mug. Add ¼ cup milk mixture to each mug, stirring well. Serve hot.
Yield: 4 (1-cup) servings.

PER SERVING: CALORIES 80 (11% FROM FAT) FAT 1.0G (SAT 0.6G) PROTEIN 2.0G CARBOHYDRATE 15.2G FIBER 0.0G CHOLESTEROL 4MG SODIUM 50MG EXCHANGE PER SERVING: 1 STARCH

RECIPE tip

Combine 2 tablespoons instant coffee granules and 3 cups hot water to make 3 cups strongly brewed coffee.

Mulled Cider Tea

6 regular-size red zinger tea
   bags

2½ cups water

4 whole allspice

4 whole cloves

2 (3-inch) sticks cinnamon

6 cups apple cider

prep: 3 minutes   cook: 10 minutes   chill: 1 hour

1 Combine tea bags and water in a medium saucepan; bring to a boil. Boil, uncovered, until liquid is reduced to 2 cups.

2 Remove tea bags, and stir in spices. Let cool; chill at least 1 hour. Remove and discard spices.

3 Combine tea mixture and apple cider in a large saucepan, stirring well. Place over medium heat until hot.
Yield: 8 (1-cup) servings.

PER SERVING: CALORIES 88 (2% FROM FAT)   FAT 0.2G (SAT 0.0G)   PROTEIN 0.1G
CARBOHYDRATE 21.8G   FIBER 0.4G   CHOLESTEROL 0MG   SODIUM 6MG
EXCHANGES PER SERVING: 1½ FRUIT

RECIPE tip

For an alcoholic version, stir 1 cup spiced rum into the entire recipe of cider tea or add 2 tablespoons spiced rum to each serving.

breads

Curried Peppercorn Rolls (page 58)

Whole Wheat Biscuits

prep: 8 minutes   rise: 10 minutes   cook: 10 minutes

½ cup warm nonfat buttermilk
   (105° to 115°)

1 package rapid-rise yeast

1¾ cups all-purpose flour

¾ cup whole wheat flour

1½ teaspoons baking powder

½ teaspoon baking soda

¼ teaspoon salt

2 teaspoons sugar

3 tablespoons reduced-calorie
   margarine

½ cup unsweetened
   applesauce

   Vegetable cooking spray

1 Combine buttermilk and yeast in a 1-cup liquid measuring cup; let stand 5 minutes.

2 Combine all-purpose flour and next 5 ingredients in a large bowl. Cut in margarine with a pastry blender until mixture is crumbly. Add buttermilk mixture and applesauce to flour mixture, stirring just until dry ingredients are moistened.

3 Turn dough out onto a lightly floured surface, and knead gently 3 or 4 times. Roll dough to ½-inch thickness; cut into rounds with a 2½-inch biscuit cutter. Place rounds on a baking sheet coated with cooking spray; cover and let rise in a warm place (85°), free from drafts, 10 minutes. Bake at 400° for 10 to 12 minutes. Yield: 1 dozen.

PER BISCUIT: CALORIES 120 (17% FROM FAT) FAT 2.2G (SAT 0.3G) PROTEIN 3.5G CARBOHYDRATE 22.1G FIBER 1.8G CHOLESTEROL 0MG SODIUM 213MG EXCHANGES PER BISCUIT: 1½ STARCH, ½ FAT

***Serve with** barbecued chicken, garlic mashed potatoes, and low-fat coleslaw.*

TIME-saver

Place cut, unbaked Whole Wheat Biscuits or Herb and Cheese Angel Biscuits (see page 50) on a cookie sheet and freeze them. Then store the frozen biscuits in a heavy-duty, zip-top plastic bag in the freezer. You can bake the biscuits right from the freezer at 400° for 12 to 15 minutes.

Herb and Cheese Angel Biscuits

prep: 13 minutes   rise: 10 minutes   cook: 14 minutes

1   cup nonfat buttermilk

2½   cups low-fat biscuit and
      baking mix

½   cup (2 ounces) shredded
      reduced-fat sharp
      Cheddar cheese

½   teaspoon fines herbes

¼   teaspoon garlic powder

1   package rapid-rise yeast

3   tablespoons reduced-calorie
      margarine

3   tablespoons all-purpose
      flour

     Vegetable cooking spray

1   tablespoon chopped fresh
      parsley or 1½ teaspoons
      dried parsley flakes

1   Place buttermilk in a 2-cup glass measure; microwave at HIGH 1 minute or until buttermilk reaches 130°.

2   Combine baking mix and next 4 ingredients in a large bowl; cut in margarine with a pastry blender until mixture resembles coarse meal. Add buttermilk, stirring with a fork just until dry ingredients are moistened.

3   Sprinkle flour evenly over work surface. Turn dough out onto floured surface, and knead 4 or 5 times. Roll dough to ½-inch thickness; cut into rounds with a 2½-inch biscuit cutter. Place rounds on a baking sheet coated with cooking spray. Coat rounds with cooking spray, and sprinkle with parsley. Cover and let rise in a warm place (85°), free from drafts, 10 minutes. Bake at 400° for 14 minutes or until biscuits are golden.
Yield: 1 dozen.

PER BISCUIT: CALORIES 140 (28% FROM FAT) FAT 4.4G (SAT 1.2G) PROTEIN 4.5G
CARBOHYDRATE 20.6G FIBER 0.2G CHOLESTEROL 4MG SODIUM 372MG
EXCHANGES PER BISCUIT: 1½ STARCH, 1 FAT

Serve with roasted chicken, brown rice, and broccoli.

Beer-Cheese Muffins

prep: 5 minutes   cook: 25 minutes

2½   cups low-fat biscuit and
      baking mix

½   cup cornmeal

¾   cup (3 ounces) shredded
      reduced-fat Cheddar
      cheese

½   cup chopped green onions
      (about 2 large)

2   teaspoons dry mustard

1   teaspoon dried dillweed

1   (12-ounce) can light beer

     Vegetable cooking spray

1   Combine first 6 ingredients; stir well. Add beer, stirring just until dry ingredients are moistened.

2   Spoon batter evenly into muffin pans coated with cooking spray, filling two-thirds full. Bake at 375° for 25 minutes or until golden. Remove from pans immediately.
Yield: 1½ dozen.

PER MUFFIN: CALORIES 94 (21% FROM FAT) FAT 2.2G (SAT 0.8G) PROTEIN 3.1G
CARBOHYDRATE 15.3G FIBER 0.4G CHOLESTEROL 3MG SODIUM 230MG
EXCHANGES PER MUFFIN: 1 STARCH, ½ FAT

Serve with tomato soup and a tossed green salad.

Chocolate-Peppermint Muffins

prep: 8 minutes   cook: 13 minutes

1 (7-ounce) package chocolate-chocolate chip muffin mix

⅓ cup fat-free milk

2 tablespoons unsweetened applesauce

1 egg, lightly beaten

⅓ cup crushed peppermint candy (about 12 round peppermint candies)

Vegetable cooking spray

1 Combine first 4 ingredients in a small bowl. Stir just until dry ingredients are moistened. Fold in peppermint candy.

2 Spoon batter into a muffin pan coated with cooking spray, filling two-thirds full. Bake at 425° for 13 to 15 minutes or until tops spring back when lightly touched. Remove from pan immediately.
Yield: 9 muffins.

PER MUFFIN: CALORIES 143 (21% FROM FAT) FAT 3.4G (SAT 1.2G) PROTEIN 2.4G CARBOHYDRATE 26.1G FIBER 0.7G CHOLESTEROL 25MG SODIUM 142MG EXCHANGES PER MUFFIN: 1½ STARCH, ½ FAT

Serve with *fat-free milk as a snack.*

WORK-saver

To crush peppermint candy, seal it in a heavy-duty, zip-top plastic bag and crush it with a smooth-bottomed meat mallet or a heavy rolling pin.

Chocolate-Peppermint Muffins

Cinnamon-Applesauce Muffins

prep: 5 minutes   cook: 15 minutes

1¾ cups self-rising flour

½ cup sugar

1½ teaspoons ground cinnamon

½ cup unsweetened
     applesauce

½ cup fat-free milk

2 tablespoons vegetable oil

1 egg, lightly beaten

   Vegetable cooking spray

1 Combine first 3 ingredients in a medium bowl. Make a well in center of mixture. Combine applesauce and next 3 ingredients; add to flour mixture, stirring just until dry ingredients are moistened.

2 Spoon batter evenly into muffin pans coated with cooking spray, filling three-fourths full. Bake at 400° for 15 minutes or until golden. Remove from pans immediately.
Yield: 1 dozen.

PER MUFFIN: CALORIES 132 (20% FROM FAT) FAT 3.0G (SAT 0.6G) PROTEIN 2.7G
CARBOHYDRATE 23.8G FIBER 0.7G CHOLESTEROL 19MG SODIUM 243MG
EXCHANGES PER MUFFIN: 1½ STARCH, ½ FAT

Serve with broiled pork loin chops, baked sweet potatoes, and green beans.

Ginger-Pineapple Muffins

prep: 5 minutes   cook: 12 minutes

1¾ cups all-purpose flour

1 teaspoon baking soda

¼ teaspoon salt

⅓ cup sugar

¼ teaspoon ground ginger

1 (8-ounce) can crushed
     pineapple in juice,
     drained

¼ cup fat-free milk

¼ cup fat-free egg substitute

3 tablespoons vegetable oil

   Vegetable cooking spray

1 Combine first 5 ingredients in a medium bowl; make a well in center of mixture. Combine pineapple and next 3 ingredients; add to flour mixture, stirring just until dry ingredients are moistened.

2 Spoon batter evenly into muffin pans coated with cooking spray, filling two-thirds full. Bake at 400° for 12 minutes or until golden. Remove from pans immediately.
Yield: 1 dozen.

PER MUFFIN: CALORIES 133 (26% FROM FAT) FAT 3.8G (SAT 0.7G) PROTEIN 2.6G
CARBOHYDRATE 22.0G FIBER 0.6G CHOLESTEROL 0MG SODIUM 165MG
EXCHANGES PER MUFFIN: 1½ STARCH, 1 FAT

Serve with broiled fish, basmati rice, and Parmesan zucchini.

Blueberry-Lemon Streusel Coffee Cake

prep: 10 minutes   cook: 27 minutes

1 (12½-ounce) package
   fat-free lemon snack
   cake mix

¾ cup water

¼ cup fat-free egg substitute

1 cup frozen blueberries

   Vegetable cooking spray

3 tablespoons firmly packed
   brown sugar

½ teaspoon ground cinnamon

2 tablespoons reduced-calorie
   margarine

1 Reserve ½ cup cake mix for topping. Combine remaining cake mix, water, and egg substitute; stir just until dry ingredients are moistened. Fold in blueberries. Pour batter into a 9-inch square pan coated with cooking spray.

2 Combine reserved cake mix, brown sugar, and cinnamon; cut in margarine with a pastry blender until mixture resembles coarse meal. Sprinkle mixture over batter in pan. Bake at 375° for 27 to 30 minutes or until golden. Cut into squares; serve warm.
Yield: 12 servings.

PER SERVING: CALORIES 141 (8% FROM FAT)   FAT 1.3G (SAT 0.2G)   PROTEIN 1.2G
CARBOHYDRATE 29.8G   FIBER 0.4G   CHOLESTEROL 0MG   SODIUM 200MG
EXCHANGES PER SERVING: 1 STARCH, 1 FRUIT

***Serve with** a brunch menu of mushroom-cheese omelets made with fat-free egg substitute, and roasted potato slices.*

RECIPE tip

We used Sweet Rewards brand of lemon snack cake mix
for this coffee cake.

Cherry Coffee Cake

Cherry Coffee Cake

prep: 15 minutes   cook: 20 minutes

½ (32-ounce) package frozen
bread dough, thawed

Vegetable cooking spray

½ cup ⅓-less-fat cream cheese
(Neufchâtel), softened

2 tablespoons sugar, divided

1 teaspoon vanilla extract

⅓ cup dried cherries

1½ tablespoons honey

1 tablespoon fat-free milk

½ cup sifted powdered sugar

2½ teaspoons fat-free milk

¼ teaspoon vanilla extract

1 Roll dough into a 12- x 8-inch rectangle on a baking sheet coated with cooking spray.

2 Combine cream cheese, 1 tablespoon sugar, and 1 teaspoon vanilla, stirring well. Spoon cheese mixture lengthwise down center third of dough. Sprinkle cherries over cheese mixture; drizzle with honey.

3 Along 12-inch sides of rectangle, cut 12 (1-inch-wide) strips from edge of filling to edge of dough. Fold strips, alternating sides, at an angle across filling. Brush top of dough with 1 tablespoon milk. Sprinkle with remaining 1 tablespoon sugar. Bake at 375° for 20 minutes or until golden.

4 Combine powdered sugar, 2½ teaspoons milk, and ¼ teaspoon vanilla, stirring well. Drizzle sugar mixture over warm coffee cake. Yield: 12 servings.

PER SERVING: CALORIES 186 (17% FROM FAT) FAT 3.6G (SAT 1.4G) PROTEIN 4.6G CARBOHYDRATE 34.0G FIBER 0.3G CHOLESTEROL 8MG SODIUM 226MG EXCHANGES PER SERVING: 1 STARCH, 1 FRUIT, 1 FAT

Serve with a breakfast menu of scrambled fat-free egg substitute with chives, and turkey bacon.

step-by-step for braided bread

The braided top of Cherry Coffee Cake makes it look special enough for the fanciest occasion. Braiding dough is easy; use floured hands to keep the dough from sticking and follow these simple steps.

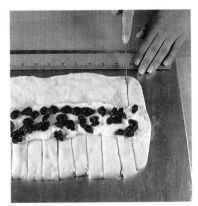

Spread the filling down the center of the dough. Cut 1-inch-wide strips on each side of the filling, starting at the edge of the filling and cutting to the outer side of the dough.

Alternating sides, fold the strips across the filling, pulling the ends at a downward angle. Tuck the edges of the last strips under the coffee cake. Sprinkle with sugar.

Drizzle the top of the warm coffee cake with the powdered sugar glaze.

Cornmeal Pancakes with Maple-Fruit Butter

prep: 12 minutes   stand: 15 minutes   cook: 7 minutes

Maple-Fruit Butter

½ cup all-purpose flour

½ cup yellow cornmeal

1 teaspoon baking powder

½ teaspoon baking soda

2 tablespoons brown sugar

1⅓ cups nonfat buttermilk

¼ cup fat-free egg substitute

1 tablespoon vegetable oil

Vegetable cooking spray

1 Prepare Maple-Fruit Butter. Set aside.

2 Combine flour and next 4 ingredients in a medium bowl; make a well in center of mixture. Combine buttermilk, egg substitute, and oil; add to flour mixture, stirring just until dry ingredients are moistened. Let batter stand 5 minutes.

3 Coat a nonstick griddle with cooking spray, and preheat to 350°. For each pancake, pour ¼ cup batter onto hot griddle. Cook pancakes until tops are covered with bubbles and edges look cooked; turn pancakes, and cook other sides. Serve each pancake with 1 tablespoon Maple-Fruit Butter, reserving remaining fruit butter for another use. Yield: 12 (4-inch) pancakes (1 pancake plus 1 tablespoon fruit butter per serving).

PER SERVING: CALORIES 97 (16% FROM FAT) FAT 1.7G (SAT 0.3G) PROTEIN 2.8G CARBOHYDRATE 18.0G FIBER 0.8G CHOLESTEROL 1MG SODIUM 132MG EXCHANGE PER SERVING: 1 STARCH

Serve with *warm cinnamon applesauce.*

Maple-Fruit Butter

½ cup pitted prunes

½ cup dried fruit bits

½ cup unsweetened orange juice

⅓ cup reduced-calorie maple-flavored pancake syrup

¼ teaspoon ground cinnamon

1 Combine first 3 ingredients in a small saucepan; bring to a boil. Cover, remove from heat, and let stand 10 minutes.

2 Position knife blade in food processor bowl; add fruit mixture. Process until smooth. Add syrup and cinnamon; process until smooth. Cover, and store in refrigerator. Yield: 1¼ cups.

PER TABLESPOON: CALORIES 31 (3% FROM FAT) FAT 0.1G (SAT 0.0G) PROTEIN 0.3G CARBOHYDRATE 7.1G FIBER 0.1G CHOLESTEROL 0MG SODIUM 7MG EXCHANGE PER TABLESPOON: ½ FRUIT

RECIPE tip

Maple-Fruit Butter looks like thick, dark apple butter. It's also delicious served with waffles, English muffins, or toast.

Cheese Grits Corn Sticks

prep: 7 minutes   cook: 15 minutes

1 (6-ounce) package buttermilk cornbread mix

¼ cup (1 ounce) shredded reduced-fat Cheddar cheese

¼ cup quick-cooking grits, uncooked

1½ cups nonfat buttermilk

2 tablespoons fat-free egg substitute

1 tablespoon vegetable oil

Vegetable cooking spray

1 Combine first 3 ingredients in a medium bowl; make a well in center of mixture. Combine buttermilk, egg substitute, and oil; add to dry ingredients, stirring just until dry ingredients are moistened.

2 Place 2 cast-iron corn stick pans coated with cooking spray in a 425° oven for 3 minutes or until hot. Remove pans from oven; spoon batter evenly into pans. Bake at 425° for 15 to 17 minutes or until golden. Remove from pans, and serve warm.
Yield: 14 corn sticks.

PER CORN STICK: CALORIES 88 (29% FROM FAT) FAT 2.8G (SAT 0.7G) PROTEIN 2.8G CARBOHYDRATE 12.4G FIBER 0.2G CHOLESTEROL 2MG SODIUM 208MG EXCHANGES PER CORN STICK: 1 STARCH, ½ FAT

Serve with *vegetable soup or chili.*

Moist Buttermilk Cornbread

prep: 7 minutes   cook: 25 minutes

Vegetable cooking spray

1 cup yellow self-rising cornmeal mix

1 small onion, chopped

½ cup nonfat buttermilk

2 tablespoons vegetable oil

1 (8¾-ounce) can no-salt-added cream-style corn

¼ cup fat-free egg substitute

1 Coat a 9-inch cast-iron skillet with cooking spray. Place skillet in a 400° oven.

2 Combine cornmeal mix and onion; stir well. Combine buttermilk and remaining 3 ingredients; add to dry ingredients, stirring just until moistened.

3 Remove skillet from oven; pour batter into skillet. Bake at 400° for 25 minutes or until golden.
Yield: 8 servings.

PER SERVING: CALORIES 120 (32% FROM FAT) FAT 4.2G (SAT 0.8G) PROTEIN 3.3G CARBOHYDRATE 18.5G FIBER 0.6G CHOLESTEROL 1MG SODIUM 220MG EXCHANGES PER SERVING: 1 STARCH, 1 FAT

Serve with *baked catfish, low-fat coleslaw, and herbed oven-roasted potato wedges.*

Curried Peppercorn Rolls

prep: 7 minutes   cook: 16 minutes

2 tablespoons creamy mustard blend

½ teaspoon coarsely ground pepper

¼ teaspoon curry powder

1 (11-ounce) can refrigerated breadstick dough

Vegetable cooking spray

1 Combine first 3 ingredients, stirring well.

2 Unroll breadstick dough onto work surface, being careful not to separate dough. Spread mustard mixture evenly over dough. Separate dough into 8 strips. Coil each strip of dough into a spiral shape. Place on a baking sheet coated with cooking spray. Bake at 350° for 16 to 18 minutes or until lightly browned.
Yield: 8 rolls.

PER ROLL: CALORIES 115 (20% FROM FAT)   FAT 2.6G (SAT 0.5G)   PROTEIN 3.0G   CARBOHYDRATE 18.9G   FIBER 0.1G   CHOLESTEROL 0MG   SODIUM 343MG   EXCHANGES PER ROLL: 1 STARCH, ½ FAT

Serve with *broiled lamb chops, couscous, and a spinach-onion salad with fat-free vinaigrette.*

RECIPE tip

We used Hellman's Dijonnaise for the creamy mustard blend in this recipe. It has no fat, no cholesterol, and only 5 calories per teaspoon.

Curried Peppercorn Rolls

Cinnamon Rolls

prep: 22 minutes   rise: 30 minutes   cook: 20 minutes

1 (16-ounce) package hot roll
     mix with yeast packet

1 cup hot water (120° to 130°)

¼ cup sugar

1 tablespoon reduced-calorie
     margarine, softened

1 egg, lightly beaten

2 tablespoons all-purpose
     flour, divided

2 tablespoons reduced-calorie
     margarine, softened

⅓ cup sugar

2 teaspoons ground cinnamon

2 tablespoons raisins

    Vegetable cooking spray

¾ cup sifted powdered sugar

1 tablespoon fat-free milk

1 Combine roll mix and yeast packet in a large bowl. Add hot water and next 3 ingredients. Stir just until dry ingredients are moistened; shape dough into a ball.

2 Sprinkle 1½ tablespoons flour evenly over work surface. Turn dough out onto floured surface. Knead until smooth and elastic (about 5 minutes). Cover and let rest 5 minutes.

3 Sprinkle remaining 1½ teaspoons flour evenly over work surface. Roll dough into a 16- x 10-inch rectangle on floured surface; spread 2 tablespoons margarine over dough. Combine ⅓ cup sugar and cinnamon; sprinkle over dough. Sprinkle with raisins.

4 Roll up dough, jellyroll fashion, beginning at long side. Pinch seam to seal. Cut roll into 1-inch slices; place 8 slices, cut sides down, into each of 2 (8-inch) round cakepans coated with cooking spray. Cover and let rise in a warm place (85°), free from drafts, 30 minutes or until doubled in bulk.

5 Bake at 375° for 20 to 22 minutes or until golden. Combine powdered sugar and milk; drizzle glaze over warm rolls.
Yield: 16 rolls.

Per Roll: Calories 188 (16% from fat)   Fat 3.4g (Sat 0.3g)   Protein 3.8g
Carbohydrate 35.8g   Fiber 0.2g   Cholesterol 16mg   Sodium 142mg
Exchanges Per Roll: 2 Starch, 1 Fat

Serve with *a breakfast menu of raspberry nonfat yogurt, crisp apple slices, and low-fat cheese.*

✳ TIME-saver

These rolls are ready to rise and bake if you prepare the dough a day in advance. Place the sliced rolls in the pans, cover, and refrigerate up to 24 hours. Then remove the pans from the refrigerator, allow the rolls to rise, and bake as directed.

Poppy Seed-Swiss Cheese Rolls

prep: 25 minutes   rise: 45 minutes   cook: 15 minutes

1 (16-ounce) package hot roll
   mix with yeast packet

1 cup (4 ounces) shredded
   reduced-fat Swiss cheese

1 tablespoon poppy seeds

2 teaspoons dry mustard

½ teaspoon garlic powder

1 cup hot water (120° to 130°)

2 tablespoons reduced-calorie
   margarine, melted

2 teaspoons Worcestershire
   sauce

1 large egg, lightly beaten

   Vegetable cooking spray

1 Combine roll mix, yeast packet, and next 4 ingredients in a large bowl; stir well. Combine water and next 3 ingredients; add to dry ingredients, stirring just until dry ingredients are moistened.

2 Turn dough out onto a lightly floured surface, and knead until smooth and elastic (about 5 minutes). Place in a bowl coated with cooking spray, turning to coat top. Cover and let rest 5 minutes.

3 Divide dough into 20 equal portions. Shape each portion into a ball, and place balls in a 13- x 9- x 2-inch pan coated with cooking spray. Cover and let rise in a warm place (85°), free from drafts, 45 minutes or until doubled in bulk. Bake at 375° for 15 to 18 minutes or until golden.
Yield: 20 rolls.

PER ROLL: CALORIES 120 (27% FROM FAT) FAT 3.6G (SAT 0.8G) PROTEIN 4.9G CARBOHYDRATE 16.8G FIBER 0.1G CHOLESTEROL 16MG SODIUM 122MG
EXCHANGES PER ROLL: 1 STARCH, ½ FAT

Serve with grilled sirloin steak, baked potatoes, and a tossed green salad.

Basil-Feta Focaccia

prep: 12 minutes   stand: 5 minutes   cook: 15 minutes

1 (6.5-ounce) package pizza
   crust mix

⅔ cup crumbled feta cheese

½ cup finely chopped onion

1 tablespoon finely chopped
   fresh basil or 1 teaspoon
   dried basil

1 teaspoon garlic powder

½ teaspoon ground pepper

½ cup hot water (120° to 130°)

   Vegetable cooking spray

1 Combine first 6 ingredients in a bowl; add hot water, stirring vigorously with a fork until blended. Coat dough with cooking spray; cover and let stand 5 minutes.

2 Press into a 10-inch circle on a baking sheet coated with cooking spray. Bake at 450° for 15 minutes or until golden. Cut into wedges.
Yield: 8 wedges.

PER WEDGE: CALORIES 106 (20% FROM FAT) FAT 2.3G (SAT 1.2G) PROTEIN 3.8G CARBOHYDRATE 17.9G FIBER 0.7G CHOLESTEROL 7MG SODIUM 213MG
EXCHANGES PER WEDGE: 1 STARCH, ½ FAT

Serve with toasted polenta slices with marinara sauce, and asparagus.

Herbed Cheese French Bread

prep: 10 minutes   cook: 5 minutes

½ cup part-skim ricotta cheese

1 tablespoon chopped fresh parsley or 1 teaspoon dried parsley flakes

1 teaspoon minced garlic (about 2 cloves)

½ teaspoon fines herbes

   Dash of ground red pepper

2 green onions, chopped

1 (16-ounce) loaf French bread

1 Combine first 6 ingredients; stir well. Slice bread in half lengthwise. Spread cheese mixture evenly over cut sides of bread.

2 Broil 5½ inches from heat (with electric oven door partially opened) for 5 minutes or until bread is lightly browned.
Yield: 16 servings.

PER SERVING: CALORIES 94 (11% FROM FAT)   FAT 1.2G (SAT 0.6G)   PROTEIN 3.5G
CARBOHYDRATE 16.3G   FIBER 0.7G   CHOLESTEROL 3MG   SODIUM 175MG
EXCHANGE PER SERVING: 1 STARCH

Serve with red beans and rice.

TIME-saver

To have bread ready to bake, wrap one or both loaf halves in foil before broiling, and freeze them. Bake frozen loaf halves at 350° for 15 minutes.

Herbed Cheese French Bread

Peppered Garlic Bread

prep: 5 minutes   cook: 15 minutes

1 (16-ounce) round loaf
   sourdough bread

¼ cup nonfat mayonnaise

2 tablespoons grated
   Parmesan cheese

1½ teaspoons ground
   pepper

1½ teaspoons garlic powder

1 Slice bread vertically into 10 slices, cutting to, but not through, bottom of loaf. Slice 6 longest slices in half for a total of 16 slices.

2 Spread one side of each bread slice evenly with mayonnaise; sprinkle with cheese, pepper, and garlic powder. Wrap loaf in aluminum foil, sealing edges. Bake at 350° for 15 minutes or until warm and toasted.
Yield: 16 servings.

PER SERVING: CALORIES 77 (9% FROM FAT) FAT 0.8G (SAT 0.1G) PROTEIN 2.9G CARBOHYDRATE 14.7G FIBER 0.5G CHOLESTEROL 0MG SODIUM 215MG EXCHANGE PER SERVING: 1 STARCH

Serve with grilled chicken or pork, a tossed green salad, and fresh strawberries and peaches.

RECIPE tip

You can substitute a 16-ounce oblong loaf of French bread for the round loaf of sourdough.

Hummus French Bread

superquick

prep: 5 minutes   cook: 10 minutes

1 (16-ounce) loaf French
   bread, split horizontally

1 (15-ounce) can garbanzo
   beans (chickpeas),
   drained

¼ cup nonfat sour cream

1½ teaspoons minced garlic
   (about 3 cloves)

1 teaspoon ground cumin

1 teaspoon fresh lemon juice

⅛ teaspoon salt

1 Place bread halves on a baking sheet. Bake at 350° for 10 minutes or until lightly toasted.

2 While bread bakes, position knife blade in food processor bowl; add beans and remaining 5 ingredients. Process 1 minute or until smooth, stopping once to scrape down sides. Spread bean mixture evenly on cut sides of bread, and slice. Yield: 16 servings.

PER SERVING: CALORIES 128 (11% FROM FAT) FAT 1.5G (SAT 0.3G) PROTEIN 4.9G CARBOHYDRATE 23.6G FIBER 1.1G CHOLESTEROL 1MG SODIUM 247MG EXCHANGES PER SERVING: 1½ STARCH

Serve with rosemary chicken, carrots, and lemon broccoli.

desserts

Orange and Cranberry Granita Compote (page 75)

Fresh Berries with Sour Cream Sauce

superquick

prep: 7 minutes

2 cups sliced fresh
    strawberries

2 cups fresh blueberries

1 (8-ounce) carton nonfat
    sour cream

2 tablespoons brown sugar

⅛ teaspoon ground cinnamon

Fresh mint sprigs (optional)

1 Combine strawberries and blueberries; spoon ½ cup fruit mixture into each of 8 individual dessert bowls.

2 Combine sour cream, brown sugar, and cinnamon; stir well. Spoon sour cream mixture evenly over fruit. Garnish with mint sprigs, if desired.
Yield: 8 servings.

PER SERVING: CALORIES 65 (4% FROM FAT) FAT 0.3G (SAT 0.0G) PROTEIN 2.5G
CARBOHYDRATE 13.1G FIBER 3.0G CHOLESTEROL 0MG SODIUM 24MG
EXCHANGE PER SERVING: 1 FRUIT

Serve with grilled chicken, herbed rice, and squash medley.

Strawberry-Rhubarb Sauce

superquick   make ahead

prep: 5 minutes   cook: 5 minutes

⅔ cup sugar

1 tablespoon cornstarch

2 tablespoons water

2 tablespoons light corn syrup

2 cups finely chopped fresh
    rhubarb (about 2 stalks)

2 cups sliced fresh
    strawberries

1 teaspoon vanilla extract

1 Combine first 4 ingredients in a large saucepan; stir well. Stir in rhubarb and strawberries. Bring to a boil over medium-high heat, stirring often. Reduce heat, and simmer, uncovered, 5 minutes or until sauce is thickened and fruit is tender, stirring often. Remove from heat, and let cool; stir in vanilla.

2 Serve sauce over low-fat frozen yogurt, angel food cake, or fresh fruit. Store sauce covered in the refrigerator for up to 1 week.
Yield: 2 cups plus 2 tablespoons sauce.

PER 2 TABLESPOONS: CALORIES 47 (2% FROM FAT) FAT 0.1G (SAT 0.0G)
PROTEIN 0.2G CARBOHYDRATE 11.7G FIBER 0.5G CHOLESTEROL 0MG SODIUM 4MG
EXCHANGE PER 2 TABLESPOONS: 1 FRUIT

Serve with oven-roasted herbed chicken, honeyed carrots, and a tossed green salad.

RECIPE tip

Make this recipe in the spring when rhubarb is in season, or use chopped frozen rhubarb.

Chocolate-Raspberry Smoothie

prep: 8 minutes

1⅓ cups fat-free milk

1½ cups chocolate nonfat
frozen yogurt, softened

⅓ cup sifted powdered sugar

⅓ cup Chambord or raspberry
nectar

2 tablespoons unsweetened
cocoa

1⅓ cups frozen unsweetened
raspberries

1 Place milk in container of an electric blender; add yogurt, powdered sugar, Chambord, and cocoa. Cover and process until smooth, stopping twice to scrape down sides.

2 With blender running, remove center cap from cover, and drop raspberries into yogurt mixture; replace cap, and process until smooth. Pour into chilled glasses. Serve immediately.
Yield: 4 (1-cup) servings.

PER SERVING: CALORIES 202 (3% FROM FAT)   FAT 0.7G (SAT 0.3G)   PROTEIN 6.3G
CARBOHYDRATE 38.1G   FIBER 2.7G   CHOLESTEROL 2MG   SODIUM 85MG
EXCHANGES PER SERVING: 2 STARCH, ½ FRUIT

Serve as a dessert beverage with beef and bean tostadas and a citrus salad.

Upside-Down Brownie Splits

prep: 8 minutes

2 cups strawberry low-fat
frozen yogurt

1 firm, ripe banana, peeled
and sliced

2 (1.4-ounce) fat-free
chocolate brownies

¼ cup fat-free chocolate-
flavored syrup

1 Scoop ½ cup yogurt into each of 4 individual dessert dishes. Top evenly with sliced banana.

2 Microwave brownies at HIGH 30 seconds or until warm. Crumble brownies evenly over sliced banana. Top each serving with 1 tablespoon chocolate syrup. Serve immediately.
Yield: 4 servings.

PER SERVING: CALORIES 233 (8% FROM FAT)   FAT 2.2G (SAT 1.3G)   PROTEIN 4.6G
CARBOHYDRATE 51.0G   FIBER 1.4G   CHOLESTEROL 9MG   SODIUM 75MG
EXCHANGES PER SERVING: 2 STARCH, 1 FRUIT, 1 FAT

Serve with baked potatoes stuffed with black beans, salsa, reduced-fat cheese, and nonfat sour cream and a fresh fruit salad.

Pineapple Sherbet Clouds

prep: 13 minutes

8 (½-inch-thick) slices angel food cake, torn into bite-size pieces

4 cups pineapple sherbet

½ cup lemon curd

½ cup fresh blueberries, blackberries, or raspberries

1 Place angel food cake pieces evenly into 8 individual dessert dishes.

2 Scoop ½ cup sherbet over cake in each dish; top each serving with 1 tablespoon lemon curd and 1 tablespoon berries. Serve immediately.
Yield: 8 servings.

PER SERVING: CALORIES 207 (5% FROM FAT) FAT 1.1G (SAT 0.5G) PROTEIN 2.0G CARBOHYDRATE 50.0G FIBER 0.6G CHOLESTEROL 3MG SODIUM 103MG
EXCHANGES PER SERVING: 2 STARCH, 1 FRUIT

Serve with *baked orange roughy or flounder, baked potatoes, and broccoli-carrot medley.*

Seven-Minute Frozen Peach Yogurt

prep: 7 minutes

1 (16-ounce) package frozen unsweetened sliced peaches

⅓ cup sugar

1 cup vanilla low-fat yogurt

¼ teaspoon almond extract

1 Position knife blade in food processor bowl; add half of frozen peaches. Process until fruit is chopped. Remove chopped peaches. Repeat procedure with remaining half of peaches; scrape sides of processor bowl. Return chopped peaches to processor bowl. Add sugar, yogurt, and almond extract; process until smooth. Serve immediately.
Yield: 7 (½-cup) servings.

PER SERVING: CALORIES 93 (5% FROM FAT) FAT 0.5G (SAT 0.3G) PROTEIN 2.0G CARBOHYDRATE 21.2G FIBER 1.0G CHOLESTEROL 2MG SODIUM 21MG
EXCHANGES PER SERVING: ½ STARCH, 1 FRUIT

Serve with *barbecued chicken, mashed potatoes with chives, and marinated vegetable salad.*

✳ RECIPE tip

For a cherry variation, substitute 1 (16-ounce) package frozen dark sweet pitted cherries for the peaches.

Peanut Butter-Banana Pudding

make ahead

prep: 10 minutes   chill: 2 to 8 hours

1   (3.4-ounce) package regular
    or fat-free French vanilla
    instant pudding mix

2   cups fat-free milk

⅓   cup reduced-fat creamy
    peanut butter spread

1   (8-ounce) carton nonfat
    sour cream

42 reduced-fat vanilla wafers,
    divided

6   small bananas, divided

1   (8-ounce) carton frozen
    nonfat whipped
    topping, thawed

1 Prepare pudding mix according to package directions, using a whisk and 2 cups fat-free milk. (Do not use an electric mixer.) Add peanut butter and sour cream, stirring well with a wire whisk. Set aside.

2 Line bottom of a 2½-quart casserole with 14 vanilla wafers. Peel and slice 4 bananas. Top wafers with one-third each of pudding mixture, banana slices, and whipped topping. Repeat layers twice using remaining wafers, pudding mixture, banana slices, and whipped topping. Cover and chill at least 2 hours. To garnish, peel and slice remaining 2 bananas; arrange slices around outer edges of dish. Yield: 12 servings.

PER SERVING: CALORIES 235 (23% FROM FAT)   FAT 5.9G (SAT 1.2G)   PROTEIN 6.4G   CARBOHYDRATE 38.5G   FIBER 2.1G   CHOLESTEROL 1MG   SODIUM 280MG
EXCHANGES PER SERVING: 1½ STARCH, 1 FAT

Serve with chicken-vegetable stew and reduced-fat crackers.

RECIPE tip

Substitute reduced-fat chocolate wafers for vanilla wafers for a chocolate-peanut butter-banana pudding version.

White Chocolate Angel Trifle

make ahead

prep: 11 minutes   chill: 30 minutes to 8 hours

1   (3.4-ounce) package regular
    or fat-free white
    chocolate instant
    pudding mix

2   cups fat-free milk

½   cup seedless raspberry
    spreadable fruit

2   tablespoons amaretto or
    ¼ teaspoon almond
    extract

1   (10.5-ounce) angel food
    cake

3   tablespoons sliced almonds,
    toasted

1 Prepare pudding mix according to package directions, using a whisk and 2 cups fat-free milk; let stand 5 minutes.

2 Combine spreadable fruit and amaretto in a small bowl, stirring with a wire whisk until smooth; set aside.

3 Cut cake into 1-inch cubes. Arrange half of cake cubes in a 2-quart trifle bowl or straight-sided glass bowl; brush with half of fruit mixture. Spoon half of pudding over cake. Repeat layers with remaining cake, fruit mixture, and pudding. Sprinkle with toasted almonds. Cover and chill at least 30 minutes. Yield: 8 servings.

PER SERVING: CALORIES 221 (9% FROM FAT)   FAT 2.2G (SAT 0.2G)   PROTEIN 4.5G   CARBOHYDRATE 44.7G   FIBER 0.9G   CHOLESTEROL 1MG   SODIUM 342MG
EXCHANGES PER SERVING: 2 STARCH, 1 FRUIT, ½ FAT

Serve with chicken salad with grapes and apples, and breadsticks.

Peanut Butter-Banana Pudding

Ladyfinger-Coffee Parfaits

prep: 25 minutes   chill: 2 to 8 hours

1½ tablespoons instant coffee granules

1 tablespoon boiling water

2 cups fat-free milk

1 (3.4-ounce) package vanilla instant pudding mix

2 cups frozen reduced-calorie whipped topping, thawed and divided

2 (3-ounce) packages ladyfingers, split and divided

⅔ cup fat-free chocolate-flavored syrup, divided

Chocolate-coated espresso coffee beans (optional)

1 Dissolve coffee granules in 1 tablespoon boiling water; let cool slightly. Combine coffee mixture, milk, and pudding mix, stirring well with a wire whisk. Cover and chill 5 minutes.

2 Fold 1½ cups whipped topping into pudding mixture. Place half of ladyfinger halves in bottom of an 11- x 7- x 1½-inch baking dish. Spread half of pudding mixture over ladyfingers; drizzle with half of chocolate syrup. Repeat layers with remaining ladyfinger halves, pudding mixture, and chocolate syrup. Cover and chill at least 2 hours.

3 To serve, spoon evenly into 8 (6-ounce) parfait glasses. Top evenly with remaining ½ cup whipped topping. Garnish with espresso beans, if desired.
Yield: 8 servings.

PER SERVING: CALORIES 217 (6% FROM FAT) FAT 1.4G (SAT 0.5G) PROTEIN 4.6G CARBOHYDRATE 45.6G FIBER 0.3G CHOLESTEROL 39MG SODIUM 292MG EXCHANGES PER SERVING: 3 STARCH

Serve with *linguine with marinara sauce and Italian bread.*

RECIPE tip

For a stronger coffee flavor, use 1 tablespoon of espresso powder instead of the instant coffee granules.

Ladyfinger-Coffee Parfaits

Praline Parfaits

¼ cup reduced-calorie maple-flavored syrup

¼ cup fat-free caramel-flavored ice cream topping

¼ teaspoon vanilla, butter, and nut flavoring

1 tablespoon chopped pecans, toasted

2 cups vanilla nonfat frozen yogurt, softened

12 reduced-fat vanilla wafers, coarsely crushed and divided

¼ cup plus 2 tablespoons frozen reduced-calorie whipped topping, thawed

6 reduced-fat vanilla wafers

1 Combine first 3 ingredients in a microwave-safe bowl. Microwave at HIGH 30 seconds. Let cool slightly. Stir in pecans.

2 Spoon 1 cup yogurt evenly into 6 (6-ounce) parfait glasses. Top evenly with half of crushed wafers and half of syrup mixture. Repeat layers with remaining yogurt, crushed wafers, and syrup mixture. Freeze at least 1 hour or until firm.

3 To serve, top each parfait with 1 tablespoon whipped topping and a wafer.
Yield: 6 servings.

PER SERVING: CALORIES 170 (12% FROM FAT)   FAT 2.3G (SAT 0.6G)   PROTEIN 2.9G
CARBOHYDRATE 34.9G   FIBER 0.1G   CHOLESTEROL 0MG   SODIUM 126MG
EXCHANGES PER SERVING: 2 STARCH

Serve with *grilled flank steak, roasted potatoes, and lemon broccoli.*

RECIPE tip

It's important to use fat-free caramel-flavored topping instead of fat-free syrup. Fat-free syrup doesn't heat successfully.

Caramel Swirl Ice Box Cake

prep: 12 minutes   freeze: 8 hours

21 ladyfingers, split and
     divided

¾ cup frozen reduced-calorie
     whipped topping,
     thawed

3½ cups vanilla low-fat frozen
      yogurt, softened

½ cup fat-free caramel syrup,
    divided

1 (10-ounce) package frozen
    raspberries in light
    syrup, thawed

1 Line an 8½- x 4½- x 3-inch loafpan with plastic wrap, smoothing plastic wrap in corners and on sides of pan. Arrange one-third of ladyfinger halves, cut sides facing in, on bottom and around sides of loafpan; set aside.

2 Fold whipped topping into yogurt. Spoon half of yogurt mixture into prepared loafpan. Spoon ¼ cup caramel syrup over yogurt mixture. Swirl caramel syrup with a knife to create a marbled effect. Arrange half of remaining ladyfinger halves on top of caramel. Repeat layers with remaining yogurt mixture, remaining ¼ cup caramel syrup, and remaining ladyfinger halves. Cover and freeze at least 8 hours.

3 To serve, invert dessert onto a serving plate, carefully peeling away plastic wrap. Cut into 10 slices, and top evenly with raspberries. Yield: 10 servings.

PER SERVING: CALORIES 193 (12% FROM FAT) FAT 2.6G (SAT 1.5G) PROTEIN 3.8G CARBOHYDRATE 39.0G FIBER 2.2G CHOLESTEROL 32MG SODIUM 176MG EXCHANGES PER SERVING: 1½ STARCH, 1 FRUIT, ½ FAT

Serve with *chicken-cheese quesadillas and rice.*

TIME-saver

Use the microwave to thaw frozen reduced-calorie whipped topping and raspberries and to soften nonfat or low-fat frozen yogurt in seconds. Follow these times:

- To thaw a 4-ounce container of frozen reduced-calorie whipped topping, microwave it, uncovered, at MEDIUM-LOW (30%) for 1 to 2 minutes or until topping is thawed.
- To thaw frozen berries, place the berries in a medium bowl and microwave them, uncovered, at MEDIUM (50%) for 5 to 6 minutes or until the berries are thawed.
- To soften frozen yogurt, microwave the container of yogurt, uncovered, at MEDIUM-LOW (30%) for 20 seconds at a time until the yogurt is softened.

Orange and Cranberry Granita Compote

Orange and Cranberry Granita Compote

prep: 12 minutes   cook: 12 minutes   freeze: 8 hours

1½ cups unsweetened orange
    juice

1 cup plus 2 tablespoons
    sugar, divided

4 cups water, divided

1½ cups cranberry juice cocktail

1 tablespoon lemon juice

Fresh mint sprigs (optional)

1 Pour orange juice through a wire-mesh strainer into a bowl; discard pulp. Set juice aside.

2 Combine ½ cup sugar and 2 cups water in a small saucepan; bring to a boil over medium heat, stirring until sugar dissolves. Remove from heat, and stir into strained orange juice. Pour mixture into a 9-inch square pan; let cool completely. Cover and freeze at least 8 hours or until firm.

3 Combine remaining ½ cup plus 2 tablespoons sugar and 2 cups water in a small saucepan; bring to a boil over medium heat, stirring until sugar dissolves. Remove from heat, and stir in cranberry juice cocktail and lemon juice. Pour mixture into a 9-inch square pan; let cool completely. Cover and freeze at least 8 hours or until firm.

4 Cut frozen orange mixture into 1-inch cubes, and place in container of a food processor. Pulse, 1 second at a time, until mixture is fluffy. Repeat procedure with cranberry mixture. To serve, spoon ¼ cup orange granita into a (6-ounce) parfait glass; spoon ¼ cup cranberry granita over orange granita. Garnish with mint sprigs, if desired. Serve immediately.
Yield: 18 (½-cup) servings.

PER SERVING: CALORIES 70 (0% FROM FAT) FAT 0.0G (SAT 0.0G) PROTEIN 0.1G
CARBOHYDRATE 18.0G FIBER 0.0G CHOLESTEROL 0MG SODIUM 1MG
EXCHANGE PER SERVING: 1 FRUIT

***Serve with** roasted chicken, parslied rice, and broccoli.*

RECIPE tip

You can choose to make just one of the granita flavors for a 4½-cup yield. Or, double the ingredients for one flavor, divide the mixture into 2 (9-inch) cakepans, and freeze them.

Apple Cobbler

prep: 14 minutes   cook: 35 minutes

4 cups peeled and thinly sliced firm, tart apple (about 4 large apples)

⅓ cup unsweetened orange juice

⅔ cup sugar, divided

1 tablespoon cornstarch

½ teaspoon ground cinnamon

¼ teaspoon ground nutmeg

1 cup all-purpose flour

1½ teaspoons baking powder

¼ teaspoon salt

¼ cup stick margarine

½ cup fat-free milk

2 teaspoons sugar

1 Combine apple slices and orange juice in a large bowl; add ⅓ cup sugar and next 3 ingredients, stirring well. Spoon mixture into an 11- x 7- x 1½-inch baking dish; set aside.

2 Combine remaining ⅓ cup sugar, flour, baking powder, and salt; cut in margarine with a pastry blender until mixture resembles coarse meal. Add milk; stir with a fork just until dry ingredients are moistened.

3 Drop batter by 8 large spoonfuls over apple mixture; sprinkle 2 teaspoons sugar over cobbler. Bake at 375° for 35 minutes. Serve warm or at room temperature.
Yield: 8 servings.

PER SERVING: CALORIES 236 (23% FROM FAT) FAT 6.1G (SAT 1.2G) PROTEIN 2.4G CARBOHYDRATE 44.4G FIBER 2.6G CHOLESTEROL 0MG SODIUM 223MG EXCHANGES PER SERVING: 2 STARCH, 1 FRUIT, 1 FAT

Serve with chicken parmigiana, egg noodles, and garden peas.

Summer's Best Berry Crisp

prep: 15 minutes   cook: 30 minutes

3 cups fresh raspberries

3 cups fresh blueberries

¼ cup sugar

Vegetable cooking spray

2 teaspoons vanilla extract

¾ cup all-purpose flour

½ cup firmly packed dark brown sugar

¼ teaspoon pumpkin pie spice

¼ cup plus 2 tablespoons reduced-calorie stick margarine

½ cup regular oats, uncooked

1 Combine berries and ¼ cup sugar in a 2-quart baking dish coated with cooking spray. Stir lightly; sprinkle with vanilla.

2 Combine flour, brown sugar, and pumpkin pie spice in a medium bowl. Cut in margarine with a pastry blender until mixture resembles coarse meal. Add oats; toss well. Sprinkle topping over berry mixture.

3 Bake, uncovered, at 400° for 30 minutes. Serve warm.
Yield: 8 servings.

PER SERVING: CALORIES 241 (24% FROM FAT) FAT 6.4G (SAT 0.9G) PROTEIN 2.8G CARBOHYDRATE 45.5G FIBER 6.6G CHOLESTEROL 0MG SODIUM 92MG EXCHANGES PER SERVING: 1 STARCH, 2 FRUIT, 1 FAT

Serve with chicken-mushroom-sweet red pepper kabobs, basmati rice, and marinated squash salad.

Orange-Baked Pears with Gingersnaps

prep: 10 minutes   cook: 35 minutes

2 (16-ounce) cans pear halves
   in juice, drained

½ cup apricot preserves

⅓ cup unsweetened orange
   juice

1 tablespoon lemon juice

2 teaspoons sugar

½ cup coarsely chopped
   gingersnap cookies
   (about 8 cookies)

1 tablespoon brown sugar

1 tablespoon reduced-calorie
   stick margarine, cut into
   small pieces

2½ cups vanilla low-fat frozen
   yogurt

1 Arrange pear halves, cut sides down, in an 11- x 7- x 1½-inch baking dish.

2 Combine preserves and next 3 ingredients in a small bowl; pour over pear halves. Combine gingersnaps, brown sugar, and margarine. Sprinkle over pear mixture. Bake at 375° for 35 minutes or until lightly browned.

3 To serve, spoon pear mixture into individual dessert dishes. Top each serving with ¼ cup frozen yogurt.
Yield: 10 servings.

PER SERVING: CALORIES 153 (13% FROM FAT) FAT 2.2G (SAT 0.9G) PROTEIN 1.6G
CARBOHYDRATE 31.5G FIBER 0.7G CHOLESTEROL 6MG SODIUM 42MG
EXCHANGES PER SERVING: 1 STARCH, 1 FRUIT

Serve with *roasted pork tenderloin, brown rice, and steamed asparagus.*

RECIPE tip

You can find the crisp, wafer-thin gingersnap cookies that work best for this recipe in the specialty cookie area of your supermarket.

Chocolate-Peanut Butter Bread Pudding

prep: 10 minutes   cook: 45 minutes

4 (1-ounce) slices reduced-
   calorie white bread,
   lightly toasted and cut
   into 1-inch cubes

Vegetable cooking spray

¼ cup semisweet chocolate
   mini-morsels

1 cup fat-free milk

¼ cup firmly packed light
   brown sugar

¼ cup fat-free egg substitute

2 tablespoons creamy peanut
   butter

1 Place toasted bread cubes in a 1-quart baking dish coated with cooking spray; sprinkle with chocolate morsels.

2 Combine milk and remaining 3 ingredients in container of an electric blender; cover and process until smooth. Pour milk mixture over bread mixture; let stand 5 minutes. Bake at 350° for 45 to 50 minutes or until pudding is firm. Serve warm.
Yield: 4 servings.

PER SERVING: CALORIES 233 (27% FROM FAT)   FAT 7.1G (SAT 2.0G)   PROTEIN 8.5G   CARBOHYDRATE 35.2G   FIBER 1.1G   CHOLESTEROL 2MG   SODIUM 243MG
EXCHANGES PER SERVING: 2 STARCH, 1 FAT

Serve with *grilled pork chops, corn on the cob, and coleslaw.*

TIME-saver

Dry, stale bread is ideal for this recipe. If you don't have any, use toasted bread slices.

Vanilla Pound Cake

prep: 10 minutes   cook: 1 hour and 10 minutes

Butter-flavored vegetable
  cooking spray

1 tablespoon fine, dry
  breadcrumbs

¼ cup plus 2 tablespoons stick
  margarine, softened

1½ cups sugar

¾ cup fat-free egg substitute

1 teaspoon vanilla extract

½ teaspoon almond extract

½ teaspoon baking soda

¾ cup reduced-fat sour cream

2 cups sifted cake flour

¼ teaspoon salt

1 Coat an 8½- x 4½- x 3-inch loafpan with cooking spray. Dust pan with breadcrumbs. Set aside.

2 Beat margarine at medium speed of an electric mixer until creamy; gradually add sugar, beating well. Add egg substitute and flavorings; beat well.

3 Stir baking soda into sour cream. Combine flour and salt; add to margarine mixture alternately with sour cream mixture, beginning and ending with flour mixture. Mix at low speed just until blended after each addition.

4 Pour batter into prepared pan. Bake at 325° for 1 hour and 10 minutes or until a wooden pick inserted in center comes out clean. Cool in pan 10 minutes. Remove cake from pan, and cool completely on a wire rack.
Yield: 16 servings.

PER SERVING: CALORIES 183 (28% FROM FAT)   FAT 5.7G (SAT 1.7G)   PROTEIN 2.7G
CARBOHYDRATE 30.4G   FIBER 0.4G   CHOLESTEROL 4MG   SODIUM 151MG
EXCHANGES PER SERVING: 2 STARCH, 1 FAT

Serve with meat loaf, garlic mashed potatoes, and herbed green beans.

RECIPE tip

For an almond-flavored cake, substitute ½ teaspoon almond extract for 1 teaspoon vanilla extract.

Turtle Cupcakes

prep: 10 minutes   cook: 25 minutes

1 (20.5-ounce) package low-fat fudge brownie mix

¼ cup finely chopped pecans

Vegetable cooking spray

⅓ cup fat-free caramel-flavored ice cream topping

1 Prepare brownie mix according to package directions; stir in pecans.

2 Place paper baking cups in muffin pans, and coat with cooking spray. Spoon half of batter into cups, filling each about one-third full. Spoon 1 teaspoon caramel topping into center of each cupcake. In each cup, drop 1 teaspoon batter from tip of a spoon, guiding the dripping batter around the caramel topping. Top evenly with remaining batter. Bake at 350° for 25 minutes. Remove from pans, and let cool completely on wire racks.
Yield: 16 cupcakes.

PER CUPCAKE: CALORIES 194 (20% FROM FAT) FAT 4.4G (SAT 0.7G) PROTEIN 2.4G
CARBOHYDRATE 35.9G FIBER 1.3G CHOLESTEROL 0MG SODIUM 73MG
EXCHANGES PER CUPCAKE: 2 STARCH, 1 FAT

Serve with *grilled turkey burgers and roasted potato wedges.*

turtle cupcake trick

These cupcakes are best when you bite into a pocket of caramel in the center. Here's the trick to keeping the caramel in the middle:

Allow 1 teaspoon of batter to drip from the tip of a spoon, guiding the dripping batter around the caramel topping to keep the topping from spreading to the outer edges.

Turtle Cupcakes

Dark Chocolate Snack Cake

prep: 15 minutes   cook: 25 minutes

⅔ cup unsweetened cocoa

½ cup all-purpose flour

½ teaspoon baking powder

¼ teaspoon baking soda

¼ teaspoon salt

3 large egg whites

1 cup sugar

1 (2½-ounce) jar baby food prunes

1 tablespoon reduced-calorie margarine, melted

1 teaspoon vanilla extract

Vegetable cooking spray

2 tablespoons sifted powdered sugar

1 Sift together first 5 ingredients; set aside.

2 Combine egg whites and 1 cup sugar; beat at medium speed of an electric mixer 3 to 4 minutes or until mixture is fluffy. Set aside.

3 Combine prunes, margarine, and vanilla. Add prune mixture to egg white mixture; beat at medium speed of mixer 1 minute or until combined. Gently fold egg white mixture into dry ingredients. Pour batter into a 9-inch square pan coated with cooking spray. Bake at 325° for 25 minutes or until a wooden pick inserted in center comes out clean. Let cool completely in pan on a wire rack. Sprinkle with powdered sugar, and cut into 16 squares.
Yield: 16 servings.

PER SERVING: CALORIES 94 (10% FROM FAT) FAT 1.0G (SAT 0.4G) PROTEIN 2.1G CARBOHYDRATE 19.4G FIBER 0.2G CHOLESTEROL 0MG SODIUM 88MG EXCHANGE PER SERVING: 1 STARCH

***Serve with** fat-free milk as a snack.*

RECIPE tip

Using baby food prunes as a fat replacer is a favorite trick for making recipes lighter. Now, Lighter Bake, a fruit-based butter and oil replacement by Sunsweet, provides another fat-free option. One-fourth cup of this pureed fruit product may be substituted for a jar of baby food prunes.

Mississippi Mud Brownies

make ahead

prep: 5 minutes   cook: 25 minutes   stand: 50 minutes

1 (20.5-ounce) package low-
    fat fudge brownie mix

⅔ cup water

1 teaspoon vanilla extract

½ cup reduced-fat semisweet
    chocolate morsels

Vegetable cooking spray

2 cups miniature
    marshmallows

1 (16-ounce) can reduced-fat
    chocolate-flavored
    frosting

1 Combine brownie mix, ⅔ cup water, and vanilla; stir well. Fold in chocolate morsels.

2 Spread batter in a 13- x 9- x 2-inch pan coated with cooking spray. Bake at 350° for 23 minutes.

3 Sprinkle marshmallows over hot brownies; return pan to oven, and bake 2 additional minutes. Let cool completely (about 20 minutes) in pan on a wire rack. Spread frosting over brownies; let stand at least 30 minutes. Cut into 24 squares.
Yield: 2 dozen.

PER BROWNIE: CALORIES 208 (19% FROM FAT) FAT 4.4G (SAT 2.3G) PROTEIN 1.7G
CARBOHYDRATE 40.1G FIBER 0.8G CHOLESTEROL 0MG SODIUM 74MG
EXCHANGES PER BROWNIE: 2½ STARCH, 1 FAT

Serve with chilled chicken-pasta salad, bagel chips, and a fresh fruit salad.

Peanut Butter and Chocolate Thins

make ahead

prep: 15 minutes   cook: 10 minutes   chill: 1 to 8 hours

1½ cups all-purpose flour

¾ cup firmly packed brown
    sugar

¼ teaspoon salt

3 tablespoons stick margarine

1 egg, lightly beaten

2 teaspoons vanilla extract

Vegetable cooking spray

½ cup semisweet chocolate
    morsels

3 tablespoons reduced-fat
    crunchy peanut butter
    spread

1 Combine first 3 ingredients in a medium bowl. Cut in margarine with a pastry blender until mixture resembles coarse crumbs. Stir in egg and vanilla.

2 Pat dough into a 13- x 9- x 2-inch pan coated with cooking spray. Bake at 375° for 10 minutes. Remove from oven; let cool completely on a wire rack.

3 Combine chocolate morsels and peanut butter in a small saucepan. Cook over medium heat, stirring constantly, until mixture melts. Spread chocolate mixture over crust; cover and chill at least 1 hour. Cut into 24 bars. Store in refrigerator in an airtight container.
Yield: 2 dozen.

PER BAR: CALORIES 101 (33% FROM FAT) FAT 3.7G (SAT 1.2G) PROTEIN 1.7G
CARBOHYDRATE 15.7G FIBER 0.4G CHOLESTEROL 9MG SODIUM 56MG
EXCHANGES PER BAR: 1 STARCH, 1 FAT

Serve with turkey chili with beans, tossed green salad, and corn sticks.

Lemon Bars

prep: 7 minutes   cook: 43 minutes

1 cup all-purpose flour

¼ cup plus 1 tablespoon
   powdered sugar, divided

1 teaspoon grated lemon rind

¼ cup plus 1 tablespoon
   reduced-calorie stick
   margarine

   Vegetable cooking spray

1 cup sugar

½ cup fat-free egg substitute

¼ cup fresh lemon juice

1 Combine flour, ¼ cup powdered sugar, and lemon rind. Cut in margarine with a pastry blender until mixture resembles coarse crumbs. Press mixture into a 9-inch square pan coated with cooking spray. Bake at 350° for 18 minutes.

2 Combine 1 cup sugar, egg substitute, and lemon juice, stirring well with a wire whisk. Pour over baked crust. Bake 25 additional minutes. Let cool completely on a wire rack.

3 Sprinkle with remaining 1 tablespoon powdered sugar. Cut into 16 bars. Store in an airtight container.
Yield: 16 bars.

PER BAR: CALORIES 110 (20% FROM FAT) FAT 2.4G (SAT 0.3G) PROTEIN 1.6G
CARBOHYDRATE 21.3G FIBER 0.2G CHOLESTEROL 0MG SODIUM 46MG
EXCHANGES PER BAR: 1½ STARCH, ½ FAT

Serve with baked chicken breast halves, couscous, and roasted mixed vegetables.

Lemon Macaroons

prep: 10 minutes   cook: 24 minutes per batch

1½ cups flaked coconut

⅔ cup all-purpose flour

½ cup sugar

1 teaspoon lemon extract

2 egg whites, lightly beaten

   Vegetable cooking spray

1 Combine first 5 ingredients in a bowl; stir well.

2 For each cookie, spoon 2 level teaspoonfuls dough onto cookie sheets coated with cooking spray. Flatten each cookie into a ¼-inch round. Bake at 325° for 24 to 26 minutes or until edges are lightly browned. Remove from cookie sheets, and let cool on wire racks. Store in an airtight container.
Yield: 2 dozen.

PER COOKIE: CALORIES 61 (31% FROM FAT) FAT 2.1G (SAT 1.8G) PROTEIN 0.8G
CARBOHYDRATE 9.6G FIBER 0.4G CHOLESTEROL 0MG SODIUM 20MG
EXCHANGES PER COOKIE: ½ STARCH, ½ FAT

Serve with a tea party menu of flavored cream cheese-cucumber sandwiches, fresh fruit with lemon dip, and cheese muffins.

Slice and Bake Chewy Ginger Cookies

prep: 15 minutes   freeze: 8 hours   cook: 12 minutes per batch

- 2 cups all-purpose flour
- ¾ teaspoon baking powder
- ½ teaspoon baking soda
- ¼ teaspoon salt
- 1½ teaspoons ground ginger
- ½ cup golden raisins
- ¼ cup plus 2 tablespoons stick margarine, softened
- 1 cup firmly packed dark brown sugar
- 1 teaspoon vanilla extract
- 1 egg
  Vegetable cooking spray

1 Combine first 5 ingredients in a large bowl. Add raisins, stirring well. Set aside.

2 Beat margarine, sugar, and vanilla at medium speed of an electric mixer 3 minutes. Add egg; beat at high speed 1 minute. Gradually add flour mixture, beating well.

3 Divide dough in half. Roll each portion into a 12-inch log. Wrap in plastic wrap lightly coated with cooking spray. Freeze at least 8 hours.

4 Unwrap dough, and cut each log into 24 (½-inch-thick) slices. Place 1 inch apart on cookie sheets coated with cooking spray. Bake at 350° for 12 minutes. Remove from cookie sheets, and let cool completely on wire racks.
Yield: 4 dozen.

PER COOKIE: CALORIES 56 (26% FROM FAT) FAT 1.6G (SAT 0.3G) PROTEIN 0.7G CARBOHYDRATE 9.8G FIBER 0.2G CHOLESTEROL 5MG SODIUM 52MG EXCHANGE PER COOKIE: ½ STARCH

Serve with beef and pepper stir-fry and rice.

TIME-saver

If you prefer to bake a few cookies at a time, roll the dough into shorter logs.

Great Big Oatmeal-Spice Cookies

Great Big Oatmeal-Spice Cookies

prep: 17 minutes   cook: 16 minutes per batch

1 cup sugar

1 cup firmly packed brown
   sugar

⅓ cup water

⅓ cup fat-free milk

1 tablespoon vanilla extract

1 tablespoon vegetable oil

2 (2½-ounce) jars baby food
   prunes

2 cups all-purpose flour

2 teaspoons baking soda

½ teaspoon salt

1 tablespoon pumpkin pie
   spice

3 cups quick-cooking oats,
   uncooked

1 cup raisins or dried
   cranberries

   Vegetable cooking spray

1 Combine first 7 ingredients in a large bowl, stirring well with a wire whisk. Combine flour and next 3 ingredients; add to sugar mixture, stirring just until blended. Stir in oats and raisins.

2 For each cookie, pack dough into a ¼-cup measure. Drop dough, 3 inches apart, onto cookie sheets coated with cooking spray. Bake at 350° for 16 to 18 minutes or until lightly browned. Let cool on cookie sheets 1 minute. Remove from cookie sheets, and let cool completely on wire racks. (Cookies will be soft.) Store in an airtight container. Yield: 2 dozen.

PER COOKIE: CALORIES 178 (7% FROM FAT) FAT 1.4G (SAT 0.3G) PROTEIN 3.0G CARBOHYDRATE 38.9G FIBER 1.9G CHOLESTEROL 0MG SODIUM 162MG
EXCHANGES PER COOKIE: 1 STARCH, 1½ FRUIT

Serve with *fat-free milk as a snack.*

TIME-saver

Mix the dough for these cookies, then cover and store it in the refrigerator for up to 1 week. If you prefer smaller cookies, drop the dough by rounded tablespoonfuls onto cookie sheets, and bake for 10 to 12 minutes.

fish & shellfish

Lemon-Pepper Tuna Kabobs (page 101)

Crispy Cheese-Baked Catfish

prep: 14 minutes   cook: 15 minutes

½ crushed corn flakes cereal

¼ cup (1 ounce) finely shredded reduced-fat sharp Cheddar cheese

⅛ teaspoon ground pepper

1 tablespoon plus 1 teaspoon Dijon mustard

4 (4-ounce) farm-raised catfish fillets

Vegetable cooking spray

1 Combine first 3 ingredients in a small bowl, stirring well. Spread 1 teaspoon mustard on top of each fish fillet; dredge mustard-coated side of each fillet in crumb mixture.

2 Place fish, coated sides up, on a baking sheet coated with cooking spray. Bake at 425° for 15 minutes or until fish flakes easily when tested with a fork.
Yield: 4 servings.

PER SERVING: CALORIES 193 (31% FROM FAT) FAT 6.7G (SAT 1.9G) PROTEIN 23.3G
CARBOHYDRATE 8.1G FIBER 0.1G CHOLESTEROL 71MG SODIUM 355MG
EXCHANGES PER SERVING: 3 LEAN MEAT, ½ STARCH

Serve with *coleslaw, corn on the cob, and corn muffins.*

Pecan-Crusted Flounder

prep: 8 minutes   cook: 15 minutes

1 slice whole wheat bread, torn

3 tablespoons chopped pecans

1 teaspoon salt-free Creole seasoning

¼ teaspoon salt

4 (4-ounce) flounder fillets

Butter-flavored vegetable cooking spray

2 tablespoons nonfat mayonnaise

½ teaspoon lemon juice

1 Position knife blade in food processor bowl; add first 4 ingredients. Process until mixture resembles crumbs. Set aside.

2 Place fish on a baking sheet coated with cooking spray. Combine mayonnaise and lemon juice. Brush mayonnaise mixture over top of fish. Sprinkle fish evenly with crumb mixture, and coat lightly with cooking spray. Bake at 450° for 15 minutes or until fish flakes easily when tested with a fork.
Yield: 4 servings.

PER SERVING: CALORIES 167 (31% FROM FAT) FAT 5.7G (SAT 0.7G) PROTEIN 22.6G
CARBOHYDRATE 6.0G FIBER 0.6G CHOLESTEROL 55MG SODIUM 371MG
EXCHANGES PER SERVING: 3 VERY LEAN MEAT, ½ STARCH, 1 FAT

Serve with *a fresh spinach-orange salad, basmati rice, and herbed French bread.*

RECIPE tip

Look for salt-free Creole seasoning in the spice or seafood section of the supermarket. In a pinch, substitute your own blend of red and black peppers, garlic powder, and dried oregano.

Flounder with Curried Papaya Salsa

prep: 16 minutes   chill: 15 minutes   cook: 6 minutes

1 cup finely chopped papaya
  (1 medium)

1 cup seeded, finely chopped
  plum tomato (about 4
  medium)

¼ cup finely chopped purple
  onion

1 tablespoon chopped fresh
  cilantro or parsley

½ teaspoon peeled, minced
  gingerroot

½ teaspoon curry powder

⅛ teaspoon salt

1½ tablespoons lime juice

6 (4-ounce) flounder fillets

  Vegetable cooking spray

1 Combine first 8 ingredients in a bowl, stirring well. Cover and chill at least 15 minutes.

2 Place fish on rack of a broiler pan coated with cooking spray. Broil 5½ inches from heat (with electric oven door partially opened) 6 minutes or until fish flakes easily when tested with a fork. Or, coat grill rack with cooking spray; place on grill over medium-hot coals (350° to 400°). Place fish on rack, and grill, covered, 3 minutes on each side or until fish flakes easily when tested with a fork. To serve, spoon papaya salsa over fish.
Yield: 6 servings.

PER SERVING: CALORIES 141 (11% FROM FAT) FAT 1.8G (SAT 0.4G) PROTEIN 22.3G
CARBOHYDRATE 8.9G FIBER 1.7G CHOLESTEROL 60MG SODIUM 147MG
EXCHANGES PER SERVING: 3 VERY LEAN MEAT, ½ FRUIT

Serve with *yellow rice and green beans.*

how to seed a papaya

Wait to seed a papaya until it's ripe so the sweet-tangy flavor will be at its best. When you give a ripe papaya a gentle squeeze, it will feel soft, like a ripe avocado. To speed the ripening process, place it in a paper bag for a day or two.

Cut the papaya in half vertically with a large, sharp knife.

Scoop out the seeds with a spoon, scraping clean the cavity of each half.

Broiled Flounder with Chili Cream

prep: 6 minutes   marinate: 15 minutes   cook: 8 minutes

1 tablespoon lemon juice

1 tablespoon low-sodium
   soy sauce

1 tablespoon water

1 teaspoon minced garlic
   (about 2 cloves)

4 (4-ounce) flounder fillets

½ cup nonfat sour cream

1½ teaspoons hot sauce

1 teaspoon chili powder

   Vegetable cooking spray

1 Combine first 4 ingredients in a large heavy-duty, zip-top plastic bag; add fish. Seal bag; gently turn bag to coat fish. Marinate in refrigerator at least 15 minutes.

2 While fish marinates, combine sour cream, hot sauce, and chili powder in a small bowl; set aside.

3 Remove fish from marinade, discarding marinade. Place fish on rack of a broiler pan coated with cooking spray. Broil 5½ inches from heat (with electric oven door partially opened) 8 minutes or until fish flakes easily when tested with a fork. Serve with chili cream.
Yield: 4 servings.

PER SERVING: CALORIES 129 (11% FROM FAT) FAT 1.6G (SAT 0.3G) PROTEIN 23.5G
CARBOHYDRATE 2.7G FIBER 0.2G CHOLESTEROL 60MG SODIUM 195MG
EXCHANGES PER SERVING: 3 VERY LEAN MEAT

Serve with *herbed Parmesan zucchini and a fresh fruit salad.*

RECIPE tip

Almost any fish that is broiled can be grilled. Grill flounder for this recipe, covered, over medium-hot coals (350° to 400°) for 4 minutes on each side or until it flakes easily when tested with a fork.

Flounder with Mandarin Orange Relish

prep: 11 minutes   cook: 5 minutes

1 tablespoon chili powder

¼ teaspoon salt

4 (4-ounce) flounder fillets

Vegetable cooking spray

1 (11-ounce) can mandarin oranges in light syrup

¼ cup finely chopped purple onion

3 tablespoons finely chopped fresh parsley or 1 tablespoon dried parsley

1½ teaspoons honey

1 Sprinkle chili powder and salt evenly over both sides of fillets. Place fish on rack of a broiler pan coated with cooking spray. Broil 5½ inches from heat (with electric oven door partially opened) 5 to 6 minutes or until fish flakes easily when tested with a fork.

2 While fish broils, drain oranges, reserving 1 tablespoon juice. Coarsely chop orange segments. Combine orange, reserved juice, and remaining ingredients, stirring well. Top each fillet with ¼ cup relish. Yield: 4 servings.

PER SERVING: CALORIES 153 (11% FROM FAT) FAT 1.9G (SAT 0.4G) PROTEIN 21.8G CARBOHYDRATE 11.5G FIBER 0.9G CHOLESTEROL 60MG SODIUM 263MG EXCHANGES PER SERVING: 3 VERY LEAN MEAT, 1 FRUIT

Serve with curried couscous and broccoli.

Oven-Fried Fish Sticks

prep: 11 minutes   cook: 28 minutes

1½ pounds grouper or other white fish fillets

¼ cup nonfat buttermilk

½ (1-ounce) slice white sandwich bread

½ cup yellow cornmeal

1 teaspoon ground pepper

Vegetable cooking spray

½ teaspoon salt

Malt vinegar (optional)

1 Cut fillets diagonally into 1-inch-wide strips. Combine fish strips and buttermilk in a bowl, stirring gently to coat strips.

2 Tear bread into large pieces and place in container of a blender; process until crumbly. Spread ½ cup crumbs on a baking sheet and bake at 400° for 3 to 5 minutes or until toasted.

3 Combine breadcrumbs, cornmeal, and pepper in a heavy-duty, zip-top plastic bag. Add buttermilk-coated fish strips; seal bag, and gently turn bag to coat fish strips.

4 Place fish strips on a baking sheet coated with cooking spray; sprinkle with salt. Bake at 425° for 25 minutes or until fish is crisp and flakes easily when tested with a fork. Serve with malt vinegar, if desired.
Yield: 6 servings.

PER SERVING: CALORIES 157 (10% FROM FAT) FAT 1.8G (SAT 0.4G) PROTEIN 23.5G CARBOHYDRATE 10.5G FIBER 1.3G CHOLESTEROL 42MG SODIUM 289MG EXCHANGES PER SERVING: 3 VERY LEAN MEAT, 1 STARCH

Serve with broccoli slaw and roasted potato wedges.

Flounder with Mandarin Orange Relish

20 Minute Fish Dinners

Make the salad and slice a loaf of bread while these fish recipes bake. Try the recipes with grouper, sole, or tilapia, too.

Crusty Fish Fillets with Ranch Topping

prep: 5 minutes   cook: 15 minutes

  4 (4-ounce) orange roughy or flounder fillets
  3 tablespoons fat-free Ranch-style dressing
  1 cup fat-free wheat cracker crumbs (about 22 crackers)
¼ teaspoon freshly ground pepper
¼ cup finely chopped cucumber
¼ cup finely chopped tomato
  2 tablespoons fat-free Ranch-style dressing

Spread both sides of fillets with 3 tablespoons dressing. Combine cracker crumbs and pepper in a shallow dish; dredge fish in crumb mixture. Place fish in an 11- x 7- x 1½-inch baking dish coated with cooking spray.

    Bake at 400° for 15 to 20 minutes or until fish flakes easily when tested with a fork. Drizzle with 2 tablespoons dressing; top with cucumber and tomato.
Yield: 4 servings.

PER SERVING: CALORIES 181 (5% FROM FAT) FAT 1.0G (SAT 0.0G) PROTEIN 19.7G
CARBOHYDRATE 21.1G FIBER 1.4G CHOLESTEROL 23MG SODIUM 454MG
EXCHANGES PER SERVING: 2 VERY LEAN MEAT, 1½ STARCH

Italian Fish Fillets

prep: 2 minutes   cook: 15 minutes

  4 (4-ounce) orange roughy or flounder fillets
½ cup marinara sauce
¾ cup (3 ounces) shredded part-skim mozzarella cheese
  1 teaspoon dried Italian seasoning

Place fillets in an 11- x 7- x 1½-inch baking dish coated with cooking spray. Top fillets evenly with marinara sauce. Arrange cheese evenly over sauce. Sprinkle evenly with Italian seasoning.

    Bake, uncovered, at 400° for 15 minutes or until fish flakes easily when tested with a fork. (It's best not to broil this recipe; the cheese may become tough.)
Yield: 4 servings.

PER SERVING: CALORIES 159 (31% FROM FAT) FAT 5.5G (SAT 2.4G) PROTEIN 22.4G
CARBOHYDRATE 4.4G FIBER 0.3G CHOLESTEROL 35MG SODIUM 386MG
EXCHANGES PER SERVING: 3 LEAN MEAT, 1 VEGETABLE

Tomato-Basil Fish Fillets

prep: 2 minutes   cook: 15 minutes

4 (4-ounce) orange roughy or flounder fillets
2 tablespoons fat-free Italian dressing
4 basil leaves
4 (¼-inch-thick) tomato slices
   Freshly ground pepper

Place fillets in an 11- x 7- x 1½-inch baking dish coated with cooking spray. Brush dressing evenly over fillets. Divide basil leaves and tomato slices among fillets; sprinkle with pepper, if desired.

Bake at 400° for 15 minutes or until fish flakes easily when tested with a fork.

Yield: 4 servings.

PER SERVING: CALORIES 89 (10% FROM FAT) FAT 1.0G (SAT 0.0G) PROTEIN 17.0G
CARBOHYDRATE 2.2G FIBER 0.4G CHOLESTEROL 23MG SODIUM 155MG
EXCHANGES PER SERVING: 3 VERY LEAN MEAT

✳ RECIPE tip

Cook the fish in about half the time (8 to 10 minutes) under the broiler. Just coat the rack of a broiler pan with cooking spray, add the fish, and broil 5½ inches from the heat (with the electric oven door partially opened). Don't use an ordinary glass baking dish for broiling.

Lemon-Dijon Fish Fillets

prep: 5 minutes   cook: 15 minutes

4 (4-ounce) orange roughy or flounder fillets
2 teaspoons fresh lemon juice
2 tablespoons chopped fresh chives or 2 teaspoons
     freeze-dried chives
2 tablespoons reduced-fat mayonnaise
1½ tablespoons Dijon mustard
   Lemon slices (optional)

Place fillets in an 11- x 7- x 1½-inch baking dish coated with cooking spray; brush fish with lemon juice. Bake at 400° for 12 minutes.

While fish bakes, combine chives, mayonnaise, and mustard, stirring well.

Spread mayonnaise mixture evenly over fish. Bake 3 additional minutes or until fish flakes easily when tested with a fork. Garnish with lemon slices, if desired.

Yield: 4 servings.

PER SERVING: CALORIES 106 (27% FROM FAT) FAT 3.2G (SAT 0.3G) PROTEIN 16.8G
CARBOHYDRATE 1.2G FIBER 0.1G CHOLESTEROL 25MG SODIUM 294MG
EXCHANGES PER SERVING: 2½ VERY LEAN MEAT

Grilled Mediterranean Grouper

prep: 6 minutes   cook: 10 minutes

Vegetable cooking spray

½ cup ripe olives

¼ cup French bread cubes

1 tablespoon capers, drained

1 teaspoon olive oil

1 teaspoon lemon juice

1 clove garlic

4 (4-ounce) grouper fillets

1 Coat grill rack with cooking spray; place on grill over medium-hot coals (350° to 400°).

2 While grill heats, position knife blade in food processor bowl; add olives and next 5 ingredients. Process until smooth; set aside.

3 Place fillets on rack; grill, uncovered, 5 minutes on one side. Turn fillets. Spread 2 tablespoons olive mixture over each fillet. Grill 5 additional minutes or until fish flakes easily when tested with a fork. Yield: 4 servings.

PER SERVING: CALORIES 159 (24% FROM FAT) FAT 4.3G (SAT 0.8G) PROTEIN 24.3G CARBOHYDRATE 4.4G FIBER 0.6G CHOLESTEROL 45MG SODIUM 388MG EXCHANGES PER SERVING: 3 VERY LEAN MEAT, 1 VEGETABLE

Serve with a marinated mixed vegetable salad and hard rolls.

RECIPE tip

To bake the grouper, place it on the rack of a broiler pan coated with cooking spray. Spread the olive mixture over the fish, and bake at 400° for 14 minutes.

Jambalaya

prep: 15 minutes   cook: 28 minutes

1   teaspoon vegetable oil

½   cup finely chopped onion

⅓   cup finely chopped green pepper

⅓   cup finely chopped celery

1   teaspoon salt-free Creole seasoning

¼   teaspoon ground pepper

1   (15-ounce) can no-salt-added stewed tomatoes, undrained

1   (14¼-ounce) can no-salt-added chicken broth

1   cup long-grain rice, uncooked

½   cup finely chopped, lean cooked ham

10   ounces halibut, cut into bite-size pieces

1 Heat oil in a large nonstick skillet over medium-high heat until hot. Add chopped onion, green pepper, and celery; cook 7 minutes or until tender, stirring often. Add Creole seasoning and ¼ teaspoon pepper; cook 1 additional minute.

2 Stir in tomatoes and next 3 ingredients. Bring to a boil; cover, reduce heat, and simmer 15 minutes. Add fish; cover and cook 5 to 7 minutes or until fish flakes easily when tested with a fork.
Yield: 4 servings.

PER SERVING: CALORIES 316 (10% FROM FAT) FAT 3.5G (SAT 0.7G) PROTEIN 21.3G CARBOHYDRATE 47.2G FIBER 1.5G CHOLESTEROL 37MG SODIUM 182MG EXCHANGES PER SERVING: 2 LEAN MEAT, 3 STARCH

Serve with *a tossed green salad and crusty French bread.*

Sweet-and-Sour Orange Roughy

Vegetable cooking spray

1 teaspoon peanut oil

⅔ cup thinly sliced green
   onions (about 5)

⅓ cup preshredded carrot

¼ cup cider vinegar

3 tablespoons sugar

1 tablespoon low-sodium
   soy sauce

4 (4-ounce) orange roughy
   fillets

¼ cup unsweetened orange
   juice

1 teaspoon cornstarch

1 Coat a large nonstick skillet with cooking spray, add oil and place over medium-high heat until hot. Add green onions and carrot; cook 3 minutes or until vegetables are tender, stirring often.

2 Combine vinegar, sugar, and soy sauce in a small bowl, stirring until sugar dissolves. Add to carrot mixture; bring just to a boil. Add fish; cover, reduce heat, and simmer 10 minutes or until fish flakes easily when tested with a fork. Transfer fish to a serving platter; set aside and keep warm.

3 Combine orange juice and cornstarch in a small bowl, stirring until smooth. Add to liquid in skillet. Bring to a boil, and cook, stirring constantly, 2 minutes or until sauce is slightly thickened. Spoon sweet-and-sour sauce evenly over fish.
Yield: 4 servings.

PER SERVING: CALORIES 221 (33% FROM FAT)   FAT 8.0G (SAT 1.2G)   PROTEIN 22.1G
CARBOHYDRATE 14.5G   FIBER 0.7G   CHOLESTEROL 68MG   SODIUM 161MG
EXCHANGES PER SERVING: 3 LEAN MEAT, 1 FRUIT

Serve with *rice and broccoli.*

WORK-saver

Slice green onions the easy way—with kitchen scissors.
Just clip the onions over a measuring cup.

Grilled Swordfish with Mustard-Dillweed Dressing

prep: 5 minutes   cook: 14 minutes

Vegetable cooking spray

4 (4-ounce) swordfish steaks

⅓ cup plain low-fat yogurt

2 tablespoons nonfat
    mayonnaise

2 tablespoons chopped fresh
    dillweed or 2 teaspoons
    dried dillweed

2 teaspoons Dijon mustard

⅛ teaspoon salt

    Fresh dillweed sprigs
    (optional)

1 Coat grill rack with cooking spray; place on grill over medium-hot coals (350° to 400°). Place fish on rack; grill, covered, 7 minutes on each side or until fish flakes easily when tested with a fork.

2 While fish cooks, combine yogurt and next 4 ingredients in a small bowl. Serve mustard-dillweed dressing with fish. Garnish with dillweed sprigs, if desired.
Yield: 4 servings.

PER SERVING: CALORIES 162 (29% FROM FAT) FAT 5.2G (SAT 1.4G) PROTEIN 23.6G
CARBOHYDRATE 3.6G FIBER 0.1G CHOLESTEROL 45MG SODIUM 357MG
EXCHANGES PER SERVING: 3 VERY LEAN MEAT

Serve with *couscous and grilled pepper-mushroom kabobs.*

RECIPE tip

Try the dill sauce from this recipe on fresh tuna steaks.

Citrus- and Pepper-Rubbed Tuna

prep: 6 minutes   cook: 12 minutes

2 tablespoons frozen orange
    juice concentrate,
    thawed

2 tablespoons salt-free lemon-
    pepper seasoning

¼ teaspoon salt

4 (4-ounce) tuna steaks

    Vegetable cooking spray

1 Combine orange juice concentrate, lemon-pepper seasoning, and salt in a small bowl; rub evenly over both sides of fish. Arrange fish on a baking sheet coated with cooking spray.

2 Bake at 400° for 12 to 14 minutes or until fish flakes easily when tested with a fork.
Yield: 4 servings.

PER SERVING: CALORIES 187 (28% FROM FAT) FAT 5.8G (SAT 1.5G) PROTEIN 27.0G
CARBOHYDRATE 5.5G FIBER 0.9G CHOLESTEROL 43MG SODIUM 192MG
EXCHANGES PER SERVING: 4 VERY LEAN MEAT

Serve with *garlic mashed potatoes and squash medley.*

RECIPE tip

Grill tuna steaks, covered, over medium-hot coals (350° to 400°) 4 to 5 minutes on each side or until they flake easily when tested with a fork.

Lemon-Pepper Tuna Kabobs

Lemon-Pepper Tuna Kabobs

prep: 20 minutes   marinate: 10 minutes   cook: 9 minutes

2 teaspoons grated lemon rind

1 teaspoon ground pepper

½ cup dry white wine

¼ cup fresh lemon juice

2 teaspoons olive oil

1 pound tuna or halibut steaks, cut into 1-inch pieces

2 small yellow squash, cut into 1-inch pieces

1 small sweet red pepper, cut into 1-inch pieces

1 small purple onion, cut into eighths

16 small fresh mushrooms

Vegetable cooking spray

Lemon wedges (optional)

1 Combine first 5 ingredients in heavy-duty, zip-top plastic bag; add fish and vegetables. Seal bag; turn bag to coat fish. Marinate in refrigerator 10 minutes.

2 Remove fish and vegetables from marinade. Place marinade in a small saucepan; bring to a boil, and set aside.

3 Thread vegetables onto 2 (12-inch) metal skewers. Place vegetable kabobs on rack of a broiler pan coated with cooking spray. Broil 5½ inches from heat (with electric oven door partially opened) 3 minutes.

4 While vegetables broil, thread fish on 2 (12-inch) metal skewers. Add fish kabobs to rack. Broil 6 to 8 additional minutes or until vegetables are crisp-tender and fish flakes easily when tested with a fork, brushing occasionally with marinade. Remove fish and vegetables from kabobs. Serve with lemon wedges, if desired.
Yield: 4 servings.

PER SERVING: CALORIES 257 (30% FROM FAT)   FAT 8.6G (SAT 1.8G)   PROTEIN 29.3G
CARBOHYDRATE 12.1G   FIBER 3.0G   CHOLESTEROL 43MG   SODIUM 52MG
EXCHANGES PER SERVING: 3 LEAN MEAT, 2 VEGETABLE

Serve with *rice and garlic bread.*

Linguine with Clam Sauce

prep: 4 minutes   cook: 21 minutes

1 teaspoon olive oil

2 teaspoons minced garlic (about 4 cloves)

¼ teaspoon dried crushed red pepper

½ cup chopped fresh parsley or 2 tablespoons dried parsley

2 (6½-ounce) cans minced clams, undrained

½ cup dry white wine

8 ounces uncooked linguine

2 tablespoons freshly grated Parmesan cheese

1 Heat oil in a large nonstick skillet over medium-high heat until hot. Add garlic; cook, stirring constantly, 1 minute. Add red pepper, parsley, and clams. Bring to a boil; reduce heat, and simmer 5 minutes. Add wine. Bring to a boil; cover, reduce heat, and simmer 15 minutes.

2 While sauce simmers, cook pasta according to package directions, omitting salt and fat. Drain. Add cooked pasta to clam mixture, tossing to coat well. Divide mixture evenly among 4 individual serving plates. Sprinkle cheese evenly over pasta.
Yield: 4 (1½-cup) servings.

PER SERVING: CALORIES 294 (11% FROM FAT)   FAT 3.7G (SAT 1.2G)   PROTEIN 16.5G
CARBOHYDRATE 46.9G   FIBER 1.8G   CHOLESTEROL 32MG   SODIUM 603MG
EXCHANGES PER SERVING: 1 LEAN MEAT, 3 STARCH

Serve with *a tossed green salad and French baguettes.*

Grilled Shrimp Kabobs

½ cup light beer

½ cup chili sauce

⅓ cup no-salt-added ketchup

1 teaspoon hot sauce

1 pound peeled and deveined
   large fresh shrimp

⅓ cup nonfat mayonnaise

2 teaspoons prepared
   horseradish

1 medium-size sweet red
   pepper, cut into 1-inch
   pieces

1 medium-size green pepper,
   cut into 1-inch pieces

8 pearl onions

   Vegetable cooking spray

1 Combine first 4 ingredients in a large heavy-duty, zip-top plastic bag; add shrimp. Seal bag; turn bag to coat shrimp. Marinate in refrigerator 15 minutes.

2 Combine mayonnaise and horseradish; stir well. Cover and chill while shrimp marinates and cooks.

3 Remove shrimp from marinade. Place marinade in a small saucepan; bring to a boil, and set aside.

4 Thread vegetables onto 3 (12-inch) metal skewers. Coat grill rack with cooking spray; place on grill over medium-hot coals (350° to 400°). Place vegetable kabobs on rack; grill, covered, 3 minutes.

5 While vegetables cook, thread shrimp onto 5 (12-inch) metal skewers. Place shrimp kabobs on rack; grill, covered, 5 minutes or until shrimp turn pink and vegetables are crisp-tender, turning and basting occasionally with reserved marinade. Serve with mayonnaise mixture. Yield: 4 servings.

PER SERVING: CALORIES 174 (7% FROM FAT)   FAT 1.3G (SAT 0.3G)   PROTEIN 16.5G
CARBOHYDRATE 23.2G   FIBER 1.4G   CHOLESTEROL 138MG   SODIUM 885MG
EXCHANGES PER SERVING: 2 VERY LEAN MEAT, 1 STARCH, 1 VEGETABLE

Serve with *a tossed green salad and French bread.*

TIME-saver

Buy peeled and deveined shrimp from the your supermarket's seafood department, and you'll save work and time.

Stir-Fry Shrimp and Vegetables

2 bags boil-in-bag rice, uncooked

2 teaspoons dark sesame oil

12 ounces peeled and deveined medium-size fresh shrimp

1 teaspoon minced garlic (about 2 cloves)

1 (16-ounce) package frozen stir-fry vegetables, thawed

¼ cup low-sodium soy sauce

¼ cup water

2 tablespoons rice wine vinegar

2 teaspoons cornstarch

1 teaspoon ground ginger

prep: 15 minutes   cook: 14 minutes

1 Cook rice according to package directions, omitting salt and fat.

2 While rice cooks, heat oil in a large nonstick skillet over medium-high heat until hot. Add shrimp and garlic; stir-fry 3 minutes or until shrimp turn pink. Remove shrimp from skillet; set aside, and keep warm. Add vegetables to skillet; cook 10 minutes or until vegetables are crisp-tender, stirring often. Return shrimp to skillet.

3 Combine soy sauce and next 4 ingredients in a small bowl; stir well. Add soy sauce mixture to shrimp and vegetable mixture; cook 1 minute or until thickened, stirring often. Serve over rice.
Yield: 4 servings.

PER SERVING: CALORIES 379 (9% FROM FAT) FAT 4.0G (SAT 0.6G) PROTEIN 23.9G CARBOHYDRATE 59.4G FIBER 1.7G CHOLESTEROL 129MG SODIUM 536MG EXCHANGES PER SERVING: 1 LEAN MEAT, 3 STARCH, 3 VEGETABLE

Serve with *lemon sherbet and ginger cookies.*

how to devein shrimp

You can serve shrimp without deveining, but it looks better when the vein is removed.

Using a small, sharp knife, split open the back of peeled shrimp, cutting toward the tail and following the dark vein line just beneath the surface.

Lift the vein using the sharp point of the knife, and pull it out. Rinse the shrimp well.

meatless main dishes

Overnight Vegetable Lasagna (page 118)

Cheesy Bean and Rice Casserole

prep: 15 minutes   cook: 15 minutes

1 (16-ounce) package frozen rice and vegetable pilaf blend

2 tablespoons all-purpose flour

1 (12-ounce) can evaporated skimmed milk

¼ teaspoon salt

¼ teaspoon ground pepper

¼ teaspoon hot sauce

3 ounces light process cheese product, cubed (about ⅔ cup)

1 (15-ounce) can kidney beans, drained

Butter-flavored vegetable cooking spray

¼ cup fine, dry breadcrumbs

¼ teaspoon chili powder

1 Cook rice blend according to package directions; drain and set aside.

2 While rice blend cooks, combine flour and ½ cup milk; stir until smooth. Combine flour mixture, remaining 1 cup milk, salt, pepper, and hot sauce in a medium saucepan; stir well. Cook over medium heat, stirring constantly, until mixture is thickened and bubbly. Remove from heat and add cheese; stir until cheese melts.

3 Combine rice blend, cheese mixture, and beans in an 11- x 7- x 1½-inch baking dish coated with cooking spray. Combine breadcrumbs and chili powder; sprinkle over rice mixture. Coat with cooking spray and microwave at HIGH 9 minutes or until thoroughly heated.
Yield: 4 servings.

PER SERVING: CALORIES 341 (10% FROM FAT) FAT 3.7G (SAT 1.7G) PROTEIN 20.5G CARBOHYDRATE 57.8G FIBER 4.6G CHOLESTEROL 11MG SODIUM 752MG EXCHANGES PER SERVING: 4 STARCH, 1 LEAN MEAT

Serve with *sliced fresh tomatoes.*

RECIPE tip

Bake this recipe in a regular oven at 350° for 25 minutes.

Mexican Rice and Beans Salad

prep: 3 minutes   cook: 10 minutes

1½ cups instant brown rice,
uncooked

3 tablespoons nonfat sour
cream

1 tablespoon chunky salsa

⅔ cup chunky salsa

¼ cup sliced green onion
(about 1 large)

½ teaspoon salt

¼ teaspoon ground pepper

1 (15-ounce) can no-salt-
added black beans,
rinsed and drained

4 cups shredded iceberg lettuce

¼ cup (1 ounce) shredded
reduced-fat sharp
Cheddar cheese

1 Cook rice according to package directions, omitting salt and fat.

2 Combine sour cream and 1 tablespoon salsa, stirring well. Set aside.

3 Combine brown rice, ⅔ cup salsa, green onion, and next 3 ingredients in a large bowl, stirring gently. Arrange 1 cup lettuce on each of 4 individual salad plates. Spoon rice mixture evenly onto lettuce. Sprinkle evenly with cheese. Top evenly with sour cream mixture. Yield: 4 servings.

PER SERVING: CALORIES 290 (10% FROM FAT) FAT 3.2G (SAT 1.2G) PROTEIN 13.1G
CARBOHYDRATE 52.7G FIBER 6.5G CHOLESTEROL 5MG SODIUM 501MG
EXCHANGES PER SERVING: 3½ STARCH, ½ FAT

Serve with *low-fat coleslaw and cornbread.*

TIME-saver

Regular brown rice takes about 40 minutes to cook; instant brown rice cooks in just 10 minutes.

Two-Bean Salad with Feta Cheese

prep: 8 minutes   stand: 20 minutes

1 (16-ounce) can kidney
  beans, drained

1 (15-ounce) can cannellini
  beans, drained

3 ounces feta cheese, crumbled

¼ cup finely chopped purple
  onion

2 tablespoons chopped fresh
  mint or 2 teaspoons
  dried mint

1½ tablespoons sugar

½ teaspoon garlic powder

¼ teaspoon salt

¼ teaspoon ground pepper

2 tablespoons lemon juice

1 tablespoon balsamic vinegar

1 teaspoon olive oil

4 cups torn green leaf lettuce

1 Combine first 5 ingredients in a medium bowl. Combine sugar and next 6 ingredients, stirring well with a wire whisk; pour over bean mixture. Let stand at least 20 minutes.

2 Place 1 cup lettuce on each of 4 individual serving plates; spoon bean mixture evenly over lettuce.
Yield: 4 servings.

PER SERVING: CALORIES 238 (24% FROM FAT)   FAT 6.3G (SAT 3.4G)   PROTEIN 12.9G
CARBOHYDRATE 33.1G   FIBER 5.5G   CHOLESTEROL 19MG   SODIUM 660MG
EXCHANGES PER SERVING: 1 MEDIUM-FAT MEAT, 2 STARCH

Serve with *fresh cantaloupe and toasted bagel slices.*

Two-Bean Salad with Feta Cheese

Pita Bread Bowls
with Couscous Filling

Pita Bread Bowls with Couscous Filling

prep: 15 minutes

4 (7-inch) pita bread rounds

½ cup water

⅓ cup couscous, uncooked

1 (15-ounce) can garbanzo beans, drained

1 cup chopped tomato (about 1 medium)

¼ cup sliced ripe olives

¼ cup sliced green onion (about 1 large)

¼ cup raisins

1 teaspoon minced garlic (about 2 cloves)

¼ teaspoon ground cumin

¼ cup plain nonfat yogurt or nonfat sour cream

1 Press 1 pita bread round gently into a medium microwave-safe bowl. Microwave at HIGH 1½ minutes or until crisp. Repeat procedure with remaining pita bread rounds. Set aside.

2 While pitas cook, bring ½ cup water to a boil in a medium saucepan. Remove from heat. Add couscous; cover and let stand 5 minutes or until couscous is tender and liquid is absorbed. Fluff couscous with a fork, and transfer to a medium bowl.

3 Add garbanzo beans and next 6 ingredients to couscous; toss gently. Spoon couscous mixture evenly into pita bread bowls. Top each serving with 1 tablespoon yogurt.
Yield: 4 servings.

PER SERVING: CALORIES 377 (11% FROM FAT) FAT 4.4G (SAT 0.4G) PROTEIN 12.5G
CARBOHYDRATE 70.8G FIBER 10.4G CHOLESTEROL 0MG SODIUM 453MG
EXCHANGES PER SERVING: 4 STARCH, 1 VEGETABLE, ½ FAT

Serve with wedges of cantaloupe, watermelon, and honeydew melon.

Bulgur and Broccoli Skillet Dinner

prep: 10 minutes   cook: 19 minutes

2 cups vegetable broth

1 cup bulgur (cracked wheat), uncooked

2 teaspoons sesame oil

3 cups broccoli flowerets

¾ cup sliced celery

½ cup sliced green onions (about 2 large)

½ cup finely chopped sweet red pepper

1 tablespoon low-sodium soy sauce

2 tablespoons chopped, unsalted, dry roasted peanuts

¼ cup chopped fresh parsley

1 Combine broth and bulgur in a medium saucepan; bring to a boil. Cover, reduce heat, and simmer 15 minutes or until liquid is absorbed. Set aside.

2 While bulgur cooks, heat oil in a nonstick skillet over medium-high heat until hot. Add broccoli and next 3 ingredients; cook, stirring constantly, 4 minutes or until tender. Stir in soy sauce, bulgur, peanuts, and parsley.
Yield: 4 servings.

PER SERVING: CALORIES 289 (19% FROM FAT) FAT 6.0G (SAT 0.8G) PROTEIN 10.8G
CARBOHYDRATE 53.3G FIBER 13.9G CHOLESTEROL 0MG SODIUM 501MG
EXCHANGES PER SERVING: 3 STARCH, 2 VEGETABLE, 1 FAT

Serve with fresh peach slices and soft dinner rolls.

Quick Vegetable Shepherd's Pie

prep: 12 minutes   cook: 30 minutes

6 cups frozen mixed
  vegetables, thawed

1 (15-ounce) can kidney
  beans, drained

2 (8-ounce) cans no-salt-
  added tomato sauce

1 (4-ounce) can sliced
  mushrooms, drained

1 teaspoon chili powder

1 teaspoon low-sodium
  Worcestershire sauce

½ teaspoon salt

½ teaspoon ground pepper

  Butter-flavored vegetable
  cooking spray

1⅓ cups fat-free milk

2⅔ cups frozen mashed
  potatoes, thawed

½ cup nonfat sour cream

¼ teaspoon salt

  Paprika

1 Combine first 8 ingredients in a large bowl; stir well. Spoon mixture into an 11- x 7- x 1½-inch baking dish coated with cooking spray.

2 Cook milk in a medium saucepan over medium heat until very hot. (Do not boil.) Stir in mashed potatoes; cook, stirring constantly, 5 minutes or until thickened. Stir in sour cream and ¼ teaspoon salt. Spread potato mixture over vegetable mixture; sprinkle with paprika. Spray top with cooking spray.

3 Microwave at HIGH 30 minutes, rotating dish once, or until vegetables are tender and top is golden.
Yield: 6 servings.

PER SERVING: CALORIES 266 (9% FROM FAT) FAT 2.7G (SAT 0.2G) PROTEIN 13.5G
CARBOHYDRATE 48.0G FIBER 7.9G CHOLESTEROL 3MG SODIUM 641MG
EXCHANGES PER SERVING: 3 STARCH, 1 VEGETABLE, ½ FAT

Serve with *fresh citrus slices.*

RECIPE tip

Bake this recipe in a regular oven at 350° for 40 minutes. The top will be more golden brown than if you cook it in the microwave.

Cheese and Onion Quesadillas

prep: 10 minutes   cook: 17 minutes

Butter-flavored vegetable
  cooking spray

1 cup chopped onion (about
   1 medium)

4 (8-inch) fat-free flour
   tortillas

1 cup (4 ounces) shredded
   reduced-fat sharp
   Cheddar cheese

½ teaspoon ground cumin

½ cup salsa

½ cup nonfat sour cream

1 Coat a large nonstick skillet with cooking spray; place over medium-high heat until hot. Add onion; cook, stirring constantly, 5 minutes or until tender. Remove from skillet. Wipe skillet with a paper towel.

2 Coat skillet with cooking spray; place over medium heat until hot. Place one tortilla in skillet. Cook 1 minute or until bottom of tortilla is golden. Sprinkle one-fourth onion, cheese, and cumin over one side of tortilla. Fold tortilla in half. Cook tortilla 1 minute on each side or until golden and cheese melts. Repeat procedure with remaining tortillas, onion, cheese, and cumin.

3 Top each quesadilla with 2 tablespoons salsa and 2 tablespoons sour cream. Serve immediately.
Yield: 4 servings.

PER SERVING: CALORIES 237 (22% FROM FAT) FAT 5.8G (SAT 3.2G) PROTEIN 14.0G CARBOHYDRATE 31.4G FIBER 2.2G CHOLESTEROL 19MG SODIUM 650MG EXCHANGES PER SERVING: 1 MEDIUM-FAT MEAT, 2 STARCH

***Serve with** a jicama-orange salad.*

Chili-Stuffed Potatoes

prep: 12 minutes   cook: 16 minutes

4 medium baking potatoes

1 (15-ounce) can vegetarian
   chili

¼ cup (1 ounce) shredded
   reduced-fat Cheddar
   cheese

¼ cup (1 ounce) shredded
   reduced-fat Monterey
   Jack cheese

1 cup seeded and chopped
   tomato (about 1
   medium)

½ cup nonfat sour cream

¼ cup chopped fresh cilantro
   or parsley

1 Scrub potatoes; prick several times with a fork. Place potatoes 1 inch apart on a microwave-safe rack or on paper towels. Microwave at HIGH 14 to 17 minutes, rearranging once; let stand 2 minutes.

2 While potatoes cook, place chili in a small saucepan, and cook over medium-high heat until thoroughly heated, stirring occasionally.

3 Cut an X to within ½-inch of bottoms of baked potatoes. Squeeze potatoes to open; fluff with a fork. Spoon chili evenly onto potatoes; sprinkle with cheeses. Top each with ¼ cup tomato, 2 tablespoons sour cream, and 1 tablespoon cilantro.
Yield: 4 servings.

PER SERVING: CALORIES 362 (8% FROM FAT) FAT 3.1G (SAT 1.7G) PROTEIN 20.0G CARBOHYDRATE 66.6G FIBER 12.2G CHOLESTEROL 9MG SODIUM 243MG EXCHANGES PER SERVING: 1 LEAN MEAT, 4 STARCH, 1 VEGETABLE

***Serve with** glazed carrots.*

Tortellini with Marinara Sauce

Vegetable cooking spray

1 teaspoon olive oil

¾ cup chopped onion (about
     1 small)

1 teaspoon minced garlic
     (about 2 cloves)

1 (28-ounce) can crushed
     tomatoes, undrained

2 teaspoons dried Italian
     seasoning

½ teaspoon sugar

¼ teaspoon salt

2 (9-ounce) packages
     refrigerated cheese-filled
     tortellini, uncooked

¼ cup grated Parmesan cheese

1 Coat a large saucepan with cooking spray. Add oil, and place over medium-high heat until hot. Add onion and garlic; cook, stirring constantly, 4 minutes or until tender. Add tomatoes and next 3 ingredients. Bring to a boil; reduce heat to low, and simmer 20 minutes, stirring occasionally.

2 While sauce simmers, cook pasta according to package directions, omitting salt and fat. Drain.

3 To serve, place 1 cup pasta on each of 6 individual serving plates. Top each serving with ½ cup sauce, and sprinkle servings evenly with cheese.
Yield: 6 servings.

PER SERVING: CALORIES 323 (19% FROM FAT) FAT 6.7G (SAT 2.9G) PROTEIN 17.7G
CARBOHYDRATE 48.8G FIBER 1.1G CHOLESTEROL 33MG SODIUM 676MG
EXCHANGES PER SERVING: 1 HIGH-FAT MEAT, 3 STARCH, 1 VEGETABLE

Serve with *a tossed green salad and garlic bread.*

TIME-saver

Use frozen chopped onion and 2 teaspoons minced garlic from a jar instead of the fresh versions of both ingredients.

Baked Ravioli and Vegetables

prep: 10 minutes   cook: 20 minutes

10 cups water

1 (9-ounce) package refrigerated light cheese-filled ravioli, uncooked

1 (16-ounce) package frozen broccoli, cauliflower, and carrots

1 (12-ounce) can evaporated skimmed milk, divided

2 tablespoons all-purpose flour

1 teaspoon dried Italian seasoning

½ teaspoon minced garlic (about 1 clove)

¼ teaspoon salt

¼ teaspoon ground pepper

¾ cup preshredded Parmesan cheese, divided

   Vegetable cooking spray

2 tablespoons fine, dry breadcrumbs

1 Bring water to a boil in a Dutch oven. Add pasta and vegetables; cook 5 minutes. Drain.

2 While pasta and vegetables cook, combine ½ cup milk and flour; stir well. Combine flour mixture, remaining milk, Italian seasoning, and next 3 ingredients in a medium saucepan. Cook over medium heat, stirring constantly, until thickened and bubbly. Stir in ½ cup Parmesan cheese.

3 Combine pasta mixture and cheese sauce; stir well. Spoon into an 11- x 7- x 1½-inch baking dish coated with cooking spray. Sprinkle with breadcrumbs. Bake at 350° for 15 minutes. Sprinkle remaining ¼ cup cheese over breadcrumbs; bake 5 additional minutes or until lightly browned.
Yield: 6 servings.

PER SERVING: CALORIES 262 (24% FROM FAT) FAT 6.9G (SAT 4.1G) PROTEIN 18.2G CARBOHYDRATE 31.7G FIBER 3.1G CHOLESTEROL 29MG SODIUM 601G EXCHANGES PER SERVING: 2 LEAN MEAT, 2 STARCH

Serve with soft garlic breadsticks.

Baked Ravioli and Vegetables

Creamy Vegetable Pasta

prep: 20 minutes   cook: 14 minutes

8 ounces fettuccine, uncooked

1 pound fresh asparagus

¼ cup water

2 teaspoons margarine

½ teaspoon minced garlic
   (about 1 clove)

1 tablespoon all-purpose flour

1¼ cups fat-free milk

3 tablespoons light process
   cream cheese

¾ cup preshredded Parmesan
   cheese

1 (15-ounce) can black beans,
   drained

   Freshly ground pepper
   (optional)

1 Cook pasta according to package directions, omitting salt and fat. Drain.

2 While pasta cooks, snap off tough ends of asparagus. Remove scales from stalks with a vegetable peeler or knife, if desired. Cut asparagus into 1-inch pieces; place in a microwave-safe dish. Add ¼ cup water, and cover. Microwave at HIGH 2 minutes; drain.

3 Melt margarine in a medium saucepan over medium heat; add garlic. Cook, stirring constantly, 1 minute. Add flour; cook, stirring constantly, 1 minute. Gradually add milk, and cook, stirring constantly, 8 minutes or until thickened and bubbly. Stir in cream cheese; cook, stirring constantly, 2 minutes. Stir in Parmesan cheese.

4 Combine asparagus, cheese sauce, pasta, and beans in a large bowl; toss well. Sprinkle with freshly ground pepper, if desired. Yield: 6 (1⅓-cup) servings.

PER SERVING: CALORIES 298 (22% FROM FAT) FAT 7.2G (SAT 3.5G) PROTEIN 16.6G
CARBOHYDRATE 42.3G FIBER 4.1G CHOLESTEROL 15MG SODIUM 419MG
EXCHANGES PER SERVING: 1 HIGH-FAT MEAT, 2 STARCH, 2 VEGETABLE

***Serve with** French bread.*

trimming asparagus

The best fresh asparagus is available in early spring when the sweet, thin stalks are in season. You can substitute frozen asparagus in this recipe, but the texture is better when you use fresh. Here's how to prepare the fresh spears.

Snap off the tough ends of each asparagus spear.

Remove the scales, if you wish, by scraping each spear with a vegetable peeler or a knife.

Penne with Spinach and Garlic

prep: 10 minutes   cook: 10 minutes

12 ounces penne pasta,
   uncooked (about 3¼
   cups)

2 teaspoons olive oil, divided

2 teaspoons lemon juice

2 tablespoons chopped
   almonds

   Vegetable cooking spray

1 cup sliced purple onion
   (about 1 medium)

1 teaspoon minced garlic
   (about 2 cloves)

3 cups tightly packed fresh
   spinach leaves, trimmed
   and thinly sliced (about
   ½ [10-ounce] package
   trimmed, washed fresh
   spinach)

½ teaspoon salt

¼ teaspoon ground pepper

1 Cook pasta according to package directions, omitting salt and fat. Reserve 3 tablespoons pasta water; drain pasta. Combine reserved pasta water, 1 teaspoon olive oil, and lemon juice in a small bowl; set aside.

2 While pasta cooks, place a large skillet over medium-high heat until hot. Add almonds and cook, stirring constantly, 1 to 2 minutes or until toasted. Set almonds aside.

3 Coat skillet with cooking spray; add remaining 1 teaspoon oil. Return to medium-high heat until oil is hot. Cut onion slices in half; add onion and garlic to skillet. Cook, stirring constantly, 4 minutes or until tender. Add spinach, and cook, stirring constantly, 2 minutes; stir in almonds, salt, and pepper. Stir in reserved pasta water mixture. Add pasta, and toss gently. Serve immediately.
Yield: 4 (2-cup) servings.

PER SERVING: CALORIES 384 (14% FROM FAT)   FAT 6.0G (SAT 0.7G)   PROTEIN 13.2G
CARBOHYDRATE 69.2G   FIBER 4.5   CHOLESTEROL 0MG   SODIUM 328MG
EXCHANGES PER SERVING: 4 STARCH, 1 VEGETABLE, 1 FAT

Serve with *a romaine-artichoke salad and breadsticks.*

RECIPE tip

This recipe doesn't have a thick sauce. So, adding some of the pasta water back to the pasta mixture helps the pasta stay moist.

Simple Chili Spaghetti

make ahead

prep: 10 minutes   cook: 25 minutes

8 ounces spaghetti, uncooked

1 (26-ounce) jar fat-free spaghetti sauce

1 (15-ounce) can vegetarian chili

1 (4-ounce) can sliced mushrooms, drained

2 teaspoons chili powder

½ teaspoon garlic powder

Vegetable cooking spray

½ cup (2 ounces) reduced-fat shredded sharp Cheddar cheese

1 Cook pasta according to package directions, omitting salt and fat. Drain. While pasta cooks, combine spaghetti sauce and next 4 ingredients in a medium saucepan. Bring to a boil; cover, reduce heat, and simmer 10 minutes. Coat a 13- x 9- x 2-inch baking dish with cooking spray; add spaghetti, and spoon sauce over spaghetti. (Casserole may be covered and refrigerated at this point and baked later. Bake 35 minutes or until thoroughly heated.)

2 Bake at 375° for 25 minutes or until thoroughly heated. Remove from oven, and sprinkle with cheese.
Yield: 6 servings.

PER SERVING: CALORIES 272 (9% FROM FAT) FAT 2.7G (SAT 1.2G) PROTEIN 14.4G
CARBOHYDRATE 49.2G FIBER 8.5G CHOLESTEROL 6MG SODIUM 574MG
EXCHANGES PER SERVING: 1 LEAN MEAT, 3 STARCH, 1 VEGETABLE

Serve with a tossed green salad and Italian bread.

Red Pepper Pasta

prep: 7 minutes   cook: 12 minutes

8 ounces linguine, uncooked

Olive oil-flavored vegetable cooking spray

1 teaspoon olive oil

1 teaspoon minced garlic (about 2 cloves)

1 tablespoon plus 1 teaspoon chopped fresh rosemary or 1¼ teaspoons dried rosemary

1⅓ cups coarsely chopped roasted sweet red pepper (about 1 [12-ounce] jar)

2 (14.5-ounce) cans no-salt-added stewed tomatoes, undrained

½ teaspoon salt

½ teaspoon ground red pepper

½ cup grated Parmesan cheese

1 Cook pasta according to package directions, omitting salt and fat. Drain.

2 While pasta cooks, coat a large nonstick skillet with cooking spray; add oil. Place over medium-high heat until hot. Add garlic and rosemary; cook, stirring constantly, 2 minutes. Add roasted red pepper and next 3 ingredients. Bring to a boil; reduce heat, and simmer 5 to 6 minutes or until slightly thickened. Set aside, and keep warm.

3 To serve, place 1 cup pasta on each of 4 individual serving plates. Top each with 1 cup pepper mixture. Sprinkle each serving with 2 tablespoons cheese. Serve immediately.
Yield: 4 servings.

PER SERVING: CALORIES 360 (17% FROM FAT) FAT 6.6G (SAT 2.7G) PROTEIN 14.8G
CARBOHYDRATE 62.0G FIBER 3.3G CHOLESTEROL 15MG SODIUM 509MG
EXCHANGES PER SERVING: 3 STARCH, 3 VEGETABLE, 1 FAT

Serve with a fresh spinach salad and French bread.

Dijon-Artichoke Pasta

prep: 5 minutes   cook: 12 minutes

8 ounces linguine, uncooked

1 (10¾-ounce) can reduced-fat, reduced-sodium cream of mushroom soup

⅓ cup evaporated skimmed milk

⅓ cup dry white wine

2 tablespoons Dijon mustard

1 (14¼-ounce) can quartered artichoke hearts, drained

1 (4-ounce) can sliced mushrooms, drained

¼ cup freshly grated Parmesan cheese

¼ cup sliced green onion (about 1 large)

1 tablespoon chopped ripe olives

Freshly ground pepper

1 Cook pasta according to package directions, omitting salt and fat. Drain.

2 While pasta cooks, combine soup and next 3 ingredients in a microwave-safe bowl. Microwave at HIGH 3 minutes, stirring once. Add artichokes and mushrooms. Microwave at HIGH 2 minutes or until thoroughly heated, stirring once.

3 Toss artichoke mixture with pasta. Sprinkle with Parmesan cheese and remaining 3 ingredients. Serve immediately.
Yield: 4 servings.

PER SERVING: CALORIES 341 (14% FROM FAT)   FAT 5.4G (SAT 2.0G)   PROTEIN 13.7G   CARBOHYDRATE 55.9G   FIBER 2.9G   CHOLESTEROL 12MG   SODIUM 762MG
EXCHANGES PER SERVING: 3 STARCH, 2 VEGETABLE, 1 FAT

Serve with *whole wheat rolls.*

RECIPE tip

You can use 4 cups of cooked bow tie or penne pasta in place of the linguine.

Overnight Vegetable Lasagna

prep: 18 minutes   cook: 1 hour and 15 minutes

1 (14½-ounce) can stewed
   tomatoes, undrained

1½ cups fat-free, no-salt-added
   pasta sauce

2 cups nonfat cottage cheese

½ cup grated Parmesan cheese

¼ teaspoon ground pepper

   Vegetable cooking spray

9 lasagna noodles, uncooked

12 ounces fresh zucchini,
   trimmed and shredded
   (about 3 medium)

6 (1-ounce) slices provolone
   cheese, cut into strips

1 Combine tomatoes and pasta sauce; stir well, and set aside. Combine cottage cheese, Parmesan cheese, and pepper; stir well, and set aside.

2 Spoon one-third tomato mixture into bottom of a 13- x 9- x 2-inch baking dish coated with cooking spray. Place 3 uncooked lasagna noodles over tomato mixture; top with one-third zucchini. Spoon one-third cottage cheese mixture evenly over zucchini; top with 2 slices provolone cheese. Repeat layers twice with remaining tomato mixture, noodles, zucchini, cheese mixture, and provolone slices. (Casserole may be covered and refrigerated at this point and baked later. Bake 50 minutes or until thoroughly heated.)

3 Cover and bake at 350° for 45 minutes. Uncover, and bake 15 additional minutes. Let stand 15 minutes before serving.
Yield: 8 servings.

PER SERVING: CALORIES 308 (25% FROM FAT) FAT 8.5G (SAT 5.1G) PROTEIN 22.4G CARBOHYDRATE 35.7G FIBER 2.3G CHOLESTEROL 23MG SODIUM 783MG EXCHANGES PER SERVING: 2 MEDIUM-FAT MEAT, 2 STARCH, 1 VEGETABLE

Serve with *vanilla nonfat frozen yogurt with fat-free caramel-flavored syrup for dessert.*

TIME-saver

Although it takes a little over an hour to bake this casserole, total hands-on time to prepare the recipe is just 18 minutes because the pasta cooks in the casserole as it bakes. It's an ideal make-ahead dinner—just refrigerate it unbaked, then bake the next day.

Overnight Vegetable Lasagna

Roasted Green Tomato Pizza

prep: 22 minutes   cook: 10 minutes

3 medium-size plum
  tomatoes, sliced

1 medium-size green tomato,
  cut into ½-inch slices

1 small onion, cut into ½-inch
  slices

1 small Golden Delicious
  apple, cored and cut
  into ½-inch-thick slices

  Olive oil-flavored vegetable
  cooking spray

1 (10-ounce) can refrigerated
  pizza crust dough

2 (1-ounce) slices reduced-fat
  American flavor hot
  pepper cheese product,
  cut into thin strips

1 (4½-ounce) can chopped
  green chiles, drained

½ teaspoon minced garlic
  (about 1 clove)

¼ teaspoon ground pepper

1 cup (4 ounces) shredded
  50%-reduced-fat
  mozzarella cheese

1 Place slices of plum tomato, green tomato, onion, and apple on a 15- x 10- x 1-inch jellyroll pan coated with cooking spray; coat vegetables and apple with cooking spray. Bake at 500° for 10 minutes. Remove from oven; set aside. Reduce oven temperature to 425°.

2 Unroll pizza dough onto a baking sheet coated with cooking spray. Pat dough into a 15- x 12-inch rectangle. Bake at 425° for 5 minutes. Top with hot pepper cheese strips; set aside.

3 Set roasted plum tomato slices aside. Chop green tomato, onion, and apple; combine in a small bowl. Press gently with paper towels to remove excess moisture. Add chiles and garlic, stirring well.

4 Top hot pepper cheese strips with green tomato mixture; sprinkle with pepper. Top with roasted plum tomato slices and mozzarella. Bake at 425° for 10 minutes or until cheese melts. Serve immediately. Yield: 4 servings.

PER SERVING: CALORIES 347 (26% FROM FAT) FAT 9.9G (SAT 4.6G) PROTEIN 18.2G CARBOHYDRATE 47.1G FIBER 14.8G CHOLESTEROL 20MG SODIUM 514MG EXCHANGES PER SERVING: 2 MEDIUM-FAT MEAT, 2 STARCH, 1 FRUIT

Serve with *a dessert of lemon nonfat frozen yogurt.*

TIME-saver

For easy cleanup, coat your hands with cooking spray before patting the dough into a rectangle. The dough won't stick to your fingers.

roasted green tomato pizza step-by-step

Arrange hot pepper cheese strips over pizza dough.

Press green tomato mixture with a paper towel to remove excess moisture.

Top green tomato mixture with pepper, roasted tomato slices, and cheese before baking.

Thin-Crust Vegetable Pizza

prep: 20 minutes   cook: 20 minutes

1 (6½-ounce) package pizza crust mix

⅓ cup yellow cornmeal

⅔ cup hot water

Vegetable cooking spray

1 teaspoon vegetable oil

1 large onion, sliced

1 small yellow squash, sliced

1½ teaspoons salt-free herb-and-spice blend

¼ teaspoon salt

2 tablespoons fat-free Italian dressing

1 medium-size tomato, cut into 6 slices

1½ cups (6 ounces) shredded reduced-fat sharp Cheddar cheese

1 Combine pizza crust mix and cornmeal; add ⅔ cup water, stirring well. Shape into a ball; cover and let stand 5 minutes. Pat dough into a 14- x 11-inch rectangle on a large baking sheet coated with cooking spray. Bake at 450° for 5 minutes.

2 Coat a large nonstick skillet with cooking spray; add oil. Place over medium-high heat until hot. Add onion and squash; cook, stirring constantly, 10 minutes or until vegetables are tender and onion is golden. Stir in herb-and-spice blend and salt.

3 Brush crust with dressing; top with onion mixture and tomato slices. Sprinkle with cheese. Bake at 450° for 10 minutes or until crust is golden and cheese melts. Serve immediately.
Yield: 6 servings.

PER SERVING: CALORIES 260 (25% FROM FAT) FAT 7.3G (SAT 3.3G) PROTEIN 13.4G CARBOHYDRATE 14.2G FIBER 2.6G CHOLESTEROL 19MG SODIUM 529MG EXCHANGES PER SERVING: 1½ MEDIUM-FAT MEAT, 1 STARCH

Serve with *a fresh fruit salad.*

RECIPE tip

Most spice blends contain large amounts of sodium. Mrs Dash salt-free spice blends provide a delicious way to add flavor without the sodium. The small amount of salt added to this recipe is less than the amount in a traditional spice blend.

French Bread Pizza

prep: 7 minutes   cook: 10 minutes

1½ cups pizza-pasta sauce

1 (16-ounce) loaf French bread, cut in half lengthwise

1 (4-ounce) can sliced mushrooms, drained

1 (14-ounce) can artichoke hearts, drained and sliced

4 cloves garlic, sliced

½ cup seeded, chopped tomato

2 tablespoons chopped fresh basil or 2 teaspoons dried basil

½ cup (2 ounces) shredded provolone cheese

½ cup (2 ounces) shredded part-skim mozzarella cheese

1 Spread pizza sauce evenly over French bread halves. Arrange mushrooms and next 4 ingredients evenly over sauce. Sprinkle with cheeses. Bake at 450° for 10 minutes or until cheese melts and bread is lightly browned. Cut each bread half into 3 portions.
Yield: 6 servings.

PER SERVING: CALORIES 345 (15% FROM FAT)   FAT 5.9G (SAT 3.1G)   PROTEIN 15.0G   CARBOHYDRATE 54.3G   FIBER 3.8G   CHOLESTEROL 14MG   SODIUM 884MG
EXCHANGES PER SERVING: 3 STARCH, 2 VEGETABLE, 1 FAT

Serve with *a fresh spinach salad.*

WORK-saver

Here's an easy way to seed a tomato: Cut the tomato in half horizontally and then gently squeeze each half to force out the seeds. Or, use a spoon to scoop the seeds from each cavity.

Pizza Pockets

prep: 15 minutes   cook: 12 minutes

Butter-flavored vegetable
cooking spray

1 cup chopped zucchini
(about 1 small)

½ cup chopped sweet red
pepper (about ½
medium)

½ cup coarsely chopped fresh
mushrooms

2½ cups pizza-pasta sauce,
divided

1 (10-ounce) can refrigerated
pizza crust dough

1 cup (4 ounces) shredded
part-skim mozzarella
cheese

2 tablespoons grated nonfat
Parmesan cheese

1 Coat a large nonstick skillet with cooking spray; place over medium-high heat until hot. Add zucchini, red pepper, and mushrooms. Cook, stirring constantly, 5 minutes. Stir in ½ cup pizza sauce; set aside.

2 Roll crust into a 15- x 10-inch rectangle; cut into 4 (7½- x 5-inch) rectangles.

3 Spoon one fourth of vegetable mixture onto one end of each rectangle; sprinkle evenly with mozzarella cheese. Fold rectangles in half over filling; press edges together with a fork. (At this point pockets may be covered and refrigerated to bake later for 12 minutes. Or, assemble pockets, bake 6 minutes, and freeze. Thaw in refrigerator overnight before baking the remaining 6 minutes or until browned.)

4 Coat tops with cooking spray, and sprinkle with Parmesan cheese. Place on a large baking sheet coated with cooking spray. Bake at 400° for 12 minutes or until golden. Serve with remaining 2 cups warm sauce.
Yield: 4 servings.

PER SERVING: CALORIES 338 (20% FROM FAT) FAT 7.4G (SAT 2.9G) PROTEIN 16.0G
CARBOHYDRATE 50.0G FIBER 3.9G CHOLESTEROL 16MG SODIUM 840MG
EXCHANGES PER SERVING: 1 HIGH-FAT MEAT, 3 STARCH, 1 VEGETABLE

Serve with *a citrus salad.*

pizza pocket technique shots

The hardest part of making this recipe is rolling out the pizza dough. It helps to use a heavy rolling pin to roll out the dough.

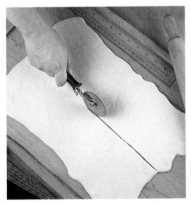

Roll the pizza crust into a 15- x 10-inch rectangle, then cut it into fourths with a pizza cutter.

Spoon the vegetable mixture onto one end of each rectangle (not the center). Fold the dough over the filling.

Press the edges of each pizza pocket with a fork to seal.

meats

Slow-Cooked Beef Burgundy (page 130)

Light-Style Bolognese Sauce

prep: 5 minutes   cook: 30 minutes

Vegetable cooking spray

1½ cups chopped onion
(about 1 medium)

2 teaspoons minced garlic
(about 4 cloves)

½ pound ground round

2 (14.5 ounce) cans no-salt-
added Italian-style
stewed tomatoes,
undrained

1 (8-ounce) can no-salt-added
tomato sauce

1 tablespoon finely chopped
fresh basil or 1 teaspoon
dried basil

1 tablespoon finely chopped
fresh oregano or 1
teaspoon dried oregano

¼ teaspoon dried crushed red
pepper

10 ounces medium egg
noodles, uncooked

¼ cup finely chopped fresh
parsley or 1½ teaspoons
dried parsley

1 Coat a large nonstick skillet with cooking spray; place over medium-high heat until hot. Add onion and garlic; cook, stirring constantly, 3 minutes or until tender. Add ground round, and cook until beef is browned, stirring until it crumbles. Drain well.

2 Add tomatoes and next 4 ingredients to beef mixture in skillet; stir well. Bring to a boil; reduce heat, and simmer, uncovered, 25 minutes, stirring occasionally.

3 While sauce simmers, cook noodles according to package directions, omitting salt and fat; drain. Place 1 cup noodles on each of 5 individual serving plates. Stir parsley into tomato sauce; spoon evenly over noodles.
Yield: 5 servings.

PER SERVING: CALORIES 368 (13% FROM FAT) FAT 5.4G (SAT 1.5G) PROTEIN 20.7G
CARBOHYDRATE 59.8G FIBER 4.0G CHOLESTEROL 82MG SODIUM 76MG
EXCHANGES PER SERVING: 1 MEDIUM-FAT MEAT, 3 STARCH, 3 VEGETABLE

Serve with *a tossed green salad and crusty French bread.*

TIME-saver

Keep this sauce handy in the freezer. If you cook regularly for two, freeze the sauce in 2½-cup portions, and you'll have two meals on hand. Or double the recipe to make 10 cups of sauce, and freeze it in 5-cup portions in heavy-duty, zip-top plastic freezer bags.

Two-Bean Chili Con Carne

prep: 13 minutes   cook: 26 minutes

Vegetable cooking spray

2 cups chopped green pepper
  (about 2 medium)

1 cup chopped onion
  (about 1 small)

1½ teaspoons minced garlic
  (about 3 cloves)

½ pound ground round

1 tablespoon salt-free
  Mexican seasoning

1 (14.5-ounce) can no-salt-
  added diced tomatoes,
  undrained

1 (15-ounce) can chili hot
  beans, undrained

1 (15-ounce) can no-salt-
  added black beans,
  rinsed and drained

½ cup medium salsa

¼ teaspoon salt

½ cup reduced-fat sour cream

1 Coat a Dutch oven with cooking spray; place over medium-high heat until hot. Add pepper, onion, and garlic; cook, stirring constantly, 3 to 5 minutes or until tender. Add ground round, and cook until beef is browned, stirring until it crumbles. Drain well.

2 Stir Mexican seasoning into beef mixture; cook 1 minute. Add tomatoes and next 4 ingredients, stirring well. Bring to a boil. Cover, reduce heat, and simmer 20 minutes, stirring occasionally.

3 Ladle chili evenly into 5 individual serving bowls. Top servings evenly with sour cream.
Yield: 5 servings.

PER SERVING: CALORIES 292 (18% FROM FAT)   FAT 5.9G (SAT 2.7G)   PROTEIN 21.0G
CARBOHYDRATE 38.0G   FIBER 8.8G   CHOLESTEROL 35MG   SODIUM 560MG
EXCHANGES PER SERVING: 2 LEAN MEAT, 2 STARCH, 2 VEGETABLE

Serve with *warm fat-free flour tortillas and fresh pineapple.*

TIME-saver

For added convenience, substitute frozen chopped green pepper and frozen chopped onion for fresh in this recipe. Keep a bag of each in the freezer, and measure out the amount you need at any time.

Quick-and-Easy Salisbury Steaks

prep: 5 minutes   cook: 14 minutes

1 pound ground round

¼ teaspoon garlic powder

¼ teaspoon salt

¼ teaspoon ground pepper

Vegetable cooking spray

1 (8-ounce) package presliced
fresh mushrooms

¼ cup chopped onion

1 tablespoon finely chopped
fresh thyme or 1
teaspoon dried thyme

2 tablespoons dry sherry or
white wine

1 (12-ounce) jar fat-free beef
gravy

Fresh thyme sprigs

1 Combine first 4 ingredients in a medium bowl; mix well. Shape mixture into 4 (½-inch-thick) patties.

2 Coat a large nonstick skillet with cooking spray; place over medium heat until hot. Add patties, and cook 4 to 5 minutes on each side or until done. Remove patties from skillet, and set aside.

3 Increase heat to medium-high; add mushrooms, onion, and thyme; cook, stirring constantly, 3 minutes or until vegetables are tender. Add sherry; cook 1 minute. Stir in gravy; return patties to skillet. Cook 2 minutes or until thoroughly heated. Garnish with thyme, if desired.
Yield: 4 servings.

PER SERVING: CALORIES 208 (31% FROM FAT) FAT 7.2G (SAT 2.5G) PROTEIN 27.1G CARBOHYDRATE 8.5G FIBER 1.0G CHOLESTEROL 70MG SODIUM 729MG EXCHANGES PER SERVING: 4 LEAN MEAT, ½ STARCH

Serve with *mashed potatoes, asparagus, and soft dinner rolls.*

Quick-and-Easy Salisbury Steaks

Barbecued Burgers

prep: 5 minutes   cook: 8 minutes

1 pound ground round

½ cup barbecue sauce, divided

2 tablespoons Italian-
    seasoned breadcrumbs

2 tablespoons dried onion
    flakes

¼ teaspoon ground pepper

    Vegetable cooking spray

4 thin slices purple onion

4 reduced-calorie whole
    wheat hamburger buns

1 Combine ground round, ¼ cup barbecue sauce, breadcrumbs, onion flakes, and pepper; shape mixture into 4 patties.

2 Coat rack of a broiler pan with cooking spray. Place patties and onion slices on rack; broil 5½ inches from heat (with electric oven door partially opened) 8 minutes, brushing occasionally with remaining ¼ cup barbecue sauce.

3 Place a patty and an onion slice on bottom half of each bun. Top with remaining bun halves.
Yield: 4 servings.

PER SERVING: CALORIES 302 (24% FROM FAT) FAT 8.2G (SAT 2.6G) PROTEIN 30.0G
CARBOHYDRATE 31.0G FIBER 6.1G CHOLESTEROL 70MG SODIUM 597MG
EXCHANGES PER SERVING: 3½ LEAN MEAT, 2 STARCH

Serve with *roasted potato wedges.*

RECIPE tip

The beef patties and onion slices may be grilled over medium-hot coals (350° to 400°) 4 minutes on each side, brushing occasionally with barbecue sauce.

Cheeseburger Meat Loaves

prep: 20 minutes   cook: 30 minutes   stand: 10 minutes

¾ pound ground round

1 cup crushed fat-free saltine crackers

¾ cup finely chopped onion (about 1 small)

½ cup finely chopped green pepper (about 1 small)

1 tablespoon low-sodium Worcestershire sauce

2 egg whites, lightly beaten

½ teaspoon minced garlic (about 1 clove)

2 (¾-ounce) slices fat-free American cheese, quartered

Vegetable cooking spray

3 tablespoons reduced-calorie ketchup

1 Combine first 7 ingredients in a large bowl; mix well. Divide meat mixture into 4 equal portions. Shape each portion around 2 pieces of cheese, forming a small loaf.

2 Place loaves in a shallow pan coated with cooking spray. Brush loaves evenly with ketchup. Bake at 350° for 30 minutes or until done. Let stand 10 minutes before serving.
Yield: 4 servings.

PER SERVING: CALORIES 220 (18% FROM FAT) FAT 4.5G (SAT 1.5G) PROTEIN 25.2G
CARBOHYDRATE 17.5G FIBER 0.8G CHOLESTEROL 51MG SODIUM 404MG
EXCHANGES PER SERVING: 3 LEAN MEAT, 1 STARCH

Serve with *green beans and glazed carrots.*

WORK-saver

Use this trick to crush crackers with no mess to clean up:
Place the crackers in a heavy-duty, zip-top plastic bag.
Seal bag, and crush crackers with a rolling pin.

Slow-Cooked Beef Burgundy

prep: 10 minutes   cook: 6 to 10 hours

¼ cup all-purpose flour

½ teaspoon salt

½ teaspoon ground pepper

1 teaspoon minced garlic (about 2 cloves)

2 pounds lean, boneless round steak, cut into 1½-inch pieces

Vegetable cooking spray

¾ cup dry red wine

¾ cup canned no-salt-added beef broth

1 tablespoon tomato paste

1 tablespoon chopped fresh thyme or 1 teaspoon dried thyme

8 ounces baby carrots (about 40 small)

1 large onion, cut into eighths

1 bay leaf

1 (8-ounce) package presliced fresh mushrooms

½ (12-ounce) package yolk-free medium egg noodles

1 Combine first 4 ingredients in a large heavy-duty, zip-top plastic bag; add beef, and seal bag. Shake to coat beef.

2 Coat a large nonstick skillet with cooking spray; place over medium-high heat until hot. Add beef, and cook 10 minutes or until browned on all sides, stirring often.

3 Transfer beef to a 4-quart electric slow cooker coated with cooking spray. Add wine and next 6 ingredients; toss well. Cover and cook 6 hours on high setting or 8 to 10 hours on low setting until meat is tender and sauce thickens. Add mushrooms 1 hour before cooking is completed. Remove and discard bay leaf. Stir thoroughly.

4 Ten minutes before sauce is done, cook noodles according to package directions, omitting salt and fat; drain. Place ½ cup noodles on each of 8 individual serving plates. Spoon beef mixture evenly over hot noodles.
Yield: 8 servings.

PER SERVING: CALORIES 299 (16% FROM FAT) FAT 5.3G (SAT 1.7G) PROTEIN 30.8G
CARBOHYDRATE 26.7G FIBER 2.6G CHOLESTEROL 65MG SODIUM 232MG
EXCHANGES PER SERVING: 3 LEAN MEAT, 2 STARCH

Serve with *a spinach salad and rye rolls.*

Slow-Cooked Beef Burgundy

Beef and Asparagus Stir-Fry

prep: 13 minutes   cook: 8 minutes

1 teaspoon sesame seeds

¾ pound fresh asparagus

Vegetable cooking spray

½ pound lean, boneless top sirloin steak, trimmed and cut into ⅛-inch-thick slices

1 cup sliced fresh mushrooms

¼ teaspoon dried crushed red pepper

3 green onions, cut diagonally into ½-inch pieces

¼ cup low-sodium teriyaki sauce

1 cup hot cooked rice (cooked without salt or fat)

1 Place a large nonstick skillet over medium-high heat until hot. Add sesame seeds. Cook, stirring constantly, 1 to 2 minutes or until toasted. Set aside.

2 Snap off tough ends of asparagus. Remove scales from stalks with a knife or vegetable peeler, if desired. Cut asparagus diagonally into 1-inch pieces. Set aside.

3 Coat skillet with cooking spray; place over medium-high heat until hot. Add beef, and cook, stirring constantly, 3 minutes or to desired degree of doneness. Drain beef, and pat dry with paper towels; wipe drippings from skillet with a paper towel.

4 Coat skillet with cooking spray; place over medium-high heat until hot. Add asparagus, mushrooms, crushed red pepper, and green onions. Cook, stirring constantly, 3 to 4 minutes or until asparagus is crisp-tender. Return beef to skillet, and add teriyaki sauce and cook, stirring constantly, 1 additional minute.

5 Place ½ cup rice on each of 2 individual serving plates. Spoon meat mixture evenly over rice; sprinkle with sesame seeds.
Yield: 2 servings.

PER SERVING: CALORIES 361 (20% FROM FAT) FAT 8.1G (SAT 2.7G) PROTEIN 34.1G
CARBOHYDRATE 37.1G FIBER 2.4G CHOLESTEROL 80MG SODIUM 715MG
EXCHANGES PER SERVING: 4 LEAN MEAT, 2 STARCH, 1 VEGETABLE

Serve with *a cucumber and onion salad.*

TIME-saver

Start cooking the rice before preparing this recipe so it will be ready when the stir-fry mixture is cooked. For speed, use boil-in-bag rice (Success or Uncle Ben's), which cooks in just 10 minutes; each regular-size bag yields 2 cups of cooked rice.

Beef Fajita Pizza

prep: 10 minutes   cook: 13 minutes

2 teaspoons chili powder

¼ teaspoon garlic powder

½ pound lean, boneless sirloin steak, trimmed

½ cup green pepper strips (about 1 small)

½ medium-size purple onion, thinly sliced and separated into rings

1 (16-ounce) Italian bread shell

½ cup chunky salsa

½ cup (2 ounces) shredded reduced-fat Cheddar cheese

1 Place a nonstick skillet over medium-high heat until hot. While skillet heats, combine chili powder and garlic powder; sprinkle over both sides of steak. Add steak to skillet; cook 4 minutes on each side. Remove steak from skillet; let stand 5 minutes. Slice steak diagonally across grain into ¼-inch slices.

2 While steak stands, arrange pepper strips and onion on bread shell. Arrange steak strips over vegetables. Spoon salsa over steak. Bake at 450° for 8 minutes; sprinkle with cheese. Bake 5 additional minutes.
Yield: 4 servings.

PER SERVING: CALORIES 452 (24% FROM FAT)   FAT 12.3G (SAT 4.9G)   PROTEIN 32.7G   CARBOHYDRATE 55.1G   FIBER 2.7G   CHOLESTEROL 54MG   SODIUM 812MG   EXCHANGES PER SERVING: 3 MEDIUM-FAT MEAT, 3 STARCH, 2 VEGETABLE

Serve with *a marinated vegetable salad.*

RECIPE tip

Use a large, prepackaged Italian bread shell, such as Boboli brand. If you prefer individual pizzas, use Boboli's individual-size shells. Store any unused shells in a heavy-duty, zip-top plastic bag in the freezer or the refrigerator.

Steak with Mushroom-Wine Sauce

prep: 4 minutes   cook: 15 minutes

4 (4-ounce) lean beef
   tenderloin steaks

½ teaspoon garlic powder

¼ teaspoon salt

¼ teaspoon freshly ground
   pepper

1 (8-ounce) package presliced
   fresh mushrooms

1½ teaspoons minced garlic
   (about 3 cloves)

½ cup canned no-salt-added
   beef broth

¼ cup dry red wine

2 teaspoons cornstarch

4 slices sourdough bread,
   toasted

1 Sprinkle steaks with garlic powder, salt, and pepper. Place a large nonstick skillet over medium-high heat until hot. Add steaks; cook 3 minutes on each side or until browned. Remove steaks from skillet, and keep warm.

2 Increase heat to medium-high; add mushrooms and garlic. Cook, stirring constantly, 5 minutes or until tender. Combine broth, wine, and cornstarch, stirring until smooth. Add to skillet; cook, stirring constantly, 2 minutes or until thickened and bubbly. Return steaks and any steak juices to skillet; cook 2 additional minutes or to desired degree of doneness.

3 Place 1 slice sourdough toast on each of 4 individual serving plates. Place 1 steak on each piece of toast, and spoon mushroom sauce over steaks.
Yield: 4 servings.

PER SERVING: CALORIES 260 (30% FROM FAT) FAT 8.6G (SAT 3.1G) PROTEIN 27.7G
CARBOHYDRATE 16.9G FIBER 1.2G CHOLESTEROL 71MG SODIUM 341MG
EXCHANGES PER SERVING: 3 LEAN MEAT, 1 STARCH

Serve with a Caesar salad and baked potatoes.

RECIPE tip

Use Marsala wine instead of dry red wine for a deliciously distinctive flavor.

Saucy Italian-Style Pot Roast

prep: 15 minutes   cook: 8 hours and 10 minutes

1 medium onion, coarsely
    chopped

1 (3-pound) lean beef rump
    roast

¼ cup all-purpose flour,
    divided

2 tablespoons finely chopped
    fresh oregano or 2
    teaspoons dried oregano

½ teaspoon salt

¼ teaspoon dried crushed red
    pepper

1 medium-size green pepper,
    coarsely chopped

1 (8-ounce) package presliced
    fresh mushrooms

2 (14½-ounce) cans Italian-
    style diced tomatoes,
    undrained

2 teaspoons minced garlic
    (about 4 cloves)

16 ounces spaghetti, uncooked

3 tablespoons water

1 Place onion in bottom of a 4-quart electric slow cooker; add beef roast. Sprinkle 2 tablespoons flour, oregano, salt, and crushed red pepper over roast. Add green pepper and next 3 ingredients to slow cooker. Cover and cook on low setting 8 hours or until roast is tender.

2 When roast is done, cook spaghetti according to package directions, omitting salt and fat; drain well.

3 While pasta cooks, remove roast from cooker, and slice diagonally across grain; keep warm. Combine remaining 2 tablespoons flour and water, stirring until smooth; add to sauce in cooker. Cook, uncovered, 10 to 15 minutes or until mixture is thickened. Serve meat and sauce over spaghetti.
Yield: 12 servings.

PER SERVING: CALORIES 330 (15% FROM FAT) FAT 5.5G (SAT 1.8G) PROTEIN 32.3G
CARBOHYDRATE 36.0G FIBER 1.9G CHOLESTEROL 65MG SODIUM 250MG
EXCHANGES PER SERVING: 3½ VERY LEAN MEAT, 2 STARCH, 1 VEGETABLE

Serve with *a tossed green salad and crusty French bread.*

RECIPE tip

Sizes of slow cookers vary. Cut the roast in pieces to fit the shape of your slow cooker, if necessary.

Ham and Potato Frittata

prep: 10 minutes   cook: 12 minutes

Butter-flavored vegetable
    cooking spray

¾ cup finely chopped reduced-
    fat, low-salt cooked ham

⅓ cup finely chopped sweet
    red pepper (about ½
    small pepper)

2 cups frozen country-style
    hash brown potatoes

½ cup sliced green onions
    (about 2 large)

¼ teaspoon salt

¼ teaspoon ground pepper

1 (8-ounce) carton fat-free
    egg substitute

⅓ cup (1.3 ounces) shredded
    reduced-fat sharp
    Cheddar cheese

1 Coat a 10-inch nonstick ovenproof skillet with cooking spray; place over medium-high heat until hot. Add ham and red pepper; cook, stirring constantly, 3 minutes. Add potatoes and next 3 ingredients; cook, stirring constantly, 4 to 5 minutes or until vegetables are tender.

2 Reduce heat to medium-low. Add egg substitute; stir gently. Cook 2 to 3 minutes or until nearly set. Place skillet in oven, and bake at 450° for 3 to 4 minutes or until set. Sprinkle with cheese while frittata is hot.
Yield: 4 servings.

PER SERVING: CALORIES 128 (25% FROM FAT) FAT 3.5G (SAT 1.6G) PROTEIN 14.8G CARBOHYDRATE 9.4G FIBER 0.6G CHOLESTEROL 22MG SODIUM 550MG
EXCHANGES PER SERVING: 2 LEAN MEAT, ½ STARCH

Serve with *fresh fruit and blueberry muffins.*

steps to a fast frittata

A frittata is simply a no-fuss omelet. The ingredients are the same, but instead of flipping the egg mixture into a half-moon, the whole recipe cooks in the pan and is served in wedges. This recipe bakes for a few minutes, so use a skillet with an ovenproof handle. If you don't have one, wrap the skillet handle in aluminum foil before baking.

Cook the ham and vegetables over medium-high heat just until tender.

Gently stir the egg substitute into the ham-vegetable mixture in the skillet, and cook over medium-low heat 2 minutes or until almost set.

Bake at 450° for 3 minutes or until the mixture is set; sprinkle cheese over the hot frittata.

Ham and Potato Frittata

Speedy Pork Tostadas

prep: 10 minutes   cook: 7 minutes

4 (8-inch) fat-free flour
    tortillas

    Vegetable cooking spray

½ pound pork tenderloin, cut
    into short, thin strips

1 teaspoon minced garlic
    (about 2 cloves)

1 teaspoon ground cumin

1 (16-ounce) can pinto beans,
    drained

½ cup chunky salsa

2 cups shredded romaine
    lettuce

½ cup (2 ounces) shredded
    reduced-fat Cheddar
    cheese

1 cup chopped tomato (about
    1 medium)

¼ cup nonfat sour cream

1 Arrange tortillas on a baking sheet; coat both sides lightly with cooking spray. Bake at 375° for 7 to 8 minutes or until golden.

2 While tortillas bake, coat a large nonstick skillet with cooking spray; place over medium-high heat until hot. Add pork, garlic, and cumin; cook 3 minutes or until pork is browned on all sides, stirring frequently. Add beans and salsa; simmer 4 minutes or until pork is tender.

3 Place tortillas on 4 individual serving plates; arrange lettuce evenly over tortillas. Top tortillas evenly with pork mixture, cheese, tomato, and sour cream.
Yield: 4 servings.

PER SERVING: CALORIES 339 (22% FROM FAT) FAT 8.2G (SAT 2.6G) PROTEIN 25.1G
CARBOHYDRATE 40.6G FIBER 5.8G CHOLESTEROL 46MG SODIUM 577MG
EXCHANGES PER SERVING: 2 LEAN MEAT, 2 STARCH, 2 VEGETABLE

Serve with melon wedges.

TIME-saver

Use minced garlic from a jar to save some chopping time. Use 1 teaspoon of minced garlic for 2 regular-size cloves.

Peppered Pork

prep: 7 minutes   cook: 15 minutes

1 (1-pound) pork tenderloin

1 teaspoon minced garlic
(about 2 cloves)

1 tablespoon finely chopped
fresh thyme or 1
teaspoon dried thyme

¼ teaspoon salt

¼ teaspoon ground pepper

Vegetable cooking spray

1 (16-ounce) package frozen
pepper stir-fry

3 tablespoons red wine
vinegar

1 tablespoon honey

1 Slice tenderloin crosswise into 1-inch slices. Spread garlic over both sides of slices; sprinkle both sides of slices with thyme, salt, and pepper.

2 Coat a large nonstick skillet with cooking spray; place over medium-high heat until hot. Add pork slices; cook 4 to 6 minutes on each side or until pork is tender. Remove pork from skillet; set aside, and keep warm.

3 Add pepper stir-fry to skillet, and cook, stirring constantly, 3 minutes. Add vinegar and honey; cook 2 minutes. Return pork slices to skillet, and cook 2 minutes or just until thoroughly heated.
Yield: 4 servings.

PER SERVING: CALORIES 202 (20% FROM FAT) FAT 4.4G (SAT 1.5G) PROTEIN 28.5G CARBOHYDRATE 11.4G FIBER 2.6G CHOLESTEROL 83MG SODIUM 246MG EXCHANGES PER SERVING: 3½ VERY LEAN MEAT, 2 VEGETABLE

Serve with *garlic mashed potatoes and yeast rolls.*

RECIPE tip

Two pork tenderloins are packaged together usually.
Freeze one tenderloin to use later, if desired.

Cowboy Pork Chops and Pinto Beans

prep: 5 minutes   cook: 10 minutes

4 (6-ounce) center-cut loin
   pork chops

2 teaspoons ground cumin,
   divided

½ teaspoon garlic powder

¼ teaspoon ground red
   pepper

¼ teaspoon salt

   Vegetable cooking spray

1 (16-ounce) can pinto beans,
   undrained

½ cup salsa

¼ cup barbecue sauce

2 green onions, sliced

1 Trim fat from chops. Sprinkle both sides of chops with 1 teaspoon cumin, garlic powder, ground red pepper, and salt.

2 Place chops on rack of a broiler pan coated with cooking spray. Broil chops 5½ inches from heat (with electric oven door partially opened) 5 minutes on each side.

3 While chops broil, combine remaining 1 teaspoon cumin, beans, and remaining 3 ingredients in a medium saucepan. Bring to a boil; reduce heat, and simmer, uncovered, 8 minutes, stirring occasionally. Serve chops with beans.
Yield: 4 servings.

PER SERVING: CALORIES 317 (34% FROM FAT)   FAT 12.1G (SAT 3.7G)   PROTEIN 28.6G
CARBOHYDRATE 22.6G   FIBER 1.0G   CHOLESTEROL 72MG   SODIUM 415MG
EXCHANGES PER SERVING: 3 MEDIUM-FAT MEAT, 1 STARCH, 1 VEGETABLE

Serve with *zucchini, watermelon wedges, and cornbread.*

RECIPE tip

These chops are especially good grilled. Grill 4 minutes on each side over medium-hot coals (350° to 400°).

*Cowboy Pork Chops
and Pinto Beans*

Venison Kabobs

1 pound lean venison, cut into
   1½-inch cubes

1 small purple onion, cut into
   1-inch pieces

1 medium-size sweet red
   pepper, cut into 1-inch
   pieces

1 medium-size green pepper,
   cut into 1-inch pieces

½ cup mango or other fruit
   chutney

⅓ cup honey mustard

1 tablespoon water

1 teaspoon minced garlic
   (about 2 cloves)

   Vegetable cooking spray

1 Thread venison, onion pieces, and pepper pieces alternately onto 4 (15-inch) metal skewers.

2 Combine chutney and next 3 ingredients in a small bowl; stir well. Brush mixture evenly on kabobs.

3 Coat rack of a broiler pan with cooking spray. Place kabobs on rack; broil 5½ inches from heat (with electric oven door partially opened) 8 to 10 minutes or to desired degree of doneness, turning occasionally.
Yield: 4 servings.

PER SERVING: CALORIES 270 (13% FROM FAT) FAT 3.9G (SAT 1.1G) PROTEIN 27.4G
CARBOHYDRATE 32.2G FIBER 2.1G CHOLESTEROL 95MG SODIUM 177MG
EXCHANGES PER SERVING: 3 VERY LEAN MEAT, 1½ STARCH, 2 VEGETABLE

Serve with *basmati rice and baked apples.*

RECIPE tip

Grill the kabobs, covered, 8 to 10 minutes over medium-hot coals (350° to 400°), if desired.

poultry

Crispy Cornmeal Chicken (page 150)

Vegetable-Chicken Soup with Dumplings

prep: 9 minutes   cook: 30 minutes

1 (16-ounce) package frozen homestyle stew vegetables with carrots, potatoes, onions, and English peas

8 cups canned no-salt-added chicken broth

3 cups preshredded cabbage

1½ cups coarsely chopped onion (1 medium)

¼ cup finely chopped fresh parsley or 1 tablespoon plus 1 teaspoon dried parsley

2 tablespoons finely chopped fresh basil or 2 teaspoons dried basil

1½ teaspoons minced garlic (about 3 cloves)

½ teaspoon ground pepper

1 (4.5-ounce) can refrigerated buttermilk biscuits

3 cups chopped deli-roasted chicken

1 Combine first 8 ingredients in a Dutch oven; bring to a boil. Cover, reduce heat to low, and simmer 20 minutes or until vegetables are tender.

2 Separate biscuits, and press each to ¼-inch thickness.

3 Remove cover from Dutch oven; increase heat to medium-high, and bring soup to a boil. Stir in chicken. Cut biscuits into ½-inch pieces using kitchen scissors. Drop biscuit pieces into boiling soup; reduce heat to medium-low, and cook, uncovered, 10 minutes, stirring occasionally.
Yield: 7 servings.

PER SERVING: CALORIES 253 (21% FROM FAT) FAT 5.8G (SAT 1.4G) PROTEIN 23.3G CARBOHYDRATE 23.0G FIBER 3.6G CHOLESTEROL 58MG SODIUM 968MG
EXCHANGES PER SERVING: 3 LEAN MEAT, 1 STARCH, 1 VEGETABLE

Serve with apple wedges and seedless grapes.

RECIPE tip

We used Pillsbury buttermilk biscuits to test this recipe. Substitute any other canned biscuit, except for the flaky-style biscuits.

Black Bean and Chicken Pizzas

prep: 5 minutes   cook: 10 minutes

2 cups shredded cooked
    chicken

1 teaspoon ground cumin

1 cup chunky salsa

4 (6-inch) Italian bread shells
    (Boboli)

1 (15-ounce) can no-salt-
    added black beans,
    rinsed and drained

¾ cup (3 ounces) shredded
    reduced-fat sharp
    Cheddar cheese

½ cup thinly sliced green
    onions (about 2 large)

¼ cup nonfat sour cream
    (optional)

1 Sprinkle chicken with cumin; toss well. Spread salsa evenly over bread shells to within ½ inch of edges; arrange chicken over salsa. Layer beans over chicken; sprinkle with cheese. Place pizzas on a large ungreased baking sheet.

2 Bake at 450° for 10 minutes or until cheese melts and crust is golden; sprinkle with green onions. Top each pizza with 1 tablespoon sour cream, if desired. Serve immediately. Yield: 4 servings.

PER SERVING: CALORIES 437 (21% FROM FAT) FAT 10.3G (SAT 4.2G) PROTEIN 42.6G
CARBOHYDRATE 41.9G FIBER 4.1G CHOLESTEROL 80MG SODIUM 806MG
EXCHANGES PER SERVING: 4 LEAN MEAT, 3 STARCH

Serve with a tossed green salad.

Speedy Herbed Chicken Hash

prep: 10 minutes   cook: 14 minutes

Vegetable cooking spray

2 teaspoons margarine

1 (26-ounce) package frozen
    country-style hash
    brown potatoes, thawed

1 (10-ounce) package chopped
    onion, celery, and pepper
    blend, thawed

2½ cups chopped cooked
    chicken

½ cup canned no-salt-added
    chicken broth

½ teaspoon ground sage

½ teaspoon dried rosemary,
    crushed

¼ teaspoon salt

¼ teaspoon ground pepper

1 Coat a large nonstick skillet with cooking spray; add margarine. Place over medium-high heat until margarine melts. Add potatoes and vegetable blend; cook 7 minutes or until potatoes begin to brown, stirring occasionally.

2 Add chicken and remaining ingredients; stir well. Cover and cook over medium-high heat 5 minutes or until thoroughly heated. Yield: 5 servings.

PER SERVING: CALORIES 290 (24% FROM FAT) FAT 7.6G (SAT 1.9G) PROTEIN 24.8G
CARBOHYDRATE 29.4G FIBER 1.6G CHOLESTEROL 69MG SODIUM 216MG
EXCHANGES PER SERVING: 3 LEAN MEAT, 2 STARCH

Serve with a spinach-mushroom salad and cornbread.

RECIPE tip

The vegetable blend is labeled "seasoning blend" and can be found with the frozen vegetables in the supermarket.

Black Bean and Chicken Pizzas

Moroccan Chicken with Couscous

prep: 7 minutes   cook: 12 minutes

1 pound skinned, boned
   chicken breast halves

½ teaspoon ground ginger

¼ teaspoon ground cumin

¼ teaspoon ground turmeric

¼ teaspoon salt

   Vegetable cooking spray

1 teaspoon vegetable oil

½ teaspoon minced garlic
   (about 1 clove)

1 (16-ounce) can no-salt-
   added chicken broth

1 cup frozen English peas,
   thawed

1 cup couscous, uncooked

¼ cup chopped fresh cilantro
   or 1 tablespoon plus 1
   teaspoon dried cilantro

1 Cut chicken lengthwise into 1-inch-wide strips. Combine ginger and next 3 ingredients. Sprinkle evenly over chicken; set aside.

2 Coat a large nonstick skillet with cooking spray; add oil, and place over medium-high heat until hot. Add chicken and garlic; cook 3 minutes or until chicken is lightly browned. Add broth and peas; bring to a boil. Reduce heat, and simmer 2 minutes or until chicken is done. Stir in couscous; cover and remove from heat. Let stand 5 minutes or until liquid is absorbed. Sprinkle with cilantro.
Yield: 4 servings.

PER SERVING: CALORIES 329 (9% FROM FAT) FAT 3.3G (SAT 0.6G) PROTEIN 34.0G
CARBOHYDRATE 38.3G FIBER 3.3G CHOLESTEROL 66MG SODIUM 506MG
EXCHANGES PER SERVING: 4 VERY LEAN MEAT, 2 STARCH, 1 VEGETABLE

***Serve with** carrots and dinner rolls.*

Hoisin Chicken Kabobs

make ahead

prep: 14 minutes   marinate: 30 minutes to 8 hours   cook: 10 minutes

¼ cup hoisin sauce

1 tablespoon rice vinegar

½ teaspoon minced garlic
   (about 1 clove)

1 pound skinned, boned
   chicken breasts, cut into
   1-inch pieces

4 large green onions, cut
   diagonally into 1-inch
   pieces

   Vegetable cooking spray

1 Combine first 3 ingredients in a large heavy-duty, zip-top plastic bag; add chicken. Seal bag, and shake gently to coat chicken. Marinate in refrigerator 30 minutes to 8 hours.

2 Remove chicken from marinade, reserving marinade. Alternately thread chicken and onions onto 4 (12-inch) metal skewers. Brush kabobs with reserved marinade.

3 Place chicken on rack of a broiler pan coated with cooking spray. Broil 5½ inches from heat (with electric oven door partially opened) 5 minutes on each side or until chicken is done.
Yield: 4 servings.

PER SERVING: CALORIES 193 (14% FROM FAT) FAT 3.1G (SAT 0.8G) PROTEIN 26.2G
CARBOHYDRATE 13.5G FIBER 0.3G CHOLESTEROL 70MG SODIUM 594MG
EXCHANGES PER SERVING: 3 VERY LEAN MEAT, 1 STARCH

***Serve with** rice and stir-fried mixed vegetables.*

Gingered Chicken Stir-Fry

prep: 5 minutes   cook: 10 minutes

1 regular-size bag boil-in-bag rice, uncooked or 2 cups hot cooked rice (cooked without salt or fat)

⅓ cup stir-fry sauce

½ teaspoon ground ginger

½ teaspoon garlic powder

Vegetable cooking spray

2 teaspoons dark sesame oil

1 pound skinned, boned chicken breasts, cut into bite-size pieces

1 (16-ounce) package frozen Oriental-style vegetables

1 Cook rice according to package directions, omitting salt and fat.

2 While rice cooks, combine stir-fry sauce, ginger, and garlic powder in a small bowl, stirring well; set aside. Coat a large nonstick skillet with cooking spray; add oil, and place over medium-high heat until hot. Add chicken, and stir-fry 4 minutes or until chicken is done. Remove from skillet; set aside.

3 Add vegetables to skillet; stir-fry 3 minutes. Stir in chicken and stir-fry sauce mixture. Cook over medium-high heat until thoroughly heated. Serve over rice.
Yield: 4 servings.

PER SERVING: CALORIES 315 (11% FROM FAT) FAT 4.0G (SAT 0.7G) PROTEIN 31.3G
CARBOHYDRATE 37.4G FIBER 2.5G CHOLESTEROL 66MG SODIUM 796MG
EXCHANGES PER SERVING: 3 VERY LEAN MEAT, 2 STARCH, 1 VEGETABLE

Serve with *fresh pineapple wedges.*

TIME-saver

Cut the cooking time for rice in half when you use boil-in-bag rice, such as Success or Uncle Ben's brand rice; it cooks in just 10 minutes. One regular-size bag of uncooked rice will give you 2 cups of cooked rice. A larger-size bag yields 3 cups of cooked rice.

Sesame Chicken Tenders

2 egg whites, lightly beaten

2 tablespoons low-sodium soy sauce

1 tablespoon honey

¾ cup crushed corn flakes cereal

1½ tablespoons sesame seeds

½ teaspoon paprika

¼ teaspoon salt

¼ teaspoon ground pepper

1 pound chicken tenderloins

Vegetable cooking spray

prep: 10 minutes   cook: 23 minutes

1 Combine first 3 ingredients in a medium bowl, stirring with a wire whisk. Combine next 5 ingredients in a small bowl.

2 Dip chicken in egg white mixture, and dredge in cereal mixture. Place chicken on a baking sheet coated with cooking spray. Bake at 400° for 23 to 25 minutes or until crispy and golden.
Yield: 4 servings.

PER SERVING: CALORIES 239 (12% FROM FAT)   FAT 3.3G (SAT 0.6G)   PROTEIN 29.7G
CARBOHYDRATE 20.4G   FIBER 0.4G   CHOLESTEROL 66MG   SODIUM 609MG
EXCHANGES PER SERVING: 3½ VERY LEAN MEAT, 1½ STARCH

***Serve with** a vegetable-pasta salad and fresh fruit.*

RECIPE tip

Serve these crispy chicken tenders with any of the following as a dip:

1 Tablespoon	Calories	Fat
Barbecue Sauce	12	0.3g
Fat-free Ranch-style Dressing	25	0.0g
Honey	64	0.0g
Honey-Mustard	30	1.5g
Ketchup	18	0.1g
Sweet-and-Sour Sauce	27	0.0g

Chicken with Curried Apricot Sauce

1 regular-size bag boil-in-bag rice, uncooked or 2 cups hot cooked rice (cooked without salt or fat)

Vegetable cooking spray

4 (4-ounce) skinned, boned chicken breast halves

½ teaspoon minced garlic (about 1 clove)

½ cup no-sugar-added apricot spread

3 tablespoons canned no-salt-added chicken broth

½ teaspoon curry powder

⅓ cup reduced-fat sour cream

½ teaspoon prepared horseradish

¼ teaspoon salt

⅛ teaspoon ground pepper

prep: 5 minutes   cook: 18 minutes

1 Cook rice according to package directions, omitting salt and fat.

2 While rice cooks, coat a large nonstick skillet with cooking spray; place over medium-high heat until hot. Add chicken, and cook 2 minutes on each side or until lightly browned. Remove chicken from skillet; set aside.

3 Add garlic to skillet; cook, stirring constantly, 1 minute. Combine apricot spread, chicken broth, and curry powder, stirring well. Add apricot mixture and chicken to skillet. Bring to a boil; cover, reduce heat, and simmer 10 minutes.

4 Uncover and stir in sour cream and remaining 3 ingredients; simmer 2 minutes. To serve, place ½ cup rice onto each of 4 individual serving plates. Top with chicken. Spoon apricot sauce evenly over chicken.
Yield: 4 servings.

PER SERVING: CALORIES 321 (11% FROM FAT) FAT 4.1G (SAT 1.9G) PROTEIN 29.1G
CARBOHYDRATE 40.1G FIBER 0.6G CHOLESTEROL 73MG SODIUM 306MG
EXCHANGES PER SERVING: 3 VERY LEAN MEAT, 2½ STARCH

Serve with *a mixed vegetable salad and baguettes.*

Spicy Orange Chicken

s u p e r q u i c k

1 tablespoon chopped fresh thyme or 1 teaspoon dried thyme

¼ teaspoon ground black pepper

¼ teaspoon ground red pepper

4 (4-ounce) skinned, boned chicken breast halves

¼ cup orange marmalade

1 tablespoon Dijon mustard

Vegetable cooking spray

prep: 5 minutes   cook: 10 minutes

1 Combine first 3 ingredients; sprinkle evenly over both sides of chicken.

2 Combine marmalade and mustard in a small bowl, stirring well. Brush both sides of chicken with half of marmalade mixture.

3 Place chicken on rack of a broiler pan coated with cooking spray. Broil 5½ inches from heat (with electric oven door partially opened) 5 minutes. Turn chicken; baste with remaining marmalade mixture, and broil 5 additional minutes or until chicken is done.
Yield: 4 servings.

PER SERVING: CALORIES 193 (16% FROM FAT) FAT 3.4G (SAT 0.8G) PROTEIN 25.8G
CARBOHYDRATE 13.9G FIBER 0.1G CHOLESTEROL 70MG SODIUM 184MG
EXCHANGES PER SERVING: 3 VERY LEAN MEAT, 1 STARCH

Serve with *couscous and broccoli.*

Crispy Cornmeal Chicken

prep: 10 minutes   cook: 10 minutes

4 (4-ounce) skinned, boned chicken breast halves

⅓ cup yellow cornmeal

1 teaspoon chili powder

¼ teaspoon garlic powder

¼ teaspoon salt

1 tablespoon all-purpose flour

2 egg whites, lightly beaten

2 teaspoons vegetable oil

½ cup salsa

1 Place chicken between 2 sheets of heavy-duty plastic wrap, and flatten to ½-inch thickness, using a meat mallet or rolling pin.

2 Combine cornmeal and next 3 ingredients in a small bowl. Sprinkle flour evenly over each chicken breast half; dip in egg whites, and dredge in cornmeal mixture.

3 Heat oil in a large nonstick skillet over medium heat until hot. Add chicken, and cook 5 to 6 minutes on each side or until chicken is done. Serve with salsa.
Yield: 4 servings.

PER SERVING: CALORIES 211 (17% FROM FAT) FAT 4.1G (SAT 0.8G) PROTEIN 29.5G CARBOHYDRATE 12.6G FIBER 1.5G CHOLESTEROL 66MG SODIUM 337MG
EXCHANGES PER SERVING: 4 VERY LEAN MEAT, 1 STARCH

Serve with *coleslaw and corn on the cob.*

TIME-saver

Place chicken breast halves, one at a time, in a heavy-duty, zip-top plastic bag. Seal the bag, and pound each chicken breast half. Use the same zip-top bag for each breast half; then discard the bag.

Honeyed Chicken

superquick

prep: 3 minutes   cook: 11 minutes

4 (4-ounce) skinned, boned chicken breast halves

2 tablespoons low-sodium soy sauce

Vegetable cooking spray

¼ cup honey

2 tablespoons fresh lime juice

¼ cup chopped green onion (about 1 large)

1 Brush both sides of each chicken breast half with soy sauce. Coat a large nonstick skillet with cooking spray; place over medium-high heat until hot. Add chicken and any remaining soy sauce to skillet; cook 5 to 6 minutes on each side or until chicken is done. Transfer to a serving platter; keep warm.

2 Add honey and lime juice to skillet; simmer 1 to 2 minutes or until thickened, stirring frequently. Pour honey mixture over chicken; sprinkle with green onion.
Yield: 4 servings.

PER SERVING: CALORIES 197 (7% FROM FAT) FAT 1.5G (SAT 0.4G) PROTEIN 26.4G CARBOHYDRATE 18.5G FIBER 0.1G CHOLESTEROL 66MG SODIUM 270MG
EXCHANGES PER SERVING: 3 VERY LEAN MEAT, 1 STARCH

Serve with *basmati rice and snow peas and peppers.*

Crispy Cornmeal Chicken

Broiled Parmesan Chicken

prep: 5 minutes   cook: 10 minutes

½ cup Italian-seasoned
   breadcrumbs

2 tablespoons grated
   Parmesan cheese

4 (4-ounce) skinned, boned
   chicken breast halves

3 tablespoons coarse-grained
   mustard

   Vegetable cooking spray

1 Combine breadcrumbs and cheese in a small bowl, stirring well. Brush both sides of each chicken breast half with mustard; dredge in breadcrumb mixture.

2 Place chicken on rack of a broiler pan coated with cooking spray. Broil 5½ inches from heat (with electric oven door partially opened) 5 minutes on each side or until chicken is done. Serve immediately.
Yield: 4 servings.

PER SERVING: CALORIES 180 (18% FROM FAT)   FAT 3.6G (SAT 1.1G)   PROTEIN 29.4G   CARBOHYDRATE 6.0G   FIBER 0.2G   CHOLESTEROL 69MG   SODIUM 492MG
EXCHANGES PER SERVING: 4 VERY LEAN MEAT, ½ STARCH

Serve with **garlic mashed potatoes and zucchini and red peppers.**

Easy Oven-Barbecued Chicken

prep: 7 minutes   cook: 45 minutes

1 teaspoon paprika

½ teaspoon rubbed sage

¼ teaspoon celery salt

6 (6-ounce) skinned chicken
   breast halves

¼ cup reduced-calorie ketchup

2 tablespoons brown sugar

1 tablespoon low-sodium
   Worcestershire sauce

1 tablespoon low-sodium soy
   sauce

½ teaspoon minced garlic
   (about 1 clove)

¼ teaspoon hot sauce

1 Line a 13- x 9- x 2-inch pan with aluminum foil. Combine first 3 ingredients; sprinkle evenly over chicken. Place chicken, bone sides up, in prepared pan.

2 Combine ketchup and remaining 5 ingredients. Brush half of ketchup mixture evenly over chicken; reserve remaining ketchup mixture. Bake, uncovered, at 375° for 25 minutes. Turn chicken, and brush with remaining ketchup mixture. Bake, uncovered, 20 additional minutes or until chicken is tender.
Yield: 6 servings.

PER SERVING: CALORIES 146 (9% FROM FAT)   FAT 1.5G (SAT 0.4G)   PROTEIN 26.3G   CARBOHYDRATE 4.6G   FIBER 0.1G   CHOLESTEROL 66MG   SODIUM 240MG
EXCHANGES PER SERVING: 4 VERY LEAN MEAT

Serve with **potato salad, marinated tomatoes, and dinner rolls.**

TIME-saver

Lining the pan with aluminum foil saves cleanup time. Use this technique for any saucy recipe that you bake.

Dutch Oven Chicken and Rice

prep: 5 minutes   cook: 50 minutes

- 2½ pounds assorted chicken pieces, skinned
- 1 teaspoon paprika
- ½ teaspoon ground pepper
- ¼ teaspoon salt
- Vegetable cooking spray
- 1½ teaspoons vegetable oil
- 1½ cups long-grain rice, uncooked
- 1 teaspoon minced garlic (about 2 cloves)
- 1 (16-ounce) can no-salt-added chicken broth
- 1 (14½-ounce) can pasta-style chunky tomatoes, undrained
- 1 green pepper, seeded and cut into thin strips
- 1½ cups frozen English peas

1 Sprinkle chicken with paprika, pepper, and salt. Coat an oven-proof Dutch oven with cooking spray. Add oil, and place over medium-high heat until hot. Add chicken to Dutch oven; cook on all sides until browned. Remove chicken from Dutch oven, and set aside.

2 Add rice and garlic to Dutch oven. Cook over medium-high heat, stirring constantly, 1 minute. Add broth, tomatoes, and green pepper. Bring mixture to a boil over high heat, stirring once. Return chicken to Dutch oven.

3 Cover and bake at 350° for 40 minutes. Stir in peas; cover and let stand 5 minutes.
Yield: 5 servings.

PER SERVING: CALORIES 428 (12% FROM FAT)   FAT 5.5G (SAT 1.3G)   PROTEIN 30.7G   CARBOHYDRATE 60.8G   FIBER 4.5G   CHOLESTEROL 76MG   SODIUM 837MG   EXCHANGES PER SERVING: 3 LEAN MEAT, 4 STARCH

***Serve with** a fresh spinach salad and apple muffins.*

RECIPE tip

If your Dutch oven doesn't have ovenproof handles, wrap the handles in heavy-duty aluminum foil and place the Dutch oven on a lower rack in the oven.

*Dutch Oven
Chicken and Rice*

Turkey Provençal

prep: 10 minutes   cook: 21 minutes

8 ounces angel hair pasta, uncooked

Olive oil-flavored vegetable cooking spray

1 teaspoon olive oil

1½ cups coarsely chopped onion (about 1 medium)

1 pound turkey tenderloins, cut into 1-inch pieces

1 teaspoon minced garlic (about 2 cloves)

1 large zucchini, cut into ½-inch pieces

2 cups low-fat mushroom and sweet pepper pasta sauce

¼ cup grated Parmesan cheese

1 Cook pasta according to package directions, omitting salt and fat. Drain, and keep warm.

2 Coat a large nonstick skillet with cooking spray. Add oil; place over medium-high heat until hot. Add onion; cook, stirring constantly, 4 minutes. Add turkey and garlic; cook 10 minutes or until turkey is done, stirring occasionally. Add zucchini; cook 2 minutes. Add pasta sauce; reduce heat, and simmer 5 minutes.

3 Place 1 cup pasta on each of 4 individual serving plates; top evenly with turkey mixture. Sprinkle evenly with cheese.
Yield: 4 servings.

PER SERVING: CALORIES 421 (15% FROM FAT) FAT 6.8G (SAT 2.2G) PROTEIN 38.8G CARBOHYDRATE 50.2G FIBER 5.7G CHOLESTEROL 74MG SODIUM 792MG EXCHANGES PER SERVING: 4 VERY LEAN MEAT, 3 STARCH, 1 VEGETABLE

Serve with *a tossed green salad and crusty French bread.*

RECIPE tip

Substitute any flavor low-fat pasta sauce for the mushroom and sweet pepper pasta sauce.

Turkey Scaloppine with Tomatoes

prep: 7 minutes   cook: 8 minutes

½ cup fine, dry breadcrumbs

1 tablespoon chopped fresh basil or 1 teaspoon dried basil

¼ teaspoon garlic powder

¼ teaspoon ground pepper

⅛ teaspoon salt

1 pound turkey breast slices

2 egg whites, lightly beaten

Olive oil-flavored vegetable cooking spray

1 teaspoon olive oil, divided

¼ cup dry vermouth

¼ cup canned no-salt-added chicken broth

1 teaspoon cornstarch

1 cup chopped tomato (about 1 small)

1 Combine first 5 ingredients in a small bowl; stir well. Dip each turkey slice in egg whites; dredge in breadcrumb mixture.

2 Coat a large nonstick skillet with cooking spray; add ½ teaspoon oil. Place over medium-high heat until hot. Add half of turkey slices; cook 2 to 3 minutes on each side or until turkey is done. Repeat procedure with remaining ½ teaspoon oil and turkey slices. Place turkey on a serving platter; set aside, and keep warm.

3 Combine vermouth, broth, and cornstarch; stir well. Add to skillet; cook over medium heat, stirring constantly, 1 minute or until slightly thickened. Add tomato; cook until thoroughly heated. Spoon over turkey. Serve immediately.
Yield: 4 servings.

PER SERVING: CALORIES 191 (16% FROM FAT) FAT 3.5G (SAT 0.8G) PROTEIN 29.6G
CARBOHYDRATE 8.1G FIBER 0.7G CHOLESTEROL 68MG SODIUM 293MG
EXCHANGES PER SERVING: 4 VERY LEAN MEAT, 1 VEGETABLE

Serve with *rice and roasted mixed vegetables.*

TIME-saver

Cook the broth mixture and chop the tomato while the turkey slices cook.

Turkey-Mushroom Strata

prep: 10 minutes   chill: at least 8 hours   cook: 40 minutes

5 (1.4-ounce) sourdough rolls

Vegetable cooking spray

1 pound turkey breakfast
   sausage

¾ cup (3 ounces) shredded
   Swiss cheese

1 (8-ounce) package presliced
   mushrooms

⅓ cup finely chopped onion
   (about ⅓ small onion)

1½ cups fat-free milk

1 cup fat-free egg substitute

½ teaspoon ground pepper

¼ teaspoon salt

¼ teaspoon dry mustard

1 Cut sourdough rolls into 1-inch cubes; layer evenly in a 13- x 9- x 2-inch baking dish coated with cooking spray. Set aside.

2 Coat a large nonstick skillet with cooking spray; place over medium-high heat until hot. Add sausage, and cook until sausage is browned, stirring until it crumbles; drain if necessary. Layer sausage and cheese over bread cubes.

3 Add mushrooms and onion to skillet; cook over medium-high heat, stirring constantly, 4 minutes or until tender. Layer over cheese in baking dish; set aside.

4 Combine milk and remaining 4 ingredients, stirring until smooth. Pour over bread-mushroom mixture in baking dish. Cover and chill at least 8 hours or overnight.

5 Bake, uncovered, at 350° for 35 minutes or until a knife inserted in center comes out clean. Let stand 5 minutes before serving.
Yield: 8 servings.

PER SERVING: CALORIES 240 (39% FROM FAT) FAT 10.3G (SAT 4.0G) PROTEIN 20.4G
CARBOHYDRATE 17.1G FIBER 1.1G CHOLESTEROL 55MG SODIUM 665MG
EXCHANGES PER SERVING: 3 LEAN MEAT, 1 STARCH

Serve with *a brunch menu of lemon asparagus and fresh fruit.*

Italian-Style Turkey Rigatoni

prep: 12 minutes   cook: 18 minutes

8 ounces rigatoni, uncooked

   Olive oil-flavored vegetable
   cooking spray

¾ pound Italian turkey
   sausage

1 cup chopped onion (about
   1 small)

1 (26-ounce) jar fat-free, no-
   salt-added pasta sauce
   (Enrico's)

¼ teaspoon dried crushed red
   pepper

2 tablespoons freshly grated
   Parmesan cheese

1 Cook pasta according to package directions, omitting salt and fat. Drain, and keep warm.

2 While pasta cooks, coat a large nonstick skillet with cooking spray; place over medium-high heat until hot. Remove casings from sausage. Add sausage and onion to skillet; cook until sausage is browned and onion is tender, stirring until sausage crumbles. Drain and pat dry with paper towels. Wipe drippings from skillet with a paper towel.

3 Return sausage mixture to skillet; add pasta sauce and red pepper. Bring to a boil; reduce heat, and simmer 10 minutes.

4 Combine pasta and sausage mixture in a large bowl, tossing well. Sprinkle with Parmesan cheese. Serve immediately.
Yield: 4 servings.

PER SERVING: CALORIES 461 (16% FROM FAT) FAT 8.0G (SAT 2.5G) PROTEIN 29.0G
CARBOHYDRATE 67.7G FIBER 8.9G CHOLESTEROL 57MG SODIUM 534MG
EXCHANGES PER SERVING: 2 MEDIUM-FAT MEAT, 4 STARCH

Serve with *a tossed green salad and garlic bread.*

RECIPE tip

Use kitchen scissors or a sharp knife to split the casings lengthwise down sausage links. Peel off the casings, then discard them.

salads & salad dressings

Summer Fruit Salad (page 164)

Chunky Salsa Dressing

superquick

prep: 2 minutes

½ cup fat-free garden tomato
   salad dressing (Paula's)

¼ cup mild salsa

1 Combine dressing and salsa in a small bowl; stir well. Serve over tossed salad greens, sliced fresh vegetables, or baked potatoes.
Yield: ¾ cup.

PER TABLESPOON: CALORIES 8 (11% FROM FAT) FAT 0.0G (SAT 0.0G) PROTEIN 0.1G
CARBOHYDRATE 1.9G FIBER 0.1G CHOLESTEROL 0MG SODIUM 71MG
EXCHANGE PER TABLESPOON: FREE

Curried Cucumber Dressing

make ahead

prep: 5 minutes   chill: 1 to 8 hours

1 cup plain nonfat yogurt

½ cup peeled, seeded, and
   finely chopped
   cucumber

¼ cup nonfat mayonnaise

¼ cup low-fat milk

½ teaspoon curry powder

¼ teaspoon salt

1 Combine all ingredients in a medium bowl, stirring well. Cover and chill at least 1 hour. Serve with sliced tomato.
Yield: 2 cups.

PER TABLESPOON: CALORIES 8 (0% FROM FAT) FAT 0.0G (SAT 0.0G) PROTEIN 0.5G
CARBOHYDRATE 1.4G FIBER 0.0G CHOLESTEROL 0MG SODIUM 72MG
EXCHANGE PER TABLESPOON: FREE

Buttermilk-Dillweed Dressing

superquick

prep: 3 minutes

1 cup nonfat buttermilk

½ cup nonfat sour cream

1 tablespoon lemon juice

1 teaspoon dried dillweed

½ teaspoon salt

¼ teaspoon ground pepper

1 Combine all ingredients in a medium bowl; stir with a wire whisk until smooth. Store in refrigerator. Serve with tossed salad greens, tuna, or vegetable salads.
Yield: 1½ cups plus 2 tablespoons.

PER TABLESPOON: CALORIES 7 (0% FROM FAT) FAT 0.0G (SAT 0.0G) PROTEIN 0.7G
CARBOHYDRATE 0.9G FIBER 0.0G CHOLESTEROL 0MG SODIUM 59MG
EXCHANGE PER TABLESPOON: FREE

5 Ways to Dress a Salad

Add one or two ingredients to fat-free Italian dressing, and you can create five ways to top your salads—all in 2 minutes or less.

Tomato Dressing

prep: 1 minute

Combine ½ cup fat-free Italian dressing and 2 tablespoons no-salt-added tomato paste in a small bowl, stirring with a wire whisk until smooth. Serve over tossed salad greens.
Yield: ½ cup plus 2 tablespoons.

PER TABLESPOON: CALORIES 8 (0% FROM FAT)
FAT 0.0G (SAT 0.0G) PROTEIN 0.1G CARBOHYDRATE 2.0G
FIBER 0.0G CHOLESTEROL 0MG SODIUM 130MG
EXCHANGE PER TABLESPOON: FREE

Mustard Vinaigrette

prep: 1 minute

Combine ½ cup fat-free Italian dressing and 1 tablespoon coarse-grained mustard in a small bowl, stirring with a wire whisk until blended. Serve over tossed salad greens or baked potatoes.
Yield: ½ cup.

PER TABLESPOON: CALORIES 10 (9% FROM FAT)
FAT 0.1G (SAT 0.0G) PROTEIN 0.1G CARBOHYDRATE 1.9G
FIBER 0.0G CHOLESTEROL 0MG SODIUM 217MG
EXCHANGE PER TABLESPOON: FREE

Basil Dressing

prep: 2 minutes

Combine ½ cup fat-free Italian dressing and
1 tablespoon finely chopped fresh basil in a small
bowl; stir well. Serve over tossed salad greens.
Yield: ½ cup.

PER TABLESPOON: CALORIES 8 (0% FROM FAT)
FAT 0.0G (SAT 0.0G)   PROTEIN 0.1G   CARBOHYDRATE 1.8G
FIBER 0.0G   CHOLESTEROL 0MG   SODIUM 161MG
EXCHANGE PER TABLESPOON: FREE

Roasted Pepper Dressing

prep: 2 minutes

Combine ½ cup fat-free Italian dressing and
2 tablespoons finely chopped roasted red
pepper in a small bowl; stir well. Serve over
tossed salad greens.
Yield: ½ cup plus 2 tablespoons.

PER TABLESPOON: CALORIES 7 (0% FROM FAT)
FAT 0.0G (SAT 0.0G)   PROTEIN 0.1G   CARBOHYDRATE 1.6G
FIBER 0.0G   CHOLESTEROL 0MG   SODIUM 129MG
EXCHANGE PER TABLESPOON: FREE

Purple Onion Dressing

prep: 2 minutes

Combine ½ cup fat-free Italian dressing,
2 tablespoons grated purple onion, and
¼ teaspoon ground pepper in a small bowl;
stir well. Serve over tossed salad greens.
Yield: ½ cup plus 2 tablespoons.

PER TABLESPOON: CALORIES 7 (0% FROM FAT)
FAT 0.0G (SAT 0.0G)   PROTEIN 0.1G   CARBOHYDRATE 1.7G
FIBER 0.1G   CHOLESTEROL 0MG   SODIUM 129MG
EXCHANGE PER TABLESPOON: FREE

Romaine Salad with Fresh Strawberries

prep: 8 minutes

4 cups torn romaine lettuce
(about 1 small head)

1 cup quartered fresh
strawberries

3 tablespoons fat-free
raspberry vinaigrette

1 Combine lettuce and strawberries in a large bowl. Pour raspberry vinaigrette over lettuce mixture, and toss well.
Yield: 4 servings.

PER SERVING: CALORIES 38 (7% FROM FAT) FAT 0.3G (SAT 0.0G) PROTEIN 1.6G
CARBOHYDRATE 8.0G FIBER 2.4G CHOLESTEROL 0MG SODIUM 75MG
EXCHANGE PER SERVING: 1 VEGETABLE

Serve with grilled herbed chicken breast halves and asparagus.

Spinach-Pear Salad

prep: 18 minutes   cook: 1 minute

1 tablespoon chopped
walnuts

4 cups fresh spinach leaves,
trimmed and chopped

2 tablespoons fat-free honey-
Dijon dressing

1 ripe pear, unpeeled, cored,
and thinly sliced

1 tablespoon crumbled blue
cheese

1 Place a heavy skillet over high heat until hot; add walnuts, and cook, stirring constantly, 1 minute or until toasted. Set aside.

2 Combine spinach and dressing; toss well. Arrange spinach mixture evenly on 5 individual salad plates. Arrange pear slices evenly over spinach mixture; sprinkle salads evenly with blue cheese and walnuts.
Yield: 5 servings.

PER SERVING: CALORIES 52 (31% FROM FAT) FAT 1.8G (SAT 0.4G) PROTEIN 1.7G
CARBOHYDRATE 8.1G FIBER 1.9G CHOLESTEROL 2MG SODIUM 77MG
EXCHANGE PER SERVING: 1 VEGETABLE

Serve with broiled lamb chops, couscous, and carrots.

TIME-saver

Buy packaged, prewashed baby spinach leaves; the stems are tender and don't need to be removed.

Romaine Salad with Fresh Strawberries

Coleslaw with Red Apple

make ahead

prep: 6 minutes   chill: 1 to 8 hours

½ (16-ounce) package finely shredded cabbage

1 small Red Delicious apple, cored and finely chopped

⅓ cup thinly sliced celery (about 1 medium rib)

½ cup fat-free sour cream and onion Ranch-style dressing

1 teaspoon sugar

2 teaspoons lemon juice

1 Combine cabbage, apple, and celery in a large bowl. Combine dressing, sugar, and lemon juice in a small bowl, stirring well. Pour dressing mixture over cabbage mixture, and toss well. Cover and chill at least 1 hour.
Yield: 4 servings.

PER SERVING: CALORIES 78 (2% FROM FAT) FAT 0.2G (SAT 0.0G) PROTEIN 0.8G CARBOHYDRATE 19.1G FIBER 2.7G CHOLESTEROL 0MG SODIUM 308MG EXCHANGES PER SERVING: 1 VEGETABLE, 1 FRUIT

*Serve with **barbecued pork chops and corn on the cob.***

Summer Fruit Salad

make ahead

prep: 7 minutes   chill: 30 minutes to 8 hours

2 medium-size fresh peaches, peeled and thinly sliced

1 cup fresh blueberries

1 cup fresh raspberries

2 tablespoons powdered sugar

2 teaspoons lemon juice

2 teaspoons Grand Marnier or other orange-flavored liqueur

⅛ teaspoon ground cinnamon

1 Combine fruit in a large bowl. Combine sugar and remaining 3 ingredients in a small bowl, stirring well. Pour sugar mixture over fruit mixture, and toss gently. Cover and chill at least 30 minutes.
Yield: 4 servings.

PER SERVING: CALORIES 86 (4% FROM FAT) FAT 0.4G (SAT 0.0G) PROTEIN 1.0G CARBOHYDRATE 20.3G FIBER 4.8G CHOLESTEROL 0MG SODIUM 3MG EXCHANGE PER SERVING: 1 FRUIT

*Serve with **grilled chicken, rice, and roasted green beans.***

Chilled Green Bean Salad

make ahead

prep: 15 minutes   chill: 2 to 8 hours

1 (9-ounce) package frozen
    French-style green beans

1 cup finely chopped tomato
    (about 1 medium)

1 cup thinly sliced cucumber
    (about 1 small)

⅓ cup finely chopped sweet
    red pepper

¼ cup fat-free Italian dressing

1 tablespoon dried parsley
    flakes

1 Cook green beans according to package directions, omitting salt; drain. Place beans in a large bowl. Add tomato and remaining ingredients; toss gently. Cover and chill at least 2 hours.
Yield: 4 servings.

PER SERVING: CALORIES 47 (8% FROM FAT) FAT 0.4G (SAT 0.1G) PROTEIN 2.0G
CARBOHYDRATE 10.4G FIBER 3.0G CHOLESTEROL 0MG SODIUM 170MG
EXCHANGES PER SERVING: 2 VEGETABLE

Serve with grilled hamburgers, corn on the cob, and fresh peaches.

TIME-saver

Slice the cucumber and chop the tomato and pepper while the beans cook.

Sweet-Hot Marinated Cucumbers

make ahead

prep: 10 minutes   chill: 30 minutes to 1 hour

2 small cucumbers

1 tablespoon sugar

2 tablespoons red wine
    vinegar

⅛ teaspoon salt

    Dash of dried crushed red
    pepper

1 Peel cucumbers, if desired; slice crosswise into ⅛-inch-thick slices.

2 Place sugar and remaining 3 ingredients in a small bowl; stir well. Add cucumber slices. Cover and chill up to 1 hour. (The longer the cucumbers are chilled, the hotter their flavor.)
Yield: 4 servings.

PER SERVING: CALORIES 24 (4% FROM FAT) FAT 0.1G (SAT 0.0G) PROTEIN 0.6G
CARBOHYDRATE 5.6G FIBER 0.8G CHOLESTEROL 0MG SODIUM 75MG
EXCHANGE PER SERVING: 1 VEGETABLE

Serve with macaroni and cheese, sliced tomato, and baked apples.

TIME-saver

For thin slices of cucumber, use the slicing blade of a food processor. The harder you push the cucumber against the slicing blade, the thicker the slices.

Cherry Tomato and Cucumber Salad

prep: 9 minutes

¼ cup plain nonfat yogurt

2 tablespoons crumbled feta cheese

¼ teaspoon salt

Dash of ground pepper

1 small clove garlic, crushed

1½ cups cherry tomatoes, halved

1 medium cucumber, quartered lengthwise and sliced crosswise (about 1½ cups)

1 Combine first 5 ingredients in a medium bowl; stir well. Add tomato and cucumber; toss gently. Serve immediately. Yield: 4 servings.

PER SERVING: CALORIES 44 (29% FROM FAT) FAT 1.4G (SAT 0.8G) PROTEIN 2.5G CARBOHYDRATE 6.1G FIBER 1.4G CHOLESTEROL 5MG SODIUM 222MG EXCHANGE PER SERVING: 1 VEGETABLE

Serve with roasted chicken, mashed potatoes, and steamed broccoli.

Baked Potato Salad with Blue Cheese

prep: 8 minutes   cook: 23 minutes   chill: 8 hours

6 (6-ounce) baking potatoes

½ cup reduced-fat sour cream

¼ cup nonfat buttermilk

2 teaspoons cider vinegar

½ teaspoon ground pepper

¼ teaspoon salt

½ cup sliced green onions (about 2 large)

½ cup chopped celery (about 1 large rib)

1 ounce crumbled blue cheese (about ¼ cup)

1 Scrub potatoes; pierce with a fork, and arrange in a circle on a paper towel in microwave oven. Microwave at HIGH 18 minutes, turning and rearranging potatoes halfway through cooking time. Cover and let stand 5 minutes. Let cool slightly. Cut unpeeled potatoes into ½-inch cubes.

2 Combine sour cream and next 4 ingredients in a large bowl, stirring until smooth. Add potato, green onions, celery, and blue cheese; toss gently to combine. Cover and chill at least 8 hours. Yield: 14 servings.

PER SERVING: CALORIES 96 (7% FROM FAT) FAT 0.7G (SAT 0.4G) PROTEIN 2.9G CARBOHYDRATE 19.7G FIBER 1.5G CHOLESTEROL 2MG SODIUM 91MG EXCHANGE PER SERVING: 1 STARCH

Serve with broiled catfish, coleslaw, and fruit salad.

RECIPE tip

If you'd rather bake potatoes the old-fashioned way, prick the potatoes with a fork, and bake at 400° for 50 minutes or until done.

Couscous with Plum Tomatoes and Black Beans

prep: 10 minutes   cook: 5 minutes

1½ cups water

½ teaspoon salt

1 cup couscous, uncooked

¼ cup lemon juice

2 teaspoons olive oil

¼ teaspoon ground pepper

1 (15-ounce) can no-salt-added black beans, drained

2 cups chopped plum tomato (about 4 large)

½ cup finely chopped fresh parsley

¼ cup finely chopped purple onion

1 Combine water and salt in a medium saucepan. Bring to a boil; stir in couscous. Remove from heat; cover and let stand 5 minutes. Fluff couscous with a fork; spoon into a large bowl.

2 While couscous cooks, combine lemon juice, olive oil, and pepper in a small bowl, stirring with a wire whisk. Add to couscous, stirring gently. Stir in beans and remaining ingredients.
Yield: 4 servings.

PER SERVING: CALORIES 286 (11% FROM FAT) FAT 3.4G (SAT 0.4G) PROTEIN 12.4G CARBOHYDRATE 54.2G FIBER 5.9G CHOLESTEROL 0MG SODIUM 323MG EXCHANGES PER SERVING: 3 STARCH, 2 VEGETABLE, ½ FAT

Serve with *warm pita bread.*

TIME-saver

Chop the tomato, onion, and parsley while the couscous cooks. To chop parsley quickly, pack the leaves into a measuring cup, and snip the parsley with kitchen scissors until it's finely chopped.

Texas Pasta-Bean Salad

prep: 6 minutes   cook: 12 minutes   chill: 1 to 8 hours

4 ounces wagon wheel pasta, uncooked

1 (15-ounce) can no-salt-added kidney beans, drained

1 (15-ounce) can no-salt-added black beans, drained

1 (8-ounce) can no-salt-added whole-kernel corn, drained

½ cup fat-free Ranch-style dressing

½ cup chopped green pepper (about ½ medium)

⅓ cup chopped purple onion

¼ cup salsa

2 slices turkey bacon, cooked and crumbled

1 Cook pasta according to package directions, omitting salt and fat. Drain.

2 While pasta cooks, combine kidney beans and next 6 ingredients. Stir in pasta, and toss well. Cover and chill at least 1 hour. Sprinkle with turkey bacon just before serving.
Yield: 6 servings.

PER SERVING: CALORIES 216 (7% FROM FAT) FAT 1.6G (SAT 0.3G) PROTEIN 10.9G CARBOHYDRATE 39.6G FIBER 4.5G CHOLESTEROL 3MG SODIUM 331MG EXCHANGES PER SERVING: 2 STARCH, 2 VEGETABLE

Serve with *herbed marinated tomatoes and cornbread.*

RECIPE tip

Substitute any similar size pasta for wagon wheel; try bow tie, elbow macaroni, or rotini.

Tuna and Bow Tie Pasta Salad

make ahead

prep: 19 minutes   cook: 7 minutes   chill: 2 to 8 hours

8 ounces bow tie pasta, uncooked

1 (9-ounce) can solid white tuna in spring water, drained and flaked

1 cup finely chopped tomato (about 1 medium)

½ cup shredded carrot

½ cup finely chopped, unpeeled cucumber (about ½ small)

¼ cup finely chopped celery (about ½ large rib)

¼ cup red wine vinegar

2 tablespoons water

1 tablespoon Dijon mustard

2 teaspoons olive oil

¼ teaspoon ground pepper

⅛ teaspoon salt

1 Cook pasta according to package directions, omitting salt and fat. Drain; rinse under cold water, and drain again. Place pasta in a large bowl. Add tuna and next 4 ingredients.

2 Combine vinegar and remaining 5 ingredients in a small bowl, stirring well. Pour vinegar mixture over pasta mixture, and toss well. Cover and chill at least 2 hours. Toss gently before serving. Yield: 6 servings.

PER SERVING: CALORIES 218 (14% FROM FAT)   FAT 3.3G (SAT 0.5G)   PROTEIN 14.8G
CARBOHYDRATE 31.4G   FIBER 1.8G   CHOLESTEROL 15MG   SODIUM 274MG
EXCHANGES PER SERVING: 1 LEAN MEAT, 2 STARCH

Serve with *fresh pear and apple slices and breadsticks.*

TIME-saver

Cook the pasta a day ahead of time. When you're ready to make the salad, rinse the pasta and assemble the salad.

Tuna-Rice Salad

1 (6.2-ounce) package quick long-grain-and-wild rice mix

1 (9-ounce) can solid white tuna in spring water, drained and flaked

½ cup chopped celery (about 1 large rib)

½ cup nonfat mayonnaise

¼ cup nonfat sour cream

2 tablespoons finely chopped onion

1 teaspoon lemon juice

1½ teaspoons finely chopped fresh oregano or ½ teaspoon dried oregano

¼ teaspoon ground pepper

Lettuce leaves

2 tablespoons chopped unsalted cashews

prep: 10 minutes   chill: 30 minutes

1 Cook rice according to package directions, omitting butter and seasoning packet. Chill at least 30 minutes.

2 Combine chilled rice, tuna, and next 7 ingredients, stirring well. Serve on a lettuce-lined serving plate; sprinkle with cashews.
Yield: 5 servings.

PER SERVING: CALORIES 226 (13% FROM FAT) FAT 3.3G (SAT 0.6G) PROTEIN 16.6G
CARBOHYDRATE 32.8G FIBER 1.3G CHOLESTEROL 21MG SODIUM 997MG
EXCHANGES PER SERVING: 2 VERY LEAN MEAT, 2 STARCH

Serve with fresh tomato slices and Melba toast rounds.

WORK-saver

Chop cashews in the food processor pulsing briefly. You'll only need to wipe clean the processor after chopping the nuts.

Coleslaw with Shrimp

prep: 5 minutes   cook: 3 minutes   chill: 1 hour

4 cups water

8 ounces peeled and deveined large fresh shrimp

½ cup nonfat mayonnaise

⅓ cup nonfat sour cream

3 tablespoons lemon juice

1 tablespoon sugar

1 teaspoon celery seeds

¼ teaspoon salt

¼ teaspoon ground pepper

1 (16-ounce) package finely shredded cabbage

¼ cup thinly sliced green pepper

¼ cup thinly sliced purple onion

1 Bring water to a boil in a medium saucepan; add shrimp. Cook 3 to 5 minutes or until shrimp turn pink. Drain well; rinse with cold water.

2 Combine mayonnaise and next 6 ingredients in a large bowl; stir with a wire whisk until smooth. Add shrimp, cabbage, green pepper, and onion; toss well. Cover and chill at least 1 hour.
Yield: 5 servings.

PER SERVING: CALORIES 115 (6% FROM FAT)   FAT 0.8G (SAT 0.2G)   PROTEIN 11.9G   CARBOHYDRATE 15.2G   FIBER 2.5G   CHOLESTEROL 88MG   SODIUM 551MG   EXCHANGES PER SERVING: 1 VERY LEAN MEAT, 1 STARCH

Serve with sliced tomato and cucumber and soft rolls.

RECIPE tip

If you buy unpeeled shrimp, purchase 12 ounces of shrimp. However, most supermarket seafood departments will sell already peeled shrimp. If you don't mind paying a little more, you can purchase the shrimp freshly boiled.

Taco Salad

prep: 8 minutes   cook: 13 minutes

¾ pound ground round

1 cup chopped onion

½ teaspoon minced garlic (about 1 clove)

1 teaspoon salt-free Mexican seasoning

1 (10-ounce) can enchilada sauce

1 (8-ounce) can no-salt-added whole-kernel corn, drained

8 cups slivered iceberg lettuce

1½ cups chopped tomato (about 2 medium)

¾ cup coarsely crushed no-oil baked tortilla chips

1 Cook beef, onion, and garlic in a large nonstick skillet over medium-high heat until browned, stirring until beef crumbles; drain.

2 Add Mexican seasoning to beef mixture in skillet; cook 1 minute. Stir in enchilada sauce and corn. Reduce heat to low, and simmer, uncovered, 5 minutes.

3 Arrange lettuce on 4 individual salad plates. Spoon beef mixture evenly over lettuce; top with tomato and chips.
Yield: 4 servings.

PER SERVING: CALORIES 310 (24% FROM FAT)   FAT 8.2G (SAT 1.9G)   PROTEIN 22.3G   CARBOHYDRATE 37.5G   FIBER 3.9G   CHOLESTEROL 52MG   SODIUM 420MG   EXCHANGES PER SERVING: 2 MEDIUM-FAT MEAT, 2 STARCH, 1 VEGETABLE

Serve with cantaloupe wedges.

Hoppin' John Salad

Hoppin' John Salad

2½ cups canned low-sodium chicken broth, divided

1 cup converted rice, uncooked

¼ cup apple cider vinegar

1½ teaspoons salt-free Cajun seasoning

2 teaspoons olive oil

½ teaspoon dried thyme

½ teaspoon minced garlic (about 1 clove)

¼ teaspoon hot sauce

1 (15.8-ounce) can black-eyed peas, drained

½ cup finely chopped celery (about 1 large rib)

½ cup thinly sliced green onions (about 2 large)

3 (1-ounce) slices lean ham, cut into thin strips

Green leaf lettuce

prep: 7 minutes   cook: 25 minutes   chill: 30 minutes to 8 hours

1 Place 2¼ cups broth in a medium saucepan; bring to a boil. Add rice, stirring well. Cover, reduce heat, and simmer 20 minutes. Remove from heat; let stand, covered, 5 minutes.

2 While rice cooks, combine remaining ¼ cup broth, vinegar, and next 5 ingredients in a small bowl; set aside.

3 Combine rice, peas, and next 3 ingredients in a large bowl. Add vinegar mixture, stirring gently to combine. Cover and chill at least 30 minutes.

4 Spoon rice mixture onto a lettuce-lined serving plate. Yield: 6 servings.

PER SERVING: CALORIES 227 (15% FROM FAT) FAT 3.7G (SAT 0.5G) PROTEIN 10.2G CARBOHYDRATE 37.9G FIBER 3.6G CHOLESTEROL 6MG SODIUM 540MG EXCHANGES PER SERVING: ½ HIGH-FAT MEAT, 2½ STARCH

Serve with *fresh pineapple slices and hard rolls.*

RECIPE tip

Hoppin' John is a Southern favorite most often served warm as a main dish. This chilled version, flavored with a vinaigrette, makes a handy make-ahead main-dish salad. If you have leftover rice, use 3 cups in this recipe.

Crunchy Chicken and Cucumber Salad

prep: 10 minutes   cook: 14 minutes

Vegetable cooking spray

1½ pounds skinned, boned
     chicken breasts

3 tablespoons rice vinegar

1½ tablespoons low-sodium soy
     sauce

1½ teaspoons sugar

1 teaspoon vegetable oil

⅛ teaspoon ground red
     pepper

1 clove garlic, crushed

1 medium cucumber, peeled,
     seeded, and finely
     chopped

6 green onions, thinly sliced

6 cups torn mixed salad
     greens

1 Coat a large nonstick skillet with cooking spray; place over medium heat until hot. Add chicken; cook 7 minutes on each side or until done. Remove chicken from skillet; let cool slightly, and coarsely chop chicken.

2 While chicken cooks, combine vinegar and next 5 ingredients in a small bowl, stirring well with a wire whisk.

3 Combine chicken, cucumber, green onions, and salad greens in a large bowl. Add vinegar mixture, and toss well. Serve immediately. Yield: 6 servings.

PER SERVING: CALORIES 171 (21% FROM FAT) FAT 4.0G (SAT 1.0G) PROTEIN 27.3G CARBOHYDRATE 4.9G FIBER 1.7G CHOLESTEROL 70MG SODIUM 169MG EXCHANGES PER SERVING: 4 VERY LEAN MEAT, 1 VEGETABLE

***Serve with** fresh orange sections and sesame breadsticks.*

RECIPE tip

Chop the vegetables and mix the dressing while the chicken cooks. If desired, you may substitute shrimp for chicken.

Curried Chicken Salad with Pineapple

prep: 8 minutes   cook: 14 minutes

Vegetable cooking spray

6   (4-ounce) skinned, boned
    chicken breast halves

2   tablespoons chopped
    almonds

1   (8-ounce) can pineapple
    tidbits in juice,
    undrained

¾   cup plain nonfat yogurt

1   teaspoon curry powder

¼   teaspoon salt

1   cup thinly sliced celery
    (about 3 medium ribs)

5   red leaf lettuce leaves

1   Coat a large nonstick skillet with cooking spray; place over medium heat until hot. Add chicken; cook 7 minutes on each side or until done. Remove chicken from skillet; let cool slightly, and coarsely chop chicken.

2   While chicken cooks, place a small heavy skillet over medium-high heat until hot. Add almonds, and cook, stirring constantly, 1 minute or until toasted. Set almonds aside.

3   Drain pineapple tidbits, reserving 3 tablespoons juice. Combine reserved pineapple juice, yogurt, curry powder, and salt in a large bowl, stirring well. Add chicken, pineapple, and celery; toss well.

4   Spoon chicken salad evenly onto 5 individual lettuce-lined salad plates. Sprinkle evenly with almonds.
Yield: 6 servings.

PER SERVING: CALORIES 192 (22% FROM FAT)   FAT 4.7G (SAT 1.0G)   PROTEIN 28.5G
CARBOHYDRATE 8.0G   FIBER 0.9G   CHOLESTEROL 72MG   SODIUM 196MG
EXCHANGES PER SERVING: 4 VERY LEAN MEAT, ½ FRUIT

Serve with *seedless red grapes and whole wheat bread.*

TIME-saver

Use leftover chopped cooked chicken or turkey. Or use deli-roasted chicken; just remember that the sodium and fat content may be higher.

side dishes

Sesame Broccoli (page 182)

Marmalade-Broiled Grapefruit

prep: 10 minutes   cook: 5 minutes

2 medium grapefruit, halved
    crosswise

1 tablespoon plus 1 teaspoon
    low-sugar orange
    marmalade

1 tablespoon plus 1 teaspoon
    brown sugar

1 Remove seeds, and loosen sections of grapefruit halves.

2 Combine marmalade and sugar; brush mixture over cut surfaces of grapefruit. Broil grapefruit 5½ inches from heat (with electric oven door partially opened) 5 minutes or until hot and bubbly.
Yield: 4 servings.

PER SERVING: CALORIES 51 (2% FROM FAT) FAT 0.1G (SAT 0.0G) PROTEIN 0.8G
CARBOHYDRATE 12.8G FIBER 0.7G CHOLESTEROL 0MG SODIUM 2MG
EXCHANGE PER SERVING: 1 FRUIT

Serve with *seasoned grilled pork tenderloin, baked potatoes, and a tossed green salad.*

Honeydew and Strawberry Cups

prep: 10 minutes

2 cups cubed honeydew
    melon

2 cups strawberry halves

¼ cup unsweetened orange
    juice

3 tablespoons low-sugar
    orange marmalade

2 tablespoons honey

1 Combine honeydew and strawberries in a bowl.

2 Combine orange juice, marmalade, and honey in a small bowl. Pour over honeydew mixture; toss gently to coat. Spoon evenly into each of 4 individual fruit cups.
Yield: 4 servings.

PER SERVING: CALORIES 87 (3% FROM FAT) FAT 0.3G (SAT 0.1G) PROTEIN 0.9G
CARBOHYDRATE 22.3G FIBER 2.3G CHOLESTEROL 0MG SODIUM 11MG
EXCHANGE PER SERVING: 1 FRUIT

Serve with *oven-fried chicken, rice, and green beans.*

RECIPE tip

Wash strawberries first, then pull the caps off and cut the berries in half so you won't rinse away the sweet juice. For the best flavor, wash and prepare the berries right before serving.

Spiced Apple Slices

prep: 10 minutes   cook: 7 minutes

1 tablespoon reduced-calorie margarine

1 pound Golden Delicious apples, cored, peeled, and cut into ¼-inch-thick slices

2 tablespoons sugar

2 tablespoons water

1 teaspoon fresh lemon juice

½ teaspoon apple pie spice

1 Melt margarine in a large skillet over medium heat; add apple. Sprinkle sugar and remaining ingredients over apple. Cook over medium heat 7 minutes or until apple is tender, stirring occasionally. Serve warm.
Yield: 3 servings.

PER SERVING: CALORIES 127 (21% FROM FAT) FAT 2.9G (SAT 0.4G) PROTEIN 0.2G
CARBOHYDRATE 27.7G FIBER 3.4G CHOLESTEROL 0MG SODIUM 37MG
EXCHANGES PER SERVING: 2 FRUIT

Serve with meat loaf, mashed potatoes, and broccoli.

RECIPE tip

If you don't have apple pie spice, make your own. One-half teaspoon of apple pie spice is equal to ¼ teaspoon ground cinnamon, ⅛ teaspoon ground nutmeg, and a dash of ground cardamom.

Cinnamon-Poached Pears

make ahead

prep: 5 minutes   cook: 18 minutes   chill: 30 minutes

1 (29-ounce) can pear halves in light syrup, undrained

¼ cup red cinnamon candies

1 tablespoon lemon juice

1 Drain pears, reserving syrup; set pears aside. Combine syrup, cinnamon candies, and lemon juice in a large saucepan; bring to a boil over medium-high heat. Cook until cinnamon candies dissolve, stirring occasionally. Add pears; bring to a boil. Cover, reduce heat, and simmer 5 minutes. Transfer pears to a medium bowl with a slotted spoon; cover and set aside.

2 Bring remaining liquid to a boil; cook over high heat 10 minutes or until liquid is reduced to about ¾ cup. Pour syrup over pears. Cover and chill at least 30 minutes.
Yield: 6 servings.

PER SERVING: CALORIES 169 (0% FROM FAT) FAT 0.0G (SAT 0.0G) PROTEIN 0.3G
CARBOHYDRATE 44.2G FIBER 3.4G CHOLESTEROL 0MG SODIUM 7MG
EXCHANGES PER SERVING: 1 STARCH, 2 FRUIT

Serve with broiled pork loin chops, gingered carrots, and a tossed green salad.

Raspberry Applesauce

prep: 5 minutes   cook: 10 minutes

1 (24-ounce) jar cinnamon-
   flavored applesauce

2 tablespoons light brown
   sugar

¾ cup frozen unsweetened
   raspberries

Fresh raspberries (optional)

Mint sprigs (optional)

Cinnamon sticks (optional)

1 Combine applesauce and sugar in a saucepan; cook over medium-high heat until hot and bubbly, stirring frequently. Remove from heat; stir in raspberries. Let stand 5 minutes. Serve warm or chilled. Garnish with fresh raspberries, mint, and cinnamon sticks, if desired.
Yield: 6 servings.

PER SERVING: CALORIES 105 (3% FROM FAT)   FAT 0.3G (SAT 0.0G)   PROTEIN 0.3G   CARBOHYDRATE 27.1G   FIBER 2.5G   CHOLESTEROL 0MG   SODIUM 5MG   EXCHANGES PER SERVING: 2 FRUIT

***Serve with** roasted turkey, baked sweet potatoes, and green peas.*

Raspberry Applesauce

Italian-Style Asparagus

prep: 5 minutes   cook: 4 minutes

1 pound fresh asparagus

1 cup finely chopped plum tomato (about 2 large)

¼ cup fat-free Italian dressing

1 tablespoon chopped fresh chives or 2 teaspoons freeze-dried chives

1 tablespoon chopped fresh parsley or 1 teaspoon dried parsley

1 Snap off tough ends of asparagus spears. Remove scales from spears with a knife or vegetable peeler, if desired. Arrange asparagus in a steamer basket over boiling water. Cover and steam 4 minutes or until asparagus is crisp-tender.

2 Place asparagus in a shallow dish; add tomato and remaining ingredients, and toss gently. Serve immediately, or cover and chill thoroughly.
Yield: 4 servings.

PER SERVING: CALORIES 36 (10% FROM FAT) FAT 0.4G (SAT 0.1G) PROTEIN 2.5G
CARBOHYDRATE 7.2G FIBER 1.4G CHOLESTEROL 0MG SODIUM 174MG
EXCHANGE PER SERVING: 1 VEGETABLE

Serve with roasted chicken breast halves and a citrus salad.

Garlic Green Beans Amandine

prep: 4 minutes   cook: 9 minutes

1 (9-ounce) package frozen French-style green beans

2 tablespoons sliced almonds

2 teaspoons reduced-calorie margarine, melted

2 cloves garlic, crushed

½ teaspoon grated lemon rind

¼ teaspoon salt

⅛ teaspoon ground pepper

1 Cook beans according to package directions. Drain well, and transfer to a bowl.

2 While beans cook, place a small heavy skillet over medium-high heat until hot. Add almonds, and cook, stirring constantly, 1 minute or until toasted. Set almonds aside.

3 Combine margarine and remaining 4 ingredients in a small bowl. Pour margarine mixture over beans, tossing gently to coat. Sprinkle with almonds.
Yield: 4 servings.

PER SERVING: CALORIES 50 (52% FROM FAT) FAT 2.9G (SAT 0.3G) PROTEIN 1.7G
CARBOHYDRATE 5.8G FIBER 2.1G CHOLESTEROL 0MG SODIUM 188MG
EXCHANGES PER SERVING: 1 VEGETABLE, ½ FAT

Serve with spaghetti with white clam sauce and crusty Italian bread.

Tarragon Green Beans

prep: 9 minutes   cook: 3 minutes

¾   pound fresh green beans

2   teaspoons margarine

2   tablespoons chopped fresh
    parsley or 2 teaspoons
    dried parsley

2   tablespoons chopped fresh
    tarragon or 2 teaspoons
    dried tarragon

¼   teaspoon salt

¼   teaspoon ground pepper

1 Trim beans, and cut into 1½-inch pieces. Cook beans in boiling water to cover 3 to 4 minutes or until crisp-tender; drain well. Add margarine and remaining ingredients; toss well. Serve immediately. Yield: 4 servings.

PER SERVING: CALORIES 33 (5% FROM FAT) FAT 1.3G (SAT 0.2G) PROTEIN 1.4G
CARBOHYDRATE 5.1G FIBER 1.5G CHOLESTEROL 0MG SODIUM 170MG
EXCHANGE PER SERVING: 1 VEGETABLE

Serve with *broiled lamb loin chops and couscous.*

RECIPE tip

Substitute any combination of marjoram, basil, dillweed, or rosemary for parsley and tarragon.

Apricot-Glazed Carrots

prep: 9 minutes   cook: 15 minutes

4   cups sliced carrot
    (about 1 pound)

1   tablespoon dark brown
    sugar

3   tablespoons apricot
    preserves

1   tablespoon reduced-calorie
    margarine

½   teaspoon salt

⅛   teaspoon ground pepper

1 Arrange carrot in a steamer basket over boiling water. Cover; steam 15 to 20 minutes or until tender. Transfer carrot to a bowl; add brown sugar and remaining ingredients, tossing gently until preserves and margarine melt and carrot is glazed. Yield: 6 servings.

PER SERVING: CALORIES 82 (15% FROM FAT) FAT 1.4G (SAT 0.2G) PROTEIN 0.9G
CARBOHYDRATE 17.6G FIBER 3.0G CHOLESTEROL 0MG SODIUM 247MG
EXCHANGE PER SERVING: 1 STARCH

Serve with *broiled flank steak and baked potatoes.*

Sesame Broccoli

prep: 15 minutes   cook: 5 minutes

4 cups fresh broccoli flowerets
    (about 1½ bunches)

3 tablespoons finely chopped
    sweet red pepper

2 teaspoons sesame seeds

2 tablespoons low-sodium soy
    sauce

1 tablespoon water

2 teaspoons sugar

¼ teaspoon ground ginger

¼ teaspoon dry mustard

1 Arrange broccoli and red pepper in a steamer basket over boiling water. Cover and steam 5 minutes or until crisp-tender; place in a medium bowl.

2 While vegetables cook, place a small, heavy skillet over medium-high heat until hot. Add sesame seeds, and cook, stirring constantly, 1 minute or until toasted. Set sesame seeds aside.

3 Combine soy sauce and remaining 4 ingredients in a small bowl, stirring well. Microwave at HIGH 45 seconds or until bubbly. Pour sauce over vegetables; sprinkle with sesame seeds, and toss gently. Yield: 6 servings.

PER SERVING: CALORIES 29 (22% FROM FAT)   FAT 0.7G (SAT 0.1G)   PROTEIN 1.8G   CARBOHYDRATE 4.6G   FIBER 1.8G   CHOLESTEROL 0MG   SODIUM 145MG   **EXCHANGE PER SERVING:** 1 VEGETABLE

Serve with *grilled teriyaki chicken and rice.*

WORK-saver

Buy bags of precut broccoli flowerets in the produce section of your supermarket.

Sesame Broccoli

Curried Cauliflower and Corn

prep: 8 minutes   cook: 13 minutes

4½ cups cauliflower flowerets
    (about 1 medium head)

1 (10-ounce) package frozen
    whole-kernel corn

1½ tablespoons margarine,
    melted

1 teaspoon curry powder

¼ teaspoon salt

⅛ teaspoon ground ginger

⅛ teaspoon ground pepper

¼ cup sliced green onion
    (about 1 large)

1 Arrange cauliflower in a steamer basket over boiling water; add corn. Cover and steam 13 minutes or until cauliflower is crisp-tender.

2 Combine margarine and next 4 ingredients in a large bowl; add cauliflower mixture and green onion, tossing gently to coat vegetables with spice mixture.
Yield: 7 servings.

PER SERVING: CALORIES 78 (35% FROM FAT) FAT 3.0G (SAT 0.8G) PROTEIN 2.8G
CARBOHYDRATE 12.7G FIBER 3.0G CHOLESTEROL 0MG SODIUM 137MG
EXCHANGES PER SERVING: 1 STARCH, ½ FAT

***Serve with** broiled pork loin chops, sliced tomatoes, and couscous.*

Cheesy Salsa Corn

superquick

prep: 2 minutes   cook: 8 minutes

1 (10-ounce) package frozen
    whole-kernel corn

3 tablespoons (1½ ounces)
    shredded reduced-fat,
    extra-sharp Cheddar
    cheese

2 tablespoons chunky salsa

⅛ teaspoon salt

1 Cook corn according to package directions, omitting salt; drain and place in a small bowl. Add cheese, salsa, and salt; toss gently. Serve immediately.
Yield: 4 servings.

PER SERVING: CALORIES 96 (24% FROM FAT) FAT 2.6G (SAT 1.3G) PROTEIN 5.3G
CARBOHYDRATE 15.5G FIBER 1.9G CHOLESTEROL 7MG SODIUM 170MG
EXCHANGES PER SERVING: 1 STARCH, ½ FAT

***Serve with** grilled swordfish, marinated cucumber-tomato salad, and soft dinner rolls.*

Curried Corn on the Cob

prep: 5 minutes   cook: 10 minutes

4 ears fresh corn (in husks)

1 tablespoon reduced-calorie margarine, melted

¼ teaspoon curry powder

⅛ teaspoon ground red pepper

Finely chopped fresh mint (optional)

1 Remove husks and silks from corn. Cook corn in boiling water to cover 10 minutes; drain.

2 While corn cooks, combine margarine, curry powder, red pepper, and mint, if desired, in a small bowl. Brush margarine mixture evenly on corn. Serve immediately.
Yield: 4 servings.

PER SERVING: CALORIES 103 (25% FROM FAT) FAT 2.9G (SAT 1.2G) PROTEIN 2.6G
CARBOHYDRATE 20.4G FIBER 3.0G CHOLESTEROL 0MG SODIUM 41MG
EXCHANGES PER SERVING: 1 STARCH, ½ FAT

Serve with *grilled turkey burgers and coleslaw.*

RECIPE tip

To check the sweetness of fresh corn, pop a kernel with your fingernail. The corn will taste sweet if the liquid from the kernel is milky white.

Skillet Mushrooms

prep: 11 minutes   cook: 3 minutes

Olive oil-flavored vegetable cooking spray

3 (8-ounce) packages medium-size fresh mushrooms, halved

2 cloves garlic, crushed

½ teaspoon dried Italian seasoning

¼ teaspoon salt

¼ teaspoon ground pepper

2 teaspoons lemon juice

1 Coat a large nonstick skillet with cooking spray; place over medium-high heat until hot. Add mushrooms and next 4 ingredients. Cook, stirring constantly, 3 minutes or until mushrooms are lightly browned and tender. Add lemon juice, tossing to combine.
Yield: 6 servings.

PER SERVING: CALORIES 32 (17% FROM FAT) FAT 0.6G (SAT 0.1G) PROTEIN 2.4G
CARBOHYDRATE 5.9G FIBER 1.5G CHOLESTEROL 0MG SODIUM 103MG
EXCHANGE PER SERVING: 1 VEGETABLE

Serve with *grilled sirloin steak, oven-roasted potatoes, and yellow and green squash.*

RECIPE tip

Crushed garlic gives a more intense bite to food than minced. Crush peeled cloves with a garlic press or with the flat side of a large knife.

Spring Peas

prep: 2 minutes   cook: 11 minutes

2 (10-ounce) packages frozen English peas

2 teaspoons reduced-calorie margarine

2 teaspoons lemon juice

1½ teaspoons finely chopped fresh thyme or ½ teaspoon dried thyme

¼ teaspoon salt

⅛ teaspoon ground pepper

1 Cook peas according to package directions, omitting salt; drain and transfer to a large bowl. Add margarine and remaining ingredients, stirring until margarine melts.
Yield: 6 servings.

PER SERVING: CALORIES 80 (14% FROM FAT) FAT 1.2G (SAT 0.2G) PROTEIN 4.9G CARBOHYDRATE 13.1G FIBER 4.3G CHOLESTEROL 0MG SODIUM 216MG
EXCHANGES PER SERVING: 2 VEGETABLE

Serve with roasted lamb and round red potato slices.

New Potatoes with Chives

prep: 5 minutes   cook: 17 minutes

2 pounds round red potatoes, quartered

2 teaspoons olive oil

2 tablespoons chopped fresh chives or 2 teaspoons freeze-dried chives

½ teaspoon salt

¼ teaspoon ground pepper

1 Arrange potato in a steamer basket over boiling water. Cover and steam 17 minutes or until tender. Place potato in a large bowl. Drizzle with olive oil, and sprinkle with chives, salt, and pepper, tossing well.
Yield: 8 servings.

PER SERVING: CALORIES 94 (11% FROM FAT) FAT 1.2G (SAT 0.2G) PROTEIN 2.5G CARBOHYDRATE 18.9G FIBER 2.1G CHOLESTEROL 0MG SODIUM 154MG
EXCHANGE PER SERVING: 1 STARCH

Serve with grilled pork tenderloin slices and broccoli-carrot medley.

Sliced Seasoned Potatoes

prep: 7 minutes   cook: 8 minutes

1½ pounds unpeeled baking
    potatoes, cut into
    ¼-inch-thick slices

¼ cup fat-free honey-Dijon
    dressing

1 tablespoon finely chopped
    fresh basil or 2
    teaspoons dried basil

¼ teaspoon salt

⅛ teaspoon ground pepper

1 Cook potato in a large saucepan in boiling water to cover 8 minutes or until tender. Drain potato well, reserving 2 tablespoons cooking liquid; place potato in a medium bowl.

2 Combine cooking liquid, dressing, and remaining 3 ingredients in a small bowl, stirring well with a wire whisk. Pour over potato; toss gently.
Yield: 4 servings.

PER SERVING: CALORIES 152 (1% FROM FAT) FAT 0.2G (SAT 0.1G) PROTEIN 4.0G
CARBOHYDRATE 33.4G FIBER 3.3G CHOLESTEROL 0MG SODIUM 329MG
EXCHANGES PER SERVING: 2 STARCH

Serve with broiled fish, asparagus, and dinner rolls.

Cheese Fries

prep: 3 minutes   cook: 13 minutes

2 tablespoons grated
    Parmesan cheese

½ teaspoon paprika

½ teaspoon salt

¼ teaspoon ground pepper

½ (32-ounce) bag frozen
    crinkle-cut French fried
    potatoes

    Vegetable cooking spray

1 Combine first 4 ingredients in a small bowl, stirring well; set aside.

2 Place French fries in a medium bowl; coat with cooking spray. Sprinkle fries with cheese mixture, tossing well.

3 Arrange French fries in a single layer on a baking sheet coated with cooking spray. Bake at 450° for 13 minutes or until tender.
Yield: 6 servings.

PER SERVING: CALORIES 139 (25% FROM FAT) FAT 3.9G (SAT 1.2G) PROTEIN 2.6G
CARBOHYDRATE 21.3G FIBER 1.9G CHOLESTEROL 1MG SODIUM 245MG
EXCHANGES PER SERVING: 1 STARCH, 1 FAT

Serve with oven-fried catfish, carrot-raisin salad, and cornbread.

Chili-Fried Potatoes

prep: 10 minutes   cook: 16 minutes

3 cups unpeeled, cubed
    baking potato (1 pound)

    Olive oil-flavored vegetable
    cooking spray

½ teaspoon olive oil

1 small onion, halved, thinly
    sliced, and separated
    into rings

1 teaspoon chili powder

¼ teaspoon salt

½ cup (2 ounces) shredded
    reduced-fat, extra-sharp
    Cheddar cheese

1 Arrange potato in a steamer basket over boiling water. Cover and steam 10 minutes or until tender. Remove from heat.

2 While potato steams, coat a large nonstick skillet with cooking spray; add oil. Place over medium-high heat until hot. Add onion, and cook, stirring constantly, 3 minutes or until tender. Add potato, chili powder, and salt. Cook 5 minutes or until potato is lightly browned, stirring often. Sprinkle cheese over potato. Cover, remove from heat, and let stand 1 minute or until cheese melts.
Yield: 4 servings.

PER SERVING: CALORIES 152 (22% FROM FAT)   FAT 3.7G (SAT 1.7G)   PROTEIN 6.9G   CARBOHYDRATE 23.8G   FIBER 2.6G   CHOLESTEROL 10MG   SODIUM 263MG   EXCHANGES PER SERVING: 1½ STARCH, 1 FAT

Serve with *broiled marinated beef and vegetable kabobs and a tossed green salad.*

Chili-Fried Potatoes

Cheese and Garlic Mashed Potatoes

prep: 10 minutes   cook: 12 minutes

2¼ cups peeled, cubed baking potato (about 1½ pounds)

½ cup fat-free milk

1 cup (4 ounces) shredded reduced-fat sharp Cheddar cheese

2 teaspoons reduced-calorie margarine

½ teaspoon minced garlic (about 1 clove)

½ teaspoon salt

⅛ teaspoon ground pepper

1 Place potato in a large saucepan; add water to cover. Bring to a boil; cover, reduce heat, and simmer 12 minutes or until tender. Drain potato; place in a large bowl.

2 Add milk and remaining ingredients. Beat at medium speed of an electric mixer until smooth.
Yield: 6 servings.

PER SERVING: CALORIES 132 (31% FROM FAT) FAT 4.6G (SAT 2.2G) PROTEIN 8.9G CARBOHYDRATE 14.8G FIBER 1.9G CHOLESTEROL 13MG SODIUM 365MG EXCHANGES PER SERVING: 1 MEDIUM-FAT MEAT, 1 STARCH

Serve with **barbecued pork chops and green beans.**

RECIPE tip

To remove the garlic odor from your cutting board, rub the cut side of a lemon over the surface, then wash the board with hot, soapy water.

Stuffed Sweet Potatoes

prep: 7 minutes   cook: 23 minutes

4 medium-size sweet potatoes

2 tablespoons sliced almonds

1 (8-ounce) can crushed pineapple in juice, drained

1 (11-ounce) can mandarin orange sections, drained

½ cup unsweetened applesauce

2 tablespoons reduced-calorie margarine

2 tablespoons brown sugar

1 teaspoon ground cinnamon

1 Scrub potatoes; pierce with a fork, and arrange in a circle on a paper towel in microwave oven. Microwave at HIGH 14 to 16 minutes or until soft. Let stand 5 minutes.

2 While potatoes cook, place a small, heavy skillet over medium-high heat. Add almonds, and cook, stirring constantly, 1 minute or until toasted. Set almonds aside.

3 Cut potatoes in half lengthwise; carefully scoop out potato pulp, leaving ¼-inch-thick shells. Set shells aside. Combine pulp, pineapple, and remaining 5 ingredients, stirring well. Spoon potato mixture into potato shells. Cover and microwave at HIGH 4 minutes or until thoroughly heated. Top with almonds.
Yield: 8 servings.

PER SERVING: CALORIES 145 (19% FROM FAT) FAT 3.0G (SAT 0.1G) PROTEIN 1.7G CARBOHYDRATE 29.0G FIBER 2.9G CHOLESTEROL 0MG SODIUM 40MG EXCHANGES PER SERVING: 1 STARCH, 1 FRUIT, ½ FAT

Serve with **cinnamon apples and broiled pork chops.**

Green and Yellow Squash Parmesan

prep: 8 minutes   cook: 18 minutes

1 teaspoon olive oil

⅔ cup finely chopped onion
   (about 1 small)

½ teaspoon minced garlic
   (about 1 clove)

1 medium zucchini, coarsely
   chopped

1 medium-size yellow squash,
   coarsely chopped

1 (14½-ounce) can Italian-
   style stewed tomatoes,
   undrained

½ teaspoon dried Italian
   seasoning

2 tablespoons freshly grated
   Parmesan cheese

1 Place oil in a large skillet over medium-high heat until hot. Add onion and garlic; cook, stirring constantly, 3 minutes or until tender. Add zucchini and next 3 ingredients; stir well. Bring to a boil; reduce heat, and simmer, uncovered, 15 minutes or until squash is tender, stirring occasionally. Sprinkle with cheese. Serve immediately. Yield: 4 servings.

PER SERVING: CALORIES 73 (28% FROM FAT) FAT 2.3G (SAT 0.8G) PROTEIN 3.5G CARBOHYDRATE 11.1G FIBER 1.7G CHOLESTEROL 2MG SODIUM 285MG EXCHANGES PER SERVING: 2 VEGETABLE, ½ FAT

***Serve with** grilled fish and marinated tomato slices.*

how to mince garlic

Use minced garlic from a jar to save time; ½ teaspoon of preminced garlic equals one clove. When you mince your own, use this easy method.

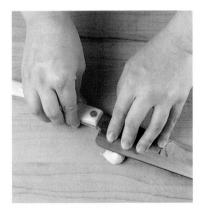

Place the flat side of a large knife over the garlic clove, and press firmly on the knife. The papery husk will be easy to remove.

Cut the peeled garlic clove into very fine pieces.

Zucchini Tabbouleh

make ahead

prep: 30 minutes

¾ cup bulgur (cracked wheat), uncooked

1 cup boiling water

⅔ cup finely chopped zucchini

⅓ cup finely chopped sweet red pepper

¼ cup finely chopped fresh parsley

¼ teaspoon salt

3 tablespoons lemon juice

1 teaspoon olive oil

1 Combine bulgur and boiling water in a large bowl; cover and let stand 30 minutes or until water is absorbed.

2 Add zucchini and next 3 ingredients to bulgur; toss well. Combine lemon juice and oil; stir well with a wire whisk. Add to zucchini mixture, tossing well. Serve at room temperature or chilled. Yield: 6 servings.

PER SERVING: CALORIES 72 (13% FROM FAT) FAT 1.0G (SAT 0.2G) PROTEIN 2.4G CARBOHYDRATE 14.7G FIBER 3.4G CHOLESTEROL 0MG SODIUM 102MG EXCHANGE PER SERVING: 1 STARCH

Serve with *broiled lamb and glazed carrots.*

TIME-saver

Chop the vegetables and mix the dressing while the bulgur stands.

Dilled Zucchini and Sun-Dried Tomatoes

superquick

prep: 5 minutes   cook: 3 minutes

6 sun-dried tomatoes

½ cup boiling water

2 pounds zucchini, cut into very thin strips

¼ cup chopped fresh dillweed or 1½ tablespoons dried dillweed

1 tablespoon rice vinegar

½ teaspoon ground red pepper

¼ teaspoon ground black pepper

⅛ teaspoon salt

1 Combine tomatoes and boiling water in a small bowl; let stand 5 minutes. Drain and chop.

2 While tomatoes soften, arrange zucchini in a steamer basket over boiling water. Cover and steam 3 minutes. Combine tomato, zucchini, dillweed, and remaining ingredients in a large bowl, tossing gently. Serve warm. Yield: 6 servings.

PER SERVING: CALORIES 36 (10% FROM FAT) FAT 0.4G (SAT 0.1G) PROTEIN 2.5G CARBOHYDRATE 7.5G FIBER 0.9G CHOLESTEROL 0MG SODIUM 153MG EXCHANGE PER SERVING: 1 VEGETABLE

Serve with *roasted turkey and garlic mashed potatoes.*

WORK-saver

Chop softened sun-dried tomatoes with kitchen scissors.

Zucchini Tabbouleh

Cottage Tomatoes

prep: 9 minutes

4 medium-size tomatoes

1 cup 1% low-fat cottage cheese

3 tablespoons chopped fresh dillweed

1½ teaspoons lemon juice

¼ teaspoon ground pepper

⅛ teaspoon salt

Paprika

1 Slice off tops of tomatoes; scoop out pulp with a small spoon, discarding pulp. Invert and drain on paper towels.

2 While tomato shells drain, combine cottage cheese and next 4 ingredients, stirring well. Spoon mixture evenly into tomato shells. Sprinkle with paprika.
Yield: 4 servings.

PER SERVING: CALORIES 57 (13% FROM FAT) FAT 0.8G (SAT 0.4G) PROTEIN 7.7G
CARBOHYDRATE 5.3G FIBER 1.0G CHOLESTEROL 2MG SODIUM 310MG
EXCHANGES PER SERVING: 1 VERY LEAN MEAT, 1 VEGETABLE

Serve with *chicken noodle soup and fat-free crackers.*

Tomatoes Gremolada

prep: 8 minutes

2 cups finely chopped plum tomato (about 4)

¼ cup chopped fresh parsley

1 teaspoon grated lemon rind

¼ teaspoon salt

⅛ teaspoon ground pepper

½ teaspoon minced garlic, (about 1 clove)

1 Combine all ingredients in a small bowl; toss gently.
Yield: 4 (½-cup) servings.

PER SERVING: CALORIES 24 (15% FROM FAT) FAT 0.4G (SAT 0.0G) PROTEIN 1.0G
CARBOHYDRATE 5.3G FIBER 1.4G CHOLESTEROL 0MG SODIUM 157MG
EXCHANGE PER SERVING: 1 VEGETABLE

Serve with *broiled fish, a tossed green salad, and hard rolls.*

RECIPE tip

Accent fish, chicken, or pasta with gremolada, a highly seasoned Italian garnish.

Plum Salsa

prep: 10 minutes   chill: 30 minutes

1 cup finely chopped plum
    tomato (about 2)

1 cup finely chopped
    unpeeled plum (about
    5 large)

¼ cup finely chopped purple
    onion

2 tablespoons finely chopped
    fresh cilantro or parsley

2 tablespoons lime juice

¼ teaspoon salt

1 jalapeño pepper, seeded
    and finely chopped

1 Combine all ingredients in a medium bowl; toss gently. Cover and chill at least 30 minutes. Serve with grilled chicken, turkey, or pork. Yield: 7 (⅓-cup) servings.

PER SERVING: CALORIES 23 (12% FROM FAT) FAT 0.3G (SAT 0.0G) PROTEIN 0.6G CARBOHYDRATE 5.4G FIBER 1.0G CHOLESTEROL 0MG SODIUM 87MG EXCHANGE PER SERVING: FREE

Serve with *grilled pork chops, zucchini slices, and roasted round red potatoes.*

RECIPE tip

If you don't have a fresh jalapeño pepper, use 1 to 2 teaspoons of drained, canned chopped green chiles.

the safe way to seed peppers

You don't have to remove the seeds from hot peppers such as jalapeños, but sauces and salsas are more attractive without them. Removing the seeds also tempers the heat. Handling hot peppers can burn your skin, so wear rubber gloves when preparing them.

Split the jalapeño lengthwise with a small sharp knife.

Use the knife tip to scrape the seeds from the pepper cavity.

15 Minute Rice Fix-Ups

You save time and add flavor to this plain ol' standby with quick-cooking boil-in-bag rice and a few common ingredients.

Greek Rice

prep: 3 minutes   cook: 10 minutes

- 1 extra-large bag boil-in-bag rice
- 1 (10-ounce) package frozen chopped spinach
- ¼ cup crumbled feta cheese
- 1 tablespoon lemon juice
- ½ teaspoon dried oregano
- ¼ teaspoon salt
- ⅛ teaspoon garlic powder
   Fresh oregano sprigs (optional)

Cook rice according to package directions, omitting salt and fat. While rice cooks, cook chopped spinach according to package directions; drain. Combine rice, spinach, cheese, lemon juice, oregano, salt, and garlic powder; toss well. Garnish with oregano sprigs, if desired.
Yield: 8 servings.

PER SERVING: CALORIES 109 (10% FROM FAT) FAT 1.2G (SAT 0.8G) PROTEIN 3.4G
CARBOHYDRATE 20.4G FIBER 1.5G CHOLESTEROL 4MG SODIUM 274MG
EXCHANGE PER SERVING: 1 STARCH

Garlic Rice

prep: 2 minutes   cook: 10 minutes

- 1 extra-large bag boil-in-bag rice
- ¼ cup grated Parmesan cheese
- 2 tablespoons chopped fresh parsley
- 1½ tablespoons reduced-calorie margarine
- 1 teaspoon minced roasted garlic

Cook rice according to package directions, omitting salt and fat. Stir in ¼ cup cheese, parsley, margarine, and roasted garlic; toss well.
Yield: 6 servings.

PER SERVING: CALORIES 153 (19% FROM FAT) FAT 3.3G (SAT 1.2G) PROTEIN 4.2G
CARBOHYDRATE 25.0G FIBER 0.5G CHOLESTEROL 4MG SODIUM 276MG
EXCHANGES PER SERVING: 1½ STARCH, ½ FAT

Lemon-Ginger Rice

prep: 2 minutes   cook: 10 minutes

   1 extra-large bag boil-in-bag rice
 ¼ cup chopped green onion (about 1 large)
   2 tablespoons lemon juice
1½ tablespoons reduced-calorie margarine
 ¾ teaspoon ground ginger
 ¼ teaspoon salt

Cook rice according to package directions, omitting salt and fat. Stir in green onion, lemon juice, margarine, ground ginger, and salt; toss well.
Yield: 6 servings.

PER SERVING: CALORIES 133 (13% FROM FAT) FAT 1.9G (SAT 0.3G) PROTEIN 2.2G
CARBOHYDRATE 25.4G FIBER 0.5G CHOLESTEROL 0MG SODIUM 286MG
EXCHANGES PER SERVING: 1½ STARCH

Southwestern Rice

prep: 5 minutes   cook: 10 minutes

   1 extra-large bag boil-in-bag rice
   1 (14½-ounce) can no-salt-added diced tomatoes, drained
 ¾ cup (3 ounces) shredded reduced-fat sharp Cheddar cheese
1½ teaspoons chili powder
 ¼ teaspoon salt

Cook rice according to package directions, omitting salt and fat. Stir in tomato, cheese, chili powder, and salt; toss well.
Yield: 9 servings.

PER SERVING: CALORIES 115 (15% FROM FAT) FAT 1.9G (SAT 1.1G) PROTEIN 4.6G
CARBOHYDRATE 18.9G FIBER 0.6G CHOLESTEROL 6MG SODIUM 249MG
EXCHANGES PER SERVING: 1½ STARCH

for extra flavor

Cook 1 cup long-grain rice according to package directions, using canned no-salt-added chicken broth instead of water and omitting salt and fat.

Broccoli, Rice, and Cheese Bake

prep: 4 minutes   cook: 25 minutes

1 regular-size bag boil-in-bag rice, uncooked

3 tablespoons all-purpose flour

1⅓ cups low-fat milk

6 ounces light loaf process cheese product, cut into 1-inch cubes (Light Velveeta)

1 (2-ounce) jar diced pimiento, drained

¼ teaspoon salt

⅛ teaspoon ground red pepper

1 (10-ounce) package frozen chopped broccoli, thawed and drained

1 Cook rice according to package directions, omitting salt and fat.

2 While rice cooks, place flour in a small, heavy saucepan. Gradually add milk, stirring with a wire whisk. Cook over medium heat, stirring constantly, 8 minutes or until thickened and bubbly. Add cheese, stirring until cheese melts. Remove from heat, and stir in pimiento, salt, and pepper.

3 Combine cheese mixture, broccoli, and rice in a large bowl, stirring well. Spoon into a 1½-quart casserole. Cover with heavy-duty plastic wrap, and vent. Microwave at HIGH 5 minutes. Let stand, covered, 10 minutes.
Yield: 8 servings.

PER SERVING: CALORIES 137 (19% FROM FAT) FAT 2.9G (SAT 1.8G) PROTEIN 8.2G
CARBOHYDRATE 20.4G FIBER 1.2G CHOLESTEROL 9MG SODIUM 418MG
EXCHANGES PER SERVING: ½ MEDIUM-FAT MEAT, 1 STARCH, 1 VEGETABLE

Serve with barbecued chicken and cornbread.

TIME-saver

Thaw the broccoli in the microwave while the rice cooks.

Cranberry-Walnut Rice

prep: 3 minutes   cook: 11 minutes

1 cup canned no-salt-added
  chicken broth

1 cup unsweetened orange
  juice

2 cups instant brown rice,
  uncooked

¼ cup chopped walnuts

⅓ cup sweetened dried
  cranberries

½ teaspoon salt

⅛ teaspoon ground pepper

1 Combine chicken broth and orange juice in a saucepan; bring to a boil. Add rice; cover, reduce heat, and simmer 10 minutes or until rice is tender and liquid is absorbed. Transfer to a large bowl.

2 While rice cooks, place a small, heavy skillet over medium-high heat. Add walnuts, and cook, stirring constantly, 1 minute or until nuts are toasted.

3 Stir nuts, cranberries, salt, and pepper into rice. Toss well.
Yield: 8 servings.

PER SERVING: CALORIES 159 (16% FROM FAT) FAT 2.9G (SAT 0.1G) PROTEIN 3.8G
CARBOHYDRATE 30.9G FIBER 2.3G CHOLESTEROL 0MG SODIUM 211MG
EXCHANGES PER SERVING: 1 STARCH, 1 FRUIT, ½ FAT

Serve with *roasted turkey, broccoli, and soft dinner rolls.*

TIME-saver

Chop and toast extra walnuts when you toast ¼ cup
for this recipe. Then store the extra nuts in a heavy-duty
zip-top plastic bag in the freezer.

Indian Rice Pilaf

1 cup long-grain rice, uncooked

1 teaspoon vegetable oil

¼ teaspoon salt

¼ teaspoon ground pepper

¼ teaspoon ground cumin

⅛ teaspoon ground cinnamon

⅛ teaspoon ground bay leaves

⅛ teaspoon ground cloves

½ cup raisins

2 cups canned no-salt-added chicken broth

prep: 5 minutes   cook: 29 minutes

1 Cook rice in oil in a medium saucepan over medium-high heat, stirring constantly, 3 to 4 minutes or until golden. Add salt and next 5 ingredients; stir well. Cook, stirring constantly, 1 minute.

2 Add raisins and chicken broth; bring to a boil. Cover, reduce heat, and simmer 15 minutes or until rice is tender and liquid is absorbed. Let stand 10 minutes.
Yield: 7 servings.

PER SERVING: CALORIES 125 (6% FROM FAT) FAT 0.9G (SAT 0.2G) PROTEIN 2.2G CARBOHYDRATE 26.0G FIBER 0.6G CHOLESTEROL 0MG SODIUM 223MG EXCHANGES PER SERVING: 1 STARCH, ½ FRUIT

Serve with *curried chicken and garden peas.*

Creamy Rice Pilaf

2 cups water

1 cup rice trio (Uncle Ben's)

½ cup frozen chopped onion, celery, and pepper blend (McKenzie's Seasoning Blend)

¼ teaspoon ground pepper

⅛ teaspoon salt

1 cup frozen English peas

1 (10¾-ounce) can reduced-fat, reduced-sodium cream of mushroom soup

prep: 5 minutes   cook: 27 minutes

1 Bring 2 cups water to a boil in a medium saucepan; add rice mix, frozen onion and pepper blend, pepper, and salt. Cover, reduce heat, and simmer 25 minutes or until rice is tender and liquid is absorbed.

2 While rice cooks, thaw peas in microwave according to package directions. Stir peas and soup into rice; cook over low heat 2 minutes or until thoroughly heated.
Yield: 8 servings.

PER SERVING: CALORIES 117 (12% FROM FAT) FAT 1.5G (SAT 0.3G) PROTEIN 3.2G CARBOHYDRATE 23.1G FIBER 0.7G CHOLESTEROL 0MG SODIUM 327MG EXCHANGE PER SERVING: 1 STARCH

Serve with *baked chicken and a tossed green salad.*

Rice with Peas and Mint

prep: 5 minutes   cook: 10 minutes

1 extra-large bag boil-in-bag rice

1 (10-ounce) package frozen English peas

¼ cup grated Parmesan cheese

2 tablespoons chopped fresh mint or 2 teaspoons dried mint

¼ teaspoon salt

1 Cook rice. Transfer to a large bowl.

2 While rice cooks, cook peas according to package directions, omitting salt and fat; drain.

3 Add peas, cheese, mint, and salt to rice. Toss well.
Yield: 9 servings.

PER SERVING: CALORIES 116 (9% FROM FAT)   FAT 1.1G (SAT 0.6G)   PROTEIN 4.4G
CARBOHYDRATE 20.9G   FIBER 1.7G   CHOLESTEROL 2MG   SODIUM 266MG
EXCHANGES PER SERVING: 1 STARCH, 1 VEGETABLE

Serve with broiled lamb loin chops and glazed carrots.

Orzo with Basil, Roasted Pepper, and Feta

prep: 10 minutes   cook: 8 minutes

1 cup orzo, uncooked

¼ cup diced roasted sweet red pepper in water

¼ cup crumbled feta cheese

¼ cup finely chopped fresh basil or 2½ tablespoons dried basil

¼ teaspoon salt

⅛ teaspoon ground pepper

1 Cook pasta according to package directions, omitting salt and fat. Drain, reserving 2 tablespoons cooking liquid. Combine pasta, 2 tablespoons cooking liquid, sweet red pepper, and remaining ingredients in a serving bowl; toss gently. Serve immediately.
Yield: 6 servings.

PER SERVING: CALORIES 139 (12% FROM FAT)   FAT 1.9G (SAT 1.0G)   PROTEIN 5.1G
CARBOHYDRATE 24.8G   FIBER 0.9G   CHOLESTEROL 6MG   SODIUM 172MG
EXCHANGES PER SERVING: 1 STARCH, 1 VEGETABLE

Serve with grilled turkey tenderloins, a tossed green salad, and garlic bread.

RECIPE tip

Adding the 2 tablespoons of cooking liquid to the drained pasta is the key to making pasta creamier, especially when the recipe doesn't include a thick, coating sauce.

Penne with Toasted Breadcrumbs and Herbs

Penne with Toasted Breadcrumbs and Herbs

prep: 5 minutes   cook: 10 minutes

½ (16-ounce) package penne (short tubular pasta), uncooked

2 teaspoons reduced-calorie margarine

1 teaspoon minced garlic (about 2 cloves)

¼ cup Italian-seasoned breadcrumbs

¼ cup chopped fresh parsley

1 tablespoon chopped fresh rosemary or 1 teaspoon dried rosemary

3 tablespoons fat-free Parmesan dressing

2 tablespoons freshly grated Parmesan cheese

1 Cook pasta according to package directions, omitting salt and fat; drain well. Transfer to a large bowl.

2 While pasta cooks, melt margarine in a small nonstick skillet over medium heat. Add garlic, and cook, stirring constantly, 1 minute. Add breadcrumbs, and cook, stirring constantly, 2 minutes or until breadcrumbs are lightly browned. Remove from heat. Stir in parsley and rosemary. Set aside.

3 Add Parmesan dressing to pasta; toss gently. Add breadcrumb mixture and cheese; toss gently. Serve immediately.
Yield: 9 servings.

PER SERVING: CALORIES 129 (13% FROM FAT)   FAT 1.9G (SAT 0.7G)   PROTEIN 5.1G
CARBOHYDRATE 22.4G   FIBER 0.7G   CHOLESTEROL 2MG   SODIUM 191MG
EXCHANGES PER SERVING: 1½ STARCH

Serve with *broiled flank steak, glazed carrots, and crusty French bread.*

RECIPE tip

Substitute any similar size shape pasta for penne, such as macaroni, ziti, bow tie, rotini, or fusilli.

the quick-chop method for parsley

Although you can chop parsley on a cutting board with a French knife, this method saves cleaning the cutting board.

Rinse and dry the parsley, then clip the leaves with kitchen scissors over a measuring cup or a measuring spoon.

soups & sandwiches

Chilled Tropical Soup

Chilled Tropical Soup

prep: 10 minutes   chill: 4 hours

2 cups unsweetened
  pineapple juice

1 (12-ounce) can papaya
  nectar

1½ cups cubed fresh pineapple

1½ cups cubed cantaloupe

2 tablespoons sugar

½ teaspoon ground ginger

1 large banana, sliced and
  divided

  Fresh mint sprigs (optional)

1 Combine first 6 ingredients in a large bowl, stirring well. Place half of fruit mixture and half of banana in container of an electric blender; cover and process on low speed until smooth. Transfer pureed mixture to a large bowl. Repeat procedure with remaining fruit mixture and banana.

2 Cover and chill at least 4 hours or up to 2 days. To serve, stir chilled soup, then ladle into individual bowls. Garnish with mint sprigs, if desired.
Yield: 5 (1-cup) servings.

PER SERVING: CALORIES 183 (3% FROM FAT) FAT 0.6G (SAT 0.1G) PROTEIN 1.2G
CARBOHYDRATE 45.8G FIBER 2.2G CHOLESTEROL 0MG SODIUM 6MG
EXCHANGES PER SERVING: 3 FRUIT

Serve as a dessert soup with tuna salad and marinated tomatoes.

Garden Gazpacho

make ahead

prep: 13 minutes   chill: 1 hour

⅔ cup roasted sweet red
  pepper in water, drained

1 teaspoon minced garlic
  (about 2 cloves)

1 (46-ounce) can vegetable
  juice, divided

1½ cups plus 2 tablespoons
  peeled, seeded, and
  finely chopped
  cucumber, divided
  (about 1 medium)

1 tablespoon red wine vinegar

½ teaspoon ground pepper

1 (15-ounce) can low-sodium
  garbanzo beans, drained

1 cup finely chopped green
  pepper (1 small)

1 Combine roasted red pepper, garlic, and 1 cup vegetable juice in container of an electric blender; cover and process until smooth. Transfer mixture to a large serving bowl; stir in remaining vegetable juice, 1 cup cucumber, and remaining 4 ingredients. Cover and chill at least 1 hour.

2 To serve, ladle soup into individual bowls. Top each serving with 1 tablespoon remaining cucumber.
Yield: 10 (1-cup) servings.

PER SERVING: CALORIES 82 (10% FROM FAT) FAT 0.9G (SAT 0.1G) PROTEIN 3.8G
CARBOHYDRATE 16.3G FIBER 1.8G CHOLESTEROL 0MG SODIUM 491MG
EXCHANGES PER SERVING: 3 VEGETABLE

Serve with chicken salad sandwiches and fresh fruit.

RECIPE tip

Substitute ⅔ cup chopped tomato for the roasted pepper in summer months, when tomatoes are sweet and juicy.

Cheddar Potato Soup

prep: 6 minutes   cook: 26 minutes

2 (16-ounce) cans no-salt-
  added chicken broth

5 cups frozen shredded
  potato

1 cup frozen chopped onion

½ teaspoon salt

½ teaspoon ground pepper

2 tablespoons all-purpose
  flour

1 (12-ounce) can evaporated
  skimmed milk

1 cup (4 ounces) shredded
  reduced-fat sharp
  Cheddar cheese

⅓ cup chopped green onion
  (about 1 large)

1 Combine first 5 ingredients in a Dutch oven; bring to a boil. Reduce heat, and simmer, uncovered, 20 minutes.

2 Combine flour and milk in a small bowl, stirring until smooth. Add to potato mixture. Cook over medium heat, stirring constantly, 5 minutes or until thickened.

3 Pour half of potato mixture into container of an electric blender; cover and process until smooth, stopping once to scrape down sides. Pour into a large bowl. Repeat procedure with remaining half of potato mixture.

4 Return mixture to Dutch oven. Add cheese; cook over medium heat, stirring until cheese melts. Ladle soup into individual bowls; sprinkle each serving evenly with green onion.
Yield: 7 (1-cup) servings.

PER SERVING: CALORIES 158 (18% FROM FAT) FAT 3.2G (SAT 1.9G) PROTEIN 10.6G
CARBOHYDRATE 17.3G FIBER 1.2G CHOLESTEROL 13MG SODIUM 623MG
EXCHANGES PER SERVING: 1 LEAN MEAT, 1 STARCH

Serve with *French bread and a fresh fruit salad.*

RECIPE tip

You can substitute ⅓ cup frozen chopped chives for green onion.

Quick Tortellini Spinach Soup

prep: 10 minutes   cook: 17 minutes

3 (14¼-ounce) cans no-salt-
    added chicken broth

¾ cup finely chopped carrot

1½ tablespoons chopped fresh
    basil or 1½ teaspoons
    dried basil

1 teaspoon minced garlic
    (about 2 cloves)

1 (9-ounce) package
    refrigerated cheese-filled
    tortellini, uncooked

2 cups loosely packed,
    coarsely chopped fresh
    spinach

½ cup sliced green onions
    (about 2 large)

¼ cup freshly grated Parmesan
    cheese

1 Combine first 4 ingredients in a large saucepan; bring to a boil. Reduce heat, and simmer, uncovered, 10 minutes.

2 Return to a boil; add tortellini, and cook 5 minutes. Add spinach and green onions; reduce heat, and simmer 2 to 3 minutes. Ladle into individual soup bowls; sprinkle soup evenly with cheese. Yield: 6 (1-cup) servings.

PER SERVING: CALORIES 186 (21% FROM FAT) FAT 4.3G (SAT 1.8G) PROTEIN 9.2G CARBOHYDRATE 24.3G FIBER 1.2G CHOLESTEROL 23MG SODIUM 321MG EXCHANGES PER SERVING: 1 STARCH, 2 VEGETABLE, 1 FAT

***Serve with** a Greek salad.*

TIME-saver

Buy packages of prewashed spinach leaves to save preparation time.

Vegetable-Beef Soup

prep: 5 minutes   cook: 25 minutes

1 pound lean beef tips

2 (14¼-ounce) cans no-salt-
    added beef broth

2 (14½-ounce) cans no-salt-
    added stewed tomatoes,
    undrained

2 (16-ounce) packages frozen
    mixed vegetables

1 cup frozen whole-kernel
    corn

½ teaspoon salt

½ teaspoon ground pepper

1½ teaspoons minced fresh
    thyme or ½ teaspoon
    dried thyme

1 Brown beef in a Dutch oven over medium-high heat, stirring frequently. Add broth and remaining ingredients, stirring well. Bring to a boil; cover, reduce heat, and simmer 20 minutes. Yield: 6 (2-cup) servings.

PER SERVING: CALORIES 286 (12% FROM FAT) FAT 3.8G (SAT 1.3G) PROTEIN 25.0G CARBOHYDRATE 37.2G FIBER 7.6G CHOLESTEROL 43MG SODIUM 378MG EXCHANGES PER SERVING: 2 LEAN MEAT, 2 STARCH, 1 VEGETABLE

***Serve with** a tossed green salad and soft breadsticks.*

TIME-saver

If you have leftover roast beef, cut it into bite-size pieces and use it instead of beef tips.

Slow-Cooked Beef and Barley Soup

prep: 7 minutes   cook: 3 hours and 10 minutes

1½ pounds lean boneless round
     steak, cut into 1-inch
     pieces

1 tablespoon all-purpose flour

¼ teaspoon salt

     Vegetable cooking spray

1 (14½-ounce) can no-salt-
     added stewed tomatoes,
     undrained

2 (14¼-ounce) cans no-salt-
     added beef broth

1 (10-ounce) package frozen
     mixed vegetables

1 cup water

1 cup frozen chopped onion

⅔ cup pearl barley

1 teaspoon salt-free herb-and-
     spice blend (Mrs Dash)

½ teaspoon salt

½ teaspoon ground pepper

1 Combine steak, flour, and ¼ teaspoon salt in a large zip-top plastic bag; shake bag to coat steak.

2 Coat a large nonstick skillet with cooking spray; place over medium-high heat until hot. Add steak; cook until browned on all sides.

3 Combine steak, tomatoes, and remaining ingredients in a 4-quart electric slow cooker. Cover and cook on high 3 to 3½ hours or on low 8 hours until steak is tender.
Yield: 10 (1-cup) servings.

Per Serving: Calories 178 (16% from fat) Fat 3.1g (Sat 1.1g) Protein 18.4g
Carbohydrate 17.6g Fiber 3.3g Cholesterol 39mg Sodium 261mg
Exchanges Per Serving: 2 Very Lean Meat, 1 Starch, 1 Vegetable

***Serve with** cornbread muffins.*

WORK-saver

Use kitchen scissors to cut the steak into 1-inch pieces; you won't have a cutting board to clean.

Basil Bean Soup with Ham

prep: 11 minutes   cook: 15 minutes

2 (16-ounce) cans no-salt-added chicken broth, divided

2 (19-ounce) cans cannellini beans, drained and divided

½ teaspoon minced garlic (about 1 clove)

1 (14½-ounce) can no-salt-added stewed tomatoes, undrained and chopped

1½ cups chopped reduced-fat, low-salt ham

¼ cup finely chopped fresh basil or 1 tablespoon dried basil

½ teaspoon ground pepper

¼ teaspoon salt

¼ cup freshly grated Parmesan cheese

Fresh basil sprigs (optional)

1 Position knife blade in food processor bowl. Combine 1 can broth, 1 can beans, and garlic in a food processor or a blender; process until smooth.

2 Pour mixture into a Dutch oven; add remaining broth, remaining beans, tomato, and next 4 ingredients. Bring to a boil; cover, reduce heat, and simmer 8 minutes, stirring occasionally. Uncover and simmer 7 minutes, stirring occasionally.

3 Ladle soup into individual bowls; sprinkle evenly with cheese. Garnish with basil sprigs, if desired.
Yield: 8 (1-cup) servings.

PER SERVING: CALORIES 144 (15% FROM FAT) FAT 2.4G (SAT 1.0G) PROTEIN 10.6G CARBOHYDRATE 18.0G FIBER 6.5G CHOLESTEROL 13MG SODIUM 739MG
EXCHANGES PER SERVING: 1 LEAN MEAT, 1 STARCH, 1 VEGETABLE

Serve with *fat-free crackers and a tossed green salad.*

TIME-saver

To chop fresh basil quickly, stack leaves in a pile, roll them up like a newspaper, and slice thinly with a large chef's knife. Then chop the thin slices using a back and forth rocking motion with the knife blade.

Quick El Paso Tomato Soup

prep: 4 minutes   cook: 5 minutes

1 (16-ounce) can no-salt-
    added chicken broth

1 (15-ounce) can chunky chili
    tomato sauce, undrained

1 cup frozen whole-kernel
    corn

¾ cup chopped cooked
    chicken breast

⅛ teaspoon salt

⅛ teaspoon hot sauce

1 Combine all ingredients in a medium saucepan; bring to a boil.
Reduce heat and simmer, uncovered, 5 minutes.
Yield: 5 (1-cup) servings.

PER SERVING: CALORIES 103 (10% FROM FAT) FAT 1.2G (SAT 0.3G) PROTEIN 9.7G
CARBOHYDRATE 11.0G FIBER 2.0G CHOLESTEROL 24MG SODIUM 721MG
EXCHANGES PER SERVING: 1 VERY LEAN MEAT, 1 STARCH

Serve with broiled cheese sandwiches and red grapes.

TIME-saver

Remove the skin and chop deli-roasted chicken breast for
this recipe. Sodium may be higher, but you'll save time if
you don't have cooked chicken on hand.

Chicken Ratatouille Stew

prep: 15 minutes   cook: 30 minutes

1 (1½-pound) deli-roasted
    chicken

6 cups peeled, cubed
    eggplant (about 1
    medium)

1¼ cups sliced zucchini
    (about 1 small)

1 cup frozen chopped green
    pepper

1 (14½-ounce) can Italian-
    style stewed tomatoes,
    undrained

1 (14¼-ounce) can no-salt-
    added chicken broth

1 teaspoon minced garlic
    (about 2 cloves)

2 tablespoons chopped fresh
    basil or 2 teaspoons
    dried basil

1 Remove and discard skin from chicken. Remove chicken from
bones, and coarsely chop chicken.

2 Combine chopped chicken, eggplant, and remaining ingredients
in a Dutch oven, stirring well. Bring to a boil; cover, reduce heat, and
simmer 30 minutes.
Yield: 8 (1-cup) servings.

PER SERVING: CALORIES 197 (29% FROM FAT) FAT 6.4G (SAT 1.8G) PROTEIN 26.0G
CARBOHYDRATE 8.0G FIBER 1.3G CHOLESTEROL 76MG SODIUM 402MG
EXCHANGES PER SERVING: 3 LEAN MEAT, 2 VEGETABLE

Serve with a tossed green salad and breadsticks.

Tex-Mex Chicken Chili Stew

prep: 7 minutes   cook: 20 minutes

1 (16-ounce) can no-salt-
    added chicken broth

1 (15-ounce) can chunky chili
    tomato sauce, undrained

1 (4½-ounce) can chopped
    green chiles, drained

1½ cups frozen chopped onion

1 cup frozen whole-kernel
    corn

2 tablespoons chili powder

1 (15-ounce) can kidney
    beans, drained

¾ pound skinned, boned
    chicken breast halves,
    cut into 1-inch pieces
    (about 3 cups)

¼ cup chopped fresh cilantro
    or parsley

1 Combine first 6 ingredients in a Dutch oven. Bring to a boil; cover, reduce heat, and simmer 10 minutes.

2 Add beans and chicken; cover and simmer 10 additional minutes. Remove from heat; add cilantro.
Yield: 8 (2-cup) servings.

PER SERVING: CALORIES 147 (6% FROM FAT)   FAT 1.0G (SAT 0.2G)   PROTEIN 14.0G
CARBOHYDRATE 19.9G   FIBER 3.9G   CHOLESTEROL 25MG   SODIUM 523MG
EXCHANGES PER SERVING: 1 VERY LEAN MEAT, 1 STARCH, 1 VEGETABLE

Serve with *warm fat-free flour tortillas and a citrus salad.*

Spicy Chicken and Pasta Stew

prep: 9 minutes   cook: 12 minutes

4 ounces bow tie or penne pasta, uncooked

2 teaspoons olive oil

¾ pound skinned, boned chicken breast halves

2 teaspoons minced garlic (about 4 cloves)

1 (16-ounce) can no-salt-added chicken broth

1 (14½-ounce) can Italian-style stewed tomatoes, undrained

½ teaspoon dried crushed red pepper

2 cups tightly packed torn fresh spinach leaves

¼ cup grated Parmesan cheese

1 Cook pasta according to package directions, omitting salt and fat; drain and set aside.

2 While pasta cooks, heat oil in a large saucepan over medium-high heat until hot. Meanwhile, cut chicken into 1-inch pieces. Add chicken and garlic to skillet; cook 5 minutes or until chicken is done, stirring occasionally. Add broth, tomatoes, and crushed pepper; bring to a boil. Reduce heat, and simmer, uncovered, 5 minutes.

3 Add pasta and spinach to saucepan. Cook 2 minutes or until spinach wilts, stirring occasionally. Ladle stew into individual bowls; sprinkle evenly with cheese.
Yield: 4 (1½-cup) servings.

PER SERVING: CALORIES 288 (18% FROM FAT) FAT 5.7G (SAT 1.8G) PROTEIN 27.6G
CARBOHYDRATE 30.2G FIBER 2.0G CHOLESTEROL 54MG SODIUM 689MG
EXCHANGES PER SERVING: 3 VERY LEAN MEAT, 2 STARCH

Serve with garlic bread.

Southwestern Turkey Stew

prep: 8 minutes   cook: 16 minutes

Vegetable cooking spray

1 teaspoon vegetable oil

¾ pound turkey tenderloin

1 cup frozen chopped green pepper

1 cup frozen chopped onion

½ teaspoon minced garlic (about 1 clove)

2 teaspoons ground cumin

1 (16-ounce) can no-salt-added chicken broth

1 (16-ounce) can kidney beans, rinsed and drained

½ cup salsa

5 lime wedges

1 Coat a large saucepan with cooking spray; add oil and place over medium-high heat until hot. Meanwhile, cut turkey into 1-inch pieces; add turkey, pepper, onion, and garlic to skillet. Cook 5 minutes or until turkey is lightly browned, stirring occasionally. Add cumin, and cook 1 minute, stirring well.

2 Add broth, beans, and salsa to saucepan. Bring to a boil; reduce heat, and simmer, uncovered, 10 minutes. Ladle stew into individual bowls. Serve with lime wedges.
Yield: 5 (1-cup) servings.

PER SERVING: CALORIES 193 (13% FROM FAT) FAT 2.7G (SAT 0.6G) PROTEIN 22.0G
CARBOHYDRATE 19.7G FIBER 3.4G CHOLESTEROL 41MG SODIUM 412MG
EXCHANGES PER SERVING: 2 VERY LEAN MEAT, 1 STARCH, 1 VEGETABLE

Serve with jalapeño cornbread.

Spicy Chicken and Pasta Stew

Creole Shrimp Stew

prep: 7 minutes   cook: 15 minutes

Vegetable cooking spray

1 teaspoon vegetable oil

½ cup chopped onion

½ cup chopped celery (about 1 large rib)

½ teaspoon salt

1½ teaspoons minced fresh thyme or ½ teaspoon dried thyme

¼ teaspoon ground pepper

2 tablespoons dry red wine

1 (14½-ounce) can no-salt-added whole tomatoes, undrained and chopped

6 ounces peeled medium-size fresh shrimp

6 ounces halibut fillets, cut into bite-size pieces

1 Coat a Dutch oven with cooking spray; add oil. Place over medium-high heat until hot. Add onion and next 4 ingredients, and cook, stirring constantly, 5 minutes. Add wine and tomato. Bring to a boil; reduce heat, and simmer, uncovered, 5 minutes.

2 Add shrimp and halibut to Dutch oven. Cover and simmer 5 additional minutes or until shrimp turn pink and fish flakes easily when tested with a fork.
Yield: 4 (1-cup) servings.

PER SERVING: CALORIES 132 (20% FROM FAT) FAT 3.0G (SAT 0.5G) PROTEIN 18.7G CARBOHYDRATE 7.3G FIBER 1.4G CHOLESTEROL 85MG SODIUM 406MG
EXCHANGES PER SERVING: 2 VERY LEAN MEAT, 1 VEGETABLE

Serve with a tossed green salad and French bread.

RECIPE tip

You can buy already peeled fresh shrimp in most supermarket seafood departments. If you buy unpeeled shrimp for this recipe, purchase 8 ounces.

Creole Shrimp Stew

5 Ideas for Peanut Butter Sandwiches

Peanut butter is the bread spread of choice for sandwiches or snacks; here's a guide to serving something besides the standard PB & J.

Peanut Butter Snack Sticks

prep: 3 minutes

Spread 1 tablespoon reduced-fat creamy or crunchy peanut butter spread over 1 slice of white sandwich bread. Top with 1 slice of whole wheat bread. Trim crusts, if desired. Cut sandwich into 3 rectangles. Serve with 3 tablespoons apple butter for dipping. Serve immediately. Yield: 3 snack servings.

PER SNACK STICK: CALORIES 111 (20% FROM FAT) FAT 2.5G (SAT 0.1G) PROTEIN 3.2G CARBOHYDRATE 20.0G FIBER 0.8G CHOLESTEROL 1MG SODIUM 123MG **EXCHANGES PER SNACK STICK:** 1 STARCH, ½ FAT

Peanut Butter, Banana, and Honey Sandwich

prep: 3 minutes

Spread 1 tablespoon reduced-fat creamy or crunchy peanut butter spread evenly over 1 slice of whole wheat bread. Top evenly with ¼ medium banana, sliced. Drizzle evenly with ¾ teaspoon honey. Top with 1 slice of whole wheat bread. Serve immediately. Yield: 1 sandwich.

PER SANDWICH: CALORIES 270 (25% FROM FAT) FAT 7.4G (SAT 1.4G) PROTEIN 10.3G CARBOHYDRATE 45.1G FIBER 3.8G CHOLESTEROL 2MG SODIUM 375MG **EXCHANGES PER SANDWICH:** 3 STARCH, 1½ FAT

Peanut Butter Siesta Sandwiches

prep: 6 minutes

Combine 1½ tablespoons reduced-fat creamy peanut butter spread, 1 teaspoon honey, and ⅛ teaspoon ground cinnamon; spread evenly over 2 (6-inch) flour tortillas. Sprinkle with 2 teaspoons granola and 2 teaspoons chopped, pitted dates; roll up, and serve immediately. Yield: 2 sandwiches.

PER SANDWICH: CALORIES 207 (29% FROM FAT) FAT 6.7G (SAT 1.9G) PROTEIN 6.3G CARBOHYDRATE 31.3G FIBER 2.3G CHOLESTEROL 0MG SODIUM 226MG EXCHANGES PER SANDWICH: 2 STARCH, 1 FAT

Crispy PB & J

prep: 5 minutes

Spread 1 tablespoon reduced-fat creamy peanut butter spread on 1 slice of white sandwich bread; sprinkle 1 tablespoon rice cereal over peanut butter. Spread 2 teaspoons grape jelly on 1 slice of white sandwich bread. Place spread sides of bread together; serve immediately. Yield: 1 sandwich.

PER SANDWICH: CALORIES 283 (23% FROM FAT) FAT 7.3G (SAT 1.4G) PROTEIN 9.0G CARBOHYDRATE 46.0G FIBER 2.2G CHOLESTEROL 2MG SODIUM 380MG EXCHANGES PER SANDWICH: 3 STARCH, 1½ FAT

Toasted Peanut Butter and Raisin Sandwiches

prep: 3 minutes

Combine 1 tablespoon reduced-fat creamy peanut butter spread and 1 teaspoon reduced-calorie maple-flavored syrup, stirring well. Spread mixture evenly on 2 slices of toasted raisin bread. Sprinkle slices evenly with 2 teaspoons raisins. Serve open-faced. Yield: 2 sandwiches.

PER SANDWICH: CALORIES 130 (25% FROM FAT) FAT 3.6G (SAT 0.7G) PROTEIN 4.0G CARBOHYDRATE 21.4G FIBER 1.7G CHOLESTEROL 1MG SODIUM 142MG EXCHANGES PER SANDWICH: 1½ STARCH, 1 FAT

Knife and Fork Barbecued Brisket Sandwiches

prep: 10 minutes   cook: 4 hours

2 large onions, thinly sliced and divided

1 (3-pound) beef brisket

1 teaspoon ground pepper

¼ teaspoon salt

2 tablespoons all-purpose flour

1 (12-ounce) bottle chili sauce

½ cup light beer

2 tablespoons brown sugar

1 tablespoon prepared horseradish

1 tablespoon minced garlic (about 6 cloves)

5 submarine rolls, split and toasted

1 Place half of onion rings in bottom of a 4-quart electric slow cooker. Trim fat from meat, and cut into large pieces to fit in slow cooker; sprinkle with pepper and salt. Dredge meat in flour; place on top of onion, sprinkling with any remaining flour. Add remaining half of onion.

2 Combine chili sauce and next 4 ingredients in a medium bowl, stirring well. Pour over meat mixture. Cover and cook on high 4 to 5 hours or until meat is tender. Remove brisket, and replace slow cooker cover.

3 Shred beef, using 2 forks; return meat to hot liquid in slow cooker, stirring well. Spoon meat mixture over toasted roll halves.
Yield: 10 servings.

PER SERVING: CALORIES 327 (23% FROM FAT) FAT 8.2G (SAT 2.1G) PROTEIN 24.3G
CARBOHYDRATE 37.6G FIBER 0.9G CHOLESTEROL 67MG SODIUM 700MG
EXCHANGES PER SERVING: 2 MEDIUM-FAT MEAT, 2½ STARCH

Serve with coleslaw.

TIME-saver

To make this recipe in advance, prepare the meat, then shred it while it's warm (it shreds easier). Refrigerate the shredded meat up to 2 days. Reheat to serve over roll halves.

Caribbean Ham Pita Pockets

superquick

prep: 10 minutes

¼ cup nonfat sour cream

2 tablespoons minced chutney

¼ teaspoon curry powder

1 (8-inch) pita bread round, cut in half

4 ounces thinly sliced reduced-fat, low-salt ham

2 slices canned pineapple in juice, drained

1 teaspoon finely chopped fresh cilantro or parsley

1 tablespoon sliced green onion

½ cup alfalfa sprouts

1 Combine first 3 ingredients in a small bowl. Spread sour cream mixture in pita halves.

2 Place ham and pineapple in pita halves; sprinkle evenly with cilantro and green onion. Top with alfalfa sprouts. Serve immediately. Yield: 2 servings.

PER SERVING: CALORIES 263 (12% FROM FAT) FAT 3.5G (SAT 1.0G) PROTEIN 14.3G CARBOHYDRATE 40.5G FIBER 3.4G CHOLESTEROL 28MG SODIUM 799MG EXCHANGES PER SERVING: 1 LEAN MEAT, 2 STARCH, 1 FRUIT

Serve with carrot and celery sticks.

Peachy Ham and Cheese Grills

superquick

prep: 3 minutes   cook: 4 minutes

2 tablespoons no-sugar-added peach fruit spread

4 (1-ounce) slices white sandwich bread

4 ounces sliced reduced-fat, low-salt ham

¼ cup (1 ounce) shredded reduced-fat Monterey Jack cheese

Butter-flavored vegetable cooking spray

1 Spread peach spread on 2 bread slices; top each evenly with ham and cheese. Top with remaining 2 bread slices. Coat sandwiches with cooking spray.

2 Coat a nonstick skillet with cooking spray, and place over medium heat until hot. Add sandwiches, and cook 2 minutes on each side or until golden.
Yield: 2 servings.

PER SERVING: CALORIES 310 (23% FROM FAT) FAT 7.9G (SAT 2.9G) PROTEIN 19.3G CARBOHYDRATE 40.0G FIBER 1.1G CHOLESTEROL 39MG SODIUM 817MG EXCHANGES PER SERVING: 2 MEDIUM-FAT MEAT, 2½ STARCH

Serve with sweet potato chips.

Open-Face Chicken Capri Baguette

Open-Face Chicken Capri Baguette

prep: 12 minutes   cook: 2 minutes

2 tablespoons nonfat
  mayonnaise

1 tablespoon Dijon mustard

1½ teaspoons balsamic vinegar

½ teaspoon minced garlic
  (about 1 clove)

1 (16-inch) French baguette,
  split lengthwise

1 cup loosely packed fresh
  basil leaves

12 ounces boneless, skinless
   roasted chicken breast,
   sliced

½ cup very thinly sliced purple
  onion, separated into
  rings (about ½ small
  onion)

3 ounces thinly sliced part-
  skim mozzarella cheese

1 Combine first 4 ingredients in a small bowl, stirring well. Spread mayonnaise mixture evenly on cut sides of baguette halves. Arrange basil leaves over mayonnaise mixture. Layer chicken, onion, and cheese on top of basil. Broil 3 inches from heat (with electric oven door partially opened) 2 minutes or until cheese melts.

2 Cut each baguette half into 3 equal pieces. Serve immediately. Yield: 6 servings.

PER SERVING: CALORIES 343 (17% FROM FAT)   FAT 6.5G (SAT 3.3G)   PROTEIN 27.9G CARBOHYDRATE 40.2G   FIBER 1.6G   CHOLESTEROL 56MG   SODIUM 831MG EXCHANGES PER SERVING: 3 LEAN MEAT, 2½ STARCH

Serve with *tomato soup.*

RECIPE tip

You can substitute fresh spinach leaves for basil leaves.

Skillet Barbecued Turkey Sandwiches

prep: 5 minutes   cook: 18 minutes

2 teaspoons reduced-calorie margarine

1 large onion, thinly sliced

½ teaspoon sugar

1 tablespoon cider vinegar

12 ounces turkey tenderloin, cut into thin slices

½ cup hickory-flavored barbecue sauce

4 (1.8-ounce) onion sandwich buns, split and toasted

1 Heat margarine in a large nonstick skillet over medium-high heat until margarine melts. Add onion slices; cook, stirring constantly, 1 minute. Cover, reduce heat, and cook 6 minutes or until tender; sprinkle with sugar. Cook, uncovered, over medium-high heat, stirring constantly, 1 minute. Add vinegar; cook 2 additional minutes, stirring occasionally. Remove onion from skillet; cover and keep warm.

2 Add turkey slices to skillet; cook over medium-high heat 3 minutes. Stir in barbecue sauce; reduce heat, and simmer, uncovered, 5 minutes or until turkey is done. Spoon turkey and sauce evenly onto bottom halves of buns; top with onion. Place top halves of buns over onion.
Yield: 4 servings.

PER SERVING: CALORIES 287 (18% FROM FAT) FAT 5.6G (SAT 0.7G) PROTEIN 25.9G
CARBOHYDRATE 31.8G FIBER 1.9G CHOLESTEROL 61MG SODIUM 578MG
EXCHANGES PER SERVING: 3 LEAN MEAT, 2 STARCH

Serve with *a tossed green salad.*

Fried Green Tomato BLTs

prep: 10 minutes   cook: 6 minutes

1 medium-size green tomato,
   cut into ¼-inch slices

⅛ teaspoon hot sauce
   (optional)

1 egg white, lightly beaten

1½ tablespoons self-rising
   cornmeal

   Vegetable cooking spray

2 leaves green leaf lettuce

2 (1-ounce) slices reduced-fat
   mozzarella cheese

2 slices turkey bacon, cooked,
   drained, and halved

4 (1-ounce) slices white
   sandwich bread, toasted

1 Sprinkle tomato slices with hot sauce, if desired; dip in egg white, and dredge in cornmeal.

2 Place slices in a single layer on a large baking sheet coated with cooking spray. Lightly coat slices with cooking spray. Broil 3 inches from heat (with electric oven door partially opened) 3 minutes on each side or until tender and golden.

3 Layer lettuce, cheese, turkey bacon, and tomato slices on 2 slices of toast. Top with remaining 2 slices of toast. Serve immediately. Yield: 2 servings.

PER SERVING: CALORIES 309 (25% FROM FAT)   FAT 8.7G (SAT 3.2G)   PROTEIN 18.4G
CARBOHYDRATE 37.7G   FIBER 2.4G   CHOLESTEROL 22MG   SODIUM 741MG
EXCHANGES PER SERVING: 1 HIGH-FAT MEAT, 2 STARCH, 1 VEGETABLE

Serve with *fresh fruit.*

how to "oven-fry" green tomatoes

You don't have to deep-fat-fry tomatoes for crispy coated slices. This method saves fat, calories, and cleanup.

Sprinkle hot sauce over the tomato slices, if desired, then dip them in beaten egg white.

Dredge each slice in cornmeal, coating well.

Arrange the coated tomato slices in a single layer on a baking sheet; coat each slice lightly with cooking spray. Broil 3 inches from the heat for 3 minutes on each side.

Fried Green Tomato BLTs

Broiled Fish Sandwiches

prep: 3 minutes   cook: 8 minutes

4 (4-ounce) orange roughy,
   flounder, or grouper
   fillets

Vegetable cooking spray

⅛ teaspoon salt

1½ teaspoons minced fresh
   dillweed or ½ teaspoon
   dried dillweed, divided

⅓ cup nonfat sour cream

¼ cup reduced-fat mayonnaise

3 tablespoons dill pickle salad
   cubes

3 tablespoons finely chopped
   purple onion

1 teaspoon lemon juice

¼ teaspoon ground red
   pepper

4 (2-ounce) French bread
   rolls, split

2 cups firmly packed finely
   shredded cabbage

1 Place fish on rack of a broiler pan coated with cooking spray. Sprinkle with half of salt and dillweed. Broil 5½ inches from heat (with electric oven door partially opened) 8 to 10 minutes or until fish flakes easily when tested with a fork.

2 While fish broils, combine sour cream and next 4 ingredients in a medium bowl; stir in red pepper and remaining half of dillweed. Spread 3 tablespoons mayonnaise mixture evenly on bottom halves of rolls; set aside.

3 Combine remaining mayonnaise mixture and cabbage in a bowl; set aside.

4 Place fillets on roll halves spread with mayonnaise mixture; top fillets with cabbage mixture. Top with remaining bun halves. Serve immediately.
Yield: 4 servings.

PER SERVING: CALORIES 307 (18% FROM FAT)   FAT 6.1G (SAT 1.0G)   PROTEIN 23.8G
CARBOHYDRATE 36.0G   FIBER 1.8G   CHOLESTEROL 29MG   SODIUM 755MG
EXCHANGES PER SERVING: 2 LEAN MEAT, 2 STARCH, 1 VEGETABLE

Serve with *fresh tomato and cucumber slices.*

RECIPE tip

If you prefer a grilled flavor, grill the fish over medium-hot coals (350° to 400°). A wire grilling basket makes it easier; just be sure to coat the basket with cooking spray. Place fish in basket, and grill 6 minutes on each side or until fish flakes easily when tested with a fork.

Vegetable Tuna Pockets

prep: 14 minutes

1 (6-ounce) can low-sodium, low-fat chunk white tuna in spring water, drained

1 (14-ounce) can artichoke hearts, drained and coarsely chopped

½ cup seeded, finely chopped cucumber (about ½ small)

½ cup seeded, finely chopped tomato (about ½ medium)

¼ cup plus 2 tablespoons fat-free Caesar salad dressing, divided

2 (8-inch) pita bread rounds, cut in half crosswise

¾ cup shredded iceberg lettuce

2 tablespoons sliced ripe olives

1 Combine first 4 ingredients in a bowl; stir in ¼ cup dressing. Spoon tuna mixture evenly into pita halves; top evenly with lettuce, remaining 2 tablespoons dressing, and olives. Serve immediately. Yield: 4 servings.

PER SERVING: CALORIES 188 (9% FROM FAT) FAT 1.9G (SAT 0.2G) PROTEIN 11.5G CARBOHYDRATE 29.9G FIBER 3.8G CHOLESTEROL 9MG SODIUM 543MG EXCHANGES PER SERVING: 1 LEAN MEAT, 2 STARCH

Serve with grapes and fresh pear slices.

RECIPE tip

For a make-ahead sandwich spread, chill the tuna mixture up to 8 hours.

Speed Cooking Guide

A lifestyle that requires little time in the kitchen calls for planning, shopping, and cooking for speed. Use the tips in this guide to help you learn to "throw together" recipes, to plan ahead so you'll have what you need, and to grocery shop in record time.

Fast Entrées

When our editors and test kitchens staffers don't have time to cook, here's what they do for dinner.

CHICKEN/TURKEY

Omit the fat and use fat-free milk to prepare a package of Alfredo sauce mix. Stir in some deli-roasted **chicken** or smoked **turkey**.

Sprinkle lemon juice and rosemary over boneless, skinless **chicken** breast halves and broil or grill the chicken.

Grill boneless, skinless **chicken** breast halves or **turkey tenderloins** over medium-hot coals. For extra flavor, toss sprigs of fresh rosemary, oregano, basil, or other strong-flavored herbs directly on the coals.

FISH

Broil **catfish** fillets sprinkled with lemon juice and Cajun seasoning blend.

Strip thick stems of rosemary and thread **fish, shrimp, chicken,** or **vegetables** onto the stems to grill or broil for kabobs.

MEAT

Brush **pork loin chops** with a mixture of plum preserves and hoisin sauce, then broil or grill the chops.

Quick Side Dishes

Asparagus: Drizzle low-fat blue cheese dressing over steamed asparagus and plum tomato slices.

Broccoli: Steam broccoli, then top it with lemon juice, flavored mustard, and melted margarine.

Carrots: Season carrot slices with honey and tarragon.

Coleslaw: Mix preshredded cabbage, chopped Red Delicious apple, and poppy seed dressing.

Corn: Add salsa and ground cumin to hot cooked whole-kernel corn.

Eggplant: Grill eggplant slices that have been marinated in balsamic vinegar.

Mashed potatoes: Stir minced garlic or chopped chives into cooked instant mashed potatoes.

Pineapple slices: Broil or grill fresh pineapple slices brushed with a honey-cinnamon mixture.

Spinach: Stir oregano and feta cheese into cooked chopped spinach.

Tomatoes: Toss tomato wedges with balsamic vinegar, ground pepper, and chopped fresh basil. Top tomato with crumbled feta cheese.

MEATLESS ENTRÉEs

Top a **baked potato** with salsa, green onions, nonfat sour cream, and shredded reduced-fat Cheddar cheese.

Brown slices of **precooked polenta** (look for packages of polenta in the produce or refrigerated sections of the supermarket), then top with low-fat pasta sauce and Parmesan cheese.

Stir cooked onion, mushrooms, green peppers, and fresh minced garlic into a jar of low-fat pasta sauce, and serve over cooked **pasta**.

Spread **pizza** or **pasta sauce** on individual pizza crusts, then top the sauce with fresh vegetables, black beans, corn, roasted chiles, or roasted garlic. Top with cheese and bake or broil until pizzas are thoroughly heated and cheese melts.

Guide to Grilling

Grill these foods, covered, over medium-hot coals, turning once, unless noted.

COOK TIME IN MINUTES	FOOD
	BEEF
12-16	Flank steak (1½ pounds)
8	Round, ground patty (3 ounces)
12	Sirloin tip steak, 1-inch kabob pieces
10	Top sirloin steak, boneless, ½-inch thick (1 pound)
	LAMB
16-20	Lean loin chop, boneless, 1-inch thick (4 ounces)
	PORK
12	Pork, boneless center-cut loin chop (4 ounces)
30 (or to 160°)	Pork loin roast, butterflied (2¼ pounds)
15 (or to 160°)	Pork tenderloin (¾ pound)
6-8	Ham, boneless steak, ½-inch thick (1 pound)
	VENISON
10	Steak, boneless loin, 1-inch thick (4 ounces)
	POULTRY
10-12	Chicken, boneless, skinless breast half (4 ounces)
30	Chicken, skinned bone-in breast half (6 ounces)
	FISH
8	Amberjack fillet, ¾-inch thick (4 ounces)
16	Catfish fillet (4 ounces)
8	Flounder, sole, perch, or orange roughy fillet (4 ounces)
10	Grouper, snapper, or sea bass fillet (4 ounces)
10-12	Salmon steak, ½-inch thick (4 ounces)
6-8	Swordfish steak, ½-inch thick (4 ounces)
10*	Trout, dressed (1 pound)
8-10	Tuna or halibut steak, ½-inch thick (4 ounces)
6	Shrimp, peeled
	VEGETABLES
15**	Corn on cob in husk (silks removed and husks soaked 5 minutes)
8-10	Mushrooms, large (on kabobs)
14-18	Onion, wedges on kabobs
15**	Onion, ½-inch-thick slices (wrapped in foil)
8-10	Onions, pearl (on kabobs)
8-10	Pepper, green, red, or yellow (1-inch pieces on kabobs)
10	Squash, medium-size halved lengthwise

* over hot coals
** do not turn

Simple Ways to Save Time

CLEANUP QUICKER

Chop a small amount of an ingredient by using a chef's knife instead of a food processor; cleanup is easier.

Rinse a measuring cup or spoon with cold water before measuring honey or another sticky ingredient, and it will slide out easily.

Drain ground meat without the mess by placing two paper towels over a sheet of foil the size of the paper towels. Press the meat with additional paper towels to absorb the fat.

Beat eggs in a mixing bowl first, then add the other ingredients to save cleaning an extra bowl.

Prevent splatters by setting a metal colander upside down over a skillet of simmering food. The colander holes allow steam to escape.

Measure ingredients onto wax paper or paper towels for easy cleanup.

Remove garlic or onion odors from a cutting board by rubbing the surface with the cut side of a lemon. Then wash the board in warm, soapy water.

Line baking pans with aluminum foil for quick and easy cleanup when cooking meat, chicken, fish, or vegetables. You'll have very little mess to clean off the pans after removing the aluminum foil.

Measure dry ingredients before wet ones so you can use the same measuring cups and spoons without washing between measuring.

COOK QUICKER

Microwave to get a jump start on cooking. Use the microwave to thaw foods or to pre-cook casseroles or meat you'll finish cooking on the grill or in the oven.

Quick-soak dried beans to cook them quickly. Combine beans and water to cover in a saucepan, then bring the water to a boil. Cover and let the beans stand for 1 hour.

Buy precut, prewashed produce such as spinach leaves, romaine hearts, mixed salad greens, mushrooms, cabbage, and carrots to save chopping and cleaning time.

Use the "meanwhile" method of cooking. While rice or pasta cooks, prepare the sauce or another part of the recipe. Anytime a portion of the recipe bakes, microwaves, simmers, or stands, use the time to prepare another part of the recipe.

Melt chocolate morsels quickly by placing them in a zip-top plastic bag. Seal the bag, and place it in a saucepan of hot water until the morsels are melted. If you're using the chocolate for drizzling, snip off a tiny corner of the bag and let the melted chocolate drip from the hole.

Alphabetize the spices and seasonings in your cupboard; they'll be easier to find.

Store your most often used cooktop utensils in a container near the stove so they're handy when you need them.

Keep all measuring items (cups, spoons) together near the area where you prepare foods for cooking.

Stock Up Before You Cook

Here's a list of basic ingredients to keep on hand for healthy, low-fat cooking from this cookbook.

IN THE PANTRY

CONDIMENTS

Chutney, fruit

Honey

Hot sauce

Jellies, apple, hot pepper

Marmalade, low-sugar orange, low-sugar apricot

Mustard, Dijon

Salsa, tomato

Soy sauce, low-sodium

Syrup, maple-flavored

Vinegars, cider, balsamic, red wine

Worcestershire sauce, low-sodium

PASTA AND RICE

Couscous, macaroni, spaghetti

Boil-in-bag rice

Brown rice, instant

CANNED/JARRED PRODUCTS

Beans, black no-salt-added, kidney no-salt-added

Corn, whole-kernel no-salt-added

Pasta sauce, low-fat or no-salt-added

Pineapple, slices or tidbits canned in juice

Tomatoes, stewed, Mexican-style, Cajun-style, Italian-style

Tomato sauce, no-salt-added

Tuna, canned in water

MISCELLANEOUS

Dressing, Italian fat-free

Oils, vegetable and olive

Potatoes, baking and round red

Pound cake, fat-free loaf

Tortilla chips, no-oil, baked

Vegetable cooking spray

IN THE REFRIGERATOR

DAIRY

Buttermilk, nonfat

Cream cheese, light or nonfat

Margarine, reduced-calorie

Mayonnaise, reduced-fat or nonfat

Milk, low-fat or fat-free

Yogurt, plain, nonfat

FRUIT

Apples

Bananas

Grapes

Lemons

Limes

Oranges

Pears

Strawberries

VEGETABLES

Broccoli flowerets

Cabbage, shredded

Cauliflower flowerets

Celery

Cucumbers

Mushrooms, fresh, sliced

Peppers, green, red, or yellow

Salad greens, packages of premixed washed

Spinach, package of washed leaves

Squash, yellow

Tomatoes, regular or plum

Vegetables, package of mixed, cut for stir-fry

MISCELLANEOUS

Garlic, minced, in a jar

Juices, apple, lemon, and orange

Pasta, fresh

Turkey bacon

IN THE FREEZER

MEAT/POULTRY

Beef, ground round

Chicken, chopped, cooked; frozen boneless, skinless breast halves

FRUIT/VEGETABLES

Onions, chopped frozen

Peaches, frozen, sliced

Peppers, chopped frozen

Seasoning blend (chopped frozen onion, peppers, celery, and parsley)

Strawberries, frozen, sliced or whole

DAIRY

Whipped topping, fat-free frozen

Yogurt, frozen, reduced-fat or nonfat

IN THE SPICE CABINET*

Basil, dried

Chili powder

Cinnamon, ground

Curry powder

Dillweed, dried

Garlic powder

Mrs Dash salt-free seasoning blends

Oregano, dried

Pepper, black, red, and crushed red

Rosemary, dried

Salt-free Creole seasoning

Salt-free Mexican seasoning

Thyme, dried

*If you have room, dried seasonings keep best in the freezer. If you store them in a cabinet, just place them in a cool area away from heat or light.

Shop for Speed

1 Enter the supermarket with a grocery list and stick to the list. You'll buy less and spend less time in the store.

2 Plan ahead so you can shop once every week or two. Avoid last minute stops to pick up an item or two; you'll spend more time and money than you planned.

3 Make your grocery list according to the order of aisles in the store. Follow that order, and you'll backtrack less.

4 If you have room for storage, stock up on standard items you know you'll use.

5 Use convenience products that combine more than one ingredient, such as spice blends (Mrs Dash has several good salt-free blends) or canned products such as Mexican-, Italian-, or Cajun-style stewed tomatoes (you get tomatoes, onions, peppers, and the seasonings in a single can). Besides saving on cooking time, these products save you storage space and the time it takes to put away groceries.

6 Have your grocer bag like items together (frozen, refrigerated, or pantry products), and put-away time in your kitchen will be quicker.

About the Recipes

Every recipe in *LOW-FAT, LOW CALORIE quick & easy cookbook* helps you meet the healthy eating recommendations of the U.S. Dietary Guidelines.

Nutrient Analysis

Use the nutrient analysis following each recipe to see how the recipe fits into your healthy eating plan.

Values are for one serving of the recipe.

Total calories for each serving

This figure tells you what percentage of calories are from fat.

PER SERVING: CALORIES 211 (11% FROM FAT) FAT 2.6G (SAT 1.2G) PROTEIN 7.8G CARBOHYDRATE 38.3G FIBER 3.2G CHOLESTEROL 6MG SODIUM 329MG

Grams are abbreviated "g."

Milligrams are abbreviated "mg."

Fat

The recommendation to keep your fat intake at 30 percent of total calories means *30 percent of your total calories for the day*. This doesn't mean that every single food you eat has to be under 30 percent.

Recipes with over 30 percent calories from fat can still be healthy. For example, salmon is higher in fat than other fish, but it is omega-3 fat, a healthier kind of fat. And for recipes with very low-calorie foods like vegetables, the total amount of fat can be low but still make up a large percentage of the calories.

Here's how the 30 percent recommendation translates to actual fat grams per day:

If you should eat 2000 calories per day. . . you can have up to 67 grams of fat

2000 calories x 30% = 600 calories

600 calories ÷ 9 calories per gram = 67 grams fat

Daily Nutrition Guide

Use the values from the U.S. Dietary Guidelines in the chart below to determine your daily nutrient needs.

	women ages 25 to 50	women over 50	men over 24
CALORIES*	2,000	2,000 OR LESS	2,700
PROTEIN	50G	50G OR LESS	63G
FAT	67G OR LESS	67G OR LESS	90G OR LESS
SATURATED FAT	22G OR LESS	22G OR LESS	30G OR LESS
CARBOHYDRATE	299G	299G	405G
FIBER	25G TO 35G	25G TO 35G	25G TO 35G
CHOLESTEROL	300MG OR LESS	300MG OR LESS	300MG OR LESS
SODIUM	2,400MG OR LESS	2,400MG OR LESS	2,400MG OR LESS

*Calorie requirements vary according to your size, weight, and level of activity. The calorie level in the chart is a general guide; you may need more calories if you are pregnant, breastfeeding, or trying to gain weight, or less if you are trying to lose or maintain weight.

Sodium

The current dietary recommendations advise us to limit our sodium to 2,400 milligrams a day. If you eat a sandwich with 800 milligrams of sodium for lunch, that's about one-third of your recommended sodium intake for the day. Keep that in mind as you make choices for the rest of the day, and try to eat low-sodium foods like fresh fruits and vegetables along with your sandwich.

We use low-fat and reduced-sodium products as often as possible in these recipes to keep fat and sodium to a minimum. But because of various food properties sometimes fat-free products cannot be substituted for low-fat versions. Low-fat and fat-free products are sometimes higher in sodium than their regular counterparts.

As you choose recipes and convenience products, read food labels and note the sodium value in the nutrient analysis following each recipe. If you must restrict sodium in your diet, here are some helpful tips to know when preparing low-fat recipes.
- In low-fat and fat-free products, sodium is sometimes higher than in the traditional versions.
- Sodium amounts are almost always high in convenience products.
- When you choose a spice blend such as lemon-pepper or Creole seasoning mix, be sure to check the ingredient label. If salt is listed first, then the product is mostly salt. Look for a no-salt-added version or one where salt is further down in the ingredient list.

Metric Equivalents

The recipes that appear in this cookbook use the standard United States method for measuring liquid and dry or solid ingredients (teaspoons, tablespoons, and cups). The information in the following charts is provided to help cooks outside the U.S. successfully use these recipes. All equivalents are approximate.

Equivalents for Different Types of Ingredients

A standard cup measure of a dry or solid ingredient will vary in weight depending on the type of ingredient.

A standard cup of liquid is the same volume for any type of liquid. Use the following chart when converting standard cup measures to grams (weight) or milliliters (volume).

Standard Cup	Fine Powder (ex. flour)	Grain (ex. rice)	Granular (ex. sugar)	Liquid Solids (ex. butter)	Liquid (ex. milk)
1	140 g	150 g	190 g	200 g	240 ml
¾	105 g	113 g	143 g	150 g	180 ml
⅔	93 g	100 g	125 g	133 g	160 ml
½	70 g	75 g	95 g	100 g	120 ml
⅓	47 g	50 g	63 g	67 g	80 ml
¼	35 g	38 g	48 g	50 g	60 ml
⅛	18 g	19 g	24 g	25 g	30 ml

Liquid Ingredients by Volume

¼ tsp				1 ml
½ tsp				2 ml
1 tsp				5 ml
3 tsp = 1 tbls		= ½ fl oz	=	15 ml
	2 tbls = ⅛ cup	= 1 fl oz	=	30 ml
	4 tbls = ¼ cup	= 2 fl oz	=	60 ml
	5⅓ tbls = ⅓ cup	= 3 fl oz	=	80 ml
	8 tbls = ½ cup	= 4 fl oz	=	120 ml
	10⅔ tbls = ⅔ cup	= 5 fl oz	=	160 ml
	12 tbls = ¾ cup	= 6 fl oz	=	180 ml
	16 tbls = 1 cup	= 8 fl oz	=	240 ml
	1 pt = 2 cups	= 16 fl oz	=	480 ml
	1 qt = 4 cups	= 32 fl oz	=	960 ml
		33 fl oz	= 1000 ml	= 1 l

Dry Ingredients by Weight

(To convert ounces to grams, multiply the number of ounces by 30.)

1 oz	=	1/16 lb	=	30 g
4 oz	=	¼ lb	=	120 g
8 oz	=	½ lb	=	240 g
12 oz	=	¾ lb	=	360 g
16 oz	=	1 lb	=	480 g

Length

(To convert inches to centimeters, multiply the number of inches by 2.5.)

1 in			=	2.5 cm		
6 in	=	½ ft	=	15 cm		
12 in	=	1 ft	=	30 cm		
36 in	=	3 ft	= 1 yd	=	90 cm	
40 in			=	100 cm	=	1 m

Cooking/Oven Temperatures

	Fahrenheit	Celsius	Gas Mark
Freeze Water	32° F	0° C	
Room Temperature	68° F	20° C	
Boil Water	212° F	100° C	
Bake	325° F	160° C	3
	350° F	180° C	4
	375° F	190° C	5
	400° F	200° C	6
	425° F	220° C	7
	450° F	230° C	8
Broil			Grill

Recipe Index

Tips Index

TIME-savers

WORK-savers

Acknowledgments

Oxmoor House wishes to thank the following merchants:

Aletha Soule, The Loom Co., New York, NY

Barbara Eigen Arts, Inc., Jersey City, NJ

Biot, New York, NY

Carolyn Rice Art Pottery, Marietta, GA

Cyclamen Studio, Inc., Berkeley, CA

Daisy Hill, Louisville, KY

Jill Rosenwald, Boston, MA

Luna Garcia, Venice, CA

Potluck, Accord, NY

Savoir Vivre International, San Francisco, CA

Smyer Glass, Benicia, CA

Union Glass, San Francisco, CA

Vietri, Hillsborough, NC

Source of Nutrient Analysis Data: Computrition, Inc.,
Chatsworth, CA and information provided by food manufacturers

✳ ✳ ✳